RELIGION IN
VICTORIAN BRITAIN

VOLUME IV
INTERPRETATIONS

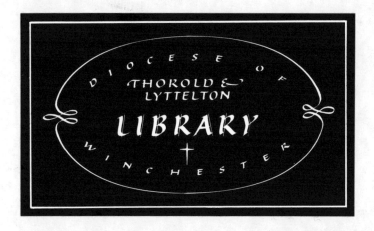

RELIGION IN VICTORIAN BRITAIN

VOLUME IV
INTERPRETATIONS

EDITED BY
GERALD PARSONS
AT THE
OPEN UNIVERSITY

MANCHESTER UNIVERSITY PRESS
MANCHESTER AND NEW YORK
IN ASSOCIATION WITH THE
OPEN UNIVERSITY
DISTRIBUTED EXCLUSIVELY IN THE USA AND CANADA
BY ST. MARTIN'S PRESS

Published by Manchester University Press
Oxford Road, Manchester M13 9PL, UK
and Room 400, 175 Fifth Avenue, New York, NY 10010, USA

Distributed exclusively in the USA and Canada by
St. Martin's Press, Inc., 175 Fifth Avenue, New York, NY 10010, USA

Reprinted 1991

British Library cataloguing in publication data
Religion in Victorian Britain.
    Vol. IV; Interpretations
    1. Great Britain. Christian church, 1837–1901
    I. Parsons, Gerald II. Open University
    274.1'081

Library of Congress cataloging in publication data
Religion in Victorian Britain.
    Includes bibliographies and index.
    Contents: v. 1. Traditions — v. 2. Controversies —
v. 3. Sources — [etc.]
    1. Great Britain — Church history — 19th century.
2. Great Britain — Religion. 3. Great Britain —
Religious life and customs. I. Parsons, Gerald.
BR759.R43   1988   274.1'081   88-12359

ISBN 0 7190 2945 7 *hardback*
      0 7190 2946 5 *paperback*

This book forms part of an Open University course A331 *Religion in Victorian Britain*.
For information about this course please write to the Student Enquiries Office, The
Open University, PO Box 71, Walton Hall, Milton Keynes, MK7 6AG, UK

Typesetting information

This book is set in 10 point Baskerville

Typeset in Hong Kong
by Graphicraft Typesetter Co., Ltd.

Printed in Great Britain
by Courier International, Tiptree, Essex

CONTENTS

PREFACE

This book is one of a four-volume series entitled *Religion in Victorian Britain*, published by Manchester University Press in association with the Open University. The four volumes form the nucleus of an Open University Course. Volumes I and II, *Traditions* and *Controversies* (edited by Gerald Parsons, 1988), consist of sets of specially written essays covering the major religious denominations and groups of the Victorian period and the issues and controversies between and within them. Volume III, *Sources* (edited by James R. Moore, 1988), is a collection of primary source material from the period, while Volume IV, *Interpretations* (edited by Gerald Parsons, 1988), is a collection of recent essays and articles in the field by other writers.

ACKNOWLEDGEMENTS

The editor wishes to acknowledge the essential contribution made to the production of this volume by other members of Open University staff: Michael Bartholomew (Staff Tutor in the History of Science and Technology), David Englander (Lecturer in European Humanities), Gillian Kay (Staff Tutor in History), Anthony Lentin (Reader in History), James R. Moore (Lecturer in the History of Science and Technology), Rosemary O'Day (Senior Lecturer in History) and Terence Thomas (Staff Tutor in Religious Studies), for their help in selecting the items for inclusion in the anthology; Barbara Humphreys and Wendy Clarke (secretaries), Jenny Cook (course manager), Tony Coulson (Library), Pam Higgins (Design Studio), Jonathan Hunt and Giles Clark (Publishing).

The author and publishers wish to thank the following who have kindly given permission for the use of copyright material: American Society of Church History for 'The Mind of Victorian Orthodoxy: Anglican Responses to 'Essays and Reviews', 1860–1864' by J. L. Altholz, *Church History*, 51, 1982, and 'The Papal Aggression of 1850: A Study in Victorian Anti-Catholicism' by W. Ralls, *Church History*, 43, 1974. Catholic Record Society for 'Ultramontanism in Yorkshire, 1850–1900' by J. F. Supple, *Recusant History*, 17, 1986. History of Science Society for 'The Victorian Conflict Between Science and Religion: A Professional Dimension' by F. M. Turner, *Isis*, 69, 1978. Holmes & Meier Publishers, Inc. for 'Victorian Ethics of Belief: A Reconsideration' by F. M. Turner and J. Von Arx from *The Secular Mind: Transformations of Faith in Modern Europe*, ed. W. W. Wagar, 1982. *The Journal of the Society for the Study of Welsh Labour History* for 'Some Working-Class Attitudes to Organised Religion in Nineteenth-Century Wales' by W. R. Lambert, *Llafur*, 1976. *Northern History* for 'Bickersteth, Bishop of Ripon: The Episcopate of a Mid-Victorian Evangelical' by D. N. Hempton, *Northern History*, 17, 1981. University of Minnesota Press for 'The Warfare of Conscience with Theology' by J. L. Altholz from *The Mind and Art of Victorian England*, ed. J. L. Altholz. 1976.

Chapter 1, from *Church Embattled*, (Newton Abbot, 1970), appears by permission of the author, to whom the publishers extend sincere apologies for failing to include the information originally.

Every effort has been made to trace all the copyright holders but if any have been inadvertently overlooked the publishers will be pleased to make the necessary arrangement at the first opportunity.

The cover illustration is taken from *Punch*, 30 June 1877.

INTRODUCTION

As the Preface has already briefly indicated, this *Reader* of essays and articles on aspects of the religious life and thought of Victorian Britain is the final part of a four-volume series designed to form the basis of an Open University Honours level undergraduate course on *Religion in Victorian Britain*.

The first two volumes of the series, entitled respectively *Religion in Victorian Britain: I Traditions* and *Religion in Victorian Britain: II Controversies*, consist of essays specifically written for this enterprise. As their titles imply, they seek to provide an account and interpretation of the major religious traditions and denominations of Victorian Britain, and to identify and examine a number of central issues and controversies in the religious life and thought of the period. The third volume in the series, *Religion in Victorian Britain: III Sources*, provides an extensive collection of primary sources for the study of religion in Victorian Britain.

Whilst in the overall series of four volumes there is an attempt to present a broad overview and interpretation of Victorian religion as a whole, the aims of the present volume are much more modest. The criteria for the selection of the essays and articles which appear in this anthology were pedagogic in nature and reflect the fact that the entire project originated in the preparation of a body of material for the teaching of undergraduates. The essays have thus been chosen to fulfill two principal pedagogic objectives.

First, they are to provide students (and other readers of the overall series of which they are a part) with examples of the scholarly discussion of traditions and issues in Victorian religious life written by authors other than those responsible for the writing of the essays in the first two volumes of the series.

Second, they have been chosen to facilitate various aspects of the actual teaching of the course for which the overall series has been written and compiled. The precise pedagogic functions of particular essays and articles which follow are therefore different. Some have been chosen primarily for the way in which they present a bold or challenging interpretation of a particular theme or issue. Others have been chosen principally for the way in which they present detailed or local case-studies which draw together a number of broader issues and themes within specific contexts.

The contrast between the two broad types of essay chosen is not, of course, total. Those which are essentially local or detailed case-studies nevertheless present particular interpretations. Similarly those which have been chosen for their vigorous presentation of a particular interpretation frequently include a wealth of detailed examples.

In the first section of the anthology there are three essays dealing with aspects of the Anglican establishment. The first provides a survey of the various parties within the Victorian Church of England, indicates the intensity of the inter-party conflicts between them, and places both the parties and their conflicts within the broader context of the various intellectual, social and political challenges which confronted the Victorian Church of England as a whole. The second essay presents a case-study of the orthodox response to what was, arguably, the greatest theological controversy of the age. In doing so, it illustrates and elucidates the nature of Victorian Anglican orthodoxy itself. The third essay in this section examines the episcopate of a particular Evangelical bishop in a provincial diocese. In so doing the essay demonstrates something of the local, diocesan impact of a number of major developments in Victorian religious life including, notably, the challenge of the 'unchurched' urban working class, the controversies over liberal theology and over Anglo-Catholic theology and ritualism, the importance of education as a religious issue, and the growth of Roman Catholicism in Victorian Britain.

In the second section there are four essays which reflect aspects of the life of other major, but non-established, Victorian religious traditions. The first presents a bold and impressive thesis concerning the nature of Victorian English Protestant Nonconformity and its characteristic strengths and weaknesses. The second essay examines the relationship between the working class and organised religion in Victorian Wales and in so doing inevitably focuses especially upon the relationship between the Welsh working classes and Welsh Nonconformity. The third essay in this section analyses the controversy over the restoration of the official hierarchy of Roman Catholic bishops to England in 1850 and places the anti-Catholicism which the incident reflected within a broader religious, social and political context. The final essay in this section examines, in the context of a particular diocese, the relationship between the ethos of the traditional English Catholic community and the newer Ultramontane style advocated by the leadership of the church in the half-century following the restoration of the hierarchy.

In the final section of the book there appear three essays which attempt to place the religious life of the era within a broader intellectual and cultural context. The first reviews the various intellectual challenges to traditional belief which arose in the Victorian period, but also clearly demonstrates the essentially *moral* nature of the conflict between traditional belief and both modern historical and scientific consciousness and a variety of theologically liberal responses to such knowledge. The second essay in this section suggests that, in the much discussed Victorian conflict between science and religion, an essential factor in the conflict was the clash between competing bodies of increasingly self-conscious professionals, each claiming authority in national cultural and intellectual life. The third essay examines the debate which took place in Victorian England over the ethics of belief. It stresses the extent to which, both in that particular debate and in the more general emergence of a more secular frame of mind of which the debate was a part, religious, intellectual, legal and political factors interacted upon each other. Both the second and third essays in this section also emphasise the importance of the *revival* which occurred in the religious life and institutions in Victorian Britain. In the view of the authors of both these essays, it was the coincidence of, on the one hand that religious revival, and on the other hand the rise of a secular intellectual elite seeking to present a new and post-Christian intellectual synthesis, which gave rise to much of the intensity of the religious controversy of the Victorian age.

M. A. CROWTHER

CHAPTER 1

CHURCH PROBLEMS AND CHURCH PARTIES

I N December 1862, Archibald Campbell Tait, Bishop of London and one of the most intelligent churchmen of his age, said in his episcopal charge to his clergy in St Paul's Cathedral:

Our Church, has, committed to it by God, in the middle of the nineteenth century, in an inquisitive and restless age, the difficult task of gathering together, fostering, developing, restraining, and guiding the Christian feelings and thoughts, and energetic life of many millions of intelligent Englishmen, impatient both of political and still more of ecclesiastical control.[1]

Tait told them that the Church had three main problems: first the spirit of free inquiry and criticism which was gradually alienating many educated people from the Church; secondly, the difficulties of an established Church in an age of freedom of worship, and in a State which was no longer wholly Anglican; and thirdly, the ever-growing population of England, in which a generation of the working class was now growing up without any knowledge of the Church or indeed of Christianity itself.

Although the order in which Tait listed these problems was perhaps accidental, it is nevertheless indicative of the Church's sense of priorities in the mid-nineteenth century. A modern reader would probably count Tait's third point, the alienation or indifference of the working class, as the Church's most difficult and important problem of that time. The Church was certainly aware of it. The investigation into the state of religious worship which had formed part of the census of 1851, however inaccurate, did show clearly that a very large proportion of the people, possibly as much as 38 per cent, attended no church, and that nearly half of the remainder were Dissenters.[2] The Church made efforts to grapple with this; from early in the century there were associations which hoped to win back the poor through education, evangelisation or charity. The National Society for Promoting the Education of the Poor in the Principles of the Established

---

(Except where otherwise stated, the place of publication is London.)

[1] Tait, A. C. *Charge*, London. 1862, p. 5.

[2] *Parl Papers*, 1852–3, Vol. lxxxix (33), p. cliii ff.

Church (founded 1811) had in its hands a great deal of responsibility for national education, and for a long time it successfully opposed any attempt to set up a centralised, secular educational system.

Churchmen rallied to provide more clergy and more churches so that the Church might expand with the population. In nearly every diocese church building was proceeding rapidly by the middle of the century, though not as rapidly as the growth of the population. Between 1801 and 1831, 500 new churches were built; between 1831 and 1851 the number was 2,029.[3] Many others were restored. In London, Bishop Blomfield was a tireless church-builder, and other bishops pledged themselves to the cause of church extension. Yet these efforts were not only failing to keep up with the population, but the new churches were often half-empty. In spite of the dedication of individuals and of organisations who undertook evangelical crusades and social work in the slums there was no cohesion in the Church.

Many churchmen of the 1860s would not have agreed that their chief problem was the indifferent masses. They believed that the Church's greatest danger lay in the increasing alienation of many educated men, stimulated by a new spirit of free inquiry into many fields of learning, including science, history and theology. No ancient belief was sacred in the eyes of the new critics, many of whom abandoned their faith or built up systems unacceptable to the Church. Science in particular was developing along new lines, but it is easy to exaggerate the effect of evolutionary theories. The publication of Darwin's *Origin of Species* in 1859 was not such a thunderbolt to the Church as might be imagined, nor did it suddenly undermine the faith of a generation. In the scientific world it certainly produced a convulsion, and a new group of scientists emerged, led by Huxley, no longer believing in the comfortable idea that the duty of science was to praise the harmony and order of God's creation.[4] The course of science had been diverted, but the Church, although startled, remained unshaken. In the first place, it was possible for the Church to point to the arguments of an older generation of scientists, men like Adam Sedgwick, who thought that Darwin's hypotheses were unsound; hence the Church periodicals devoted some space to refuting Darwin but had their attention more fully occupied in the following year by more stirring internal controversies. Secondly, Darwin was not the root cause of contemporary unbelief, though some young men like Leslie Stephen were upset by him. Darwin added scientific weight to doubts which were already felt by many.

Darwin's ideas were already in the air before he published the *Origin*; not

[3] *Ibid*, p. xli.

[4] For a discussion of changes in the nature of scientific thought before Darwin, see Gillispie, C. C. *Genesis and Geology*. Harvard, 1951.

merely the scientific air, but the entire intellectual climate of England. The theory of evolution was not incompatible with the great ideas about progress and the march of mind. Thoughtful Victorians believed that the human race was insensibly improving, with education as its great instrument. They thought that the progress of the race was shown, not only in its material welfare, but in its moral development. Britain, over a period of sixty years, seemed to have achieved standards of humanity and justice which were unequalled in the world, and which were now being conferred on the backward peoples of the Empire. Under British law there was no discrimination of persons (except for women); political reform was approaching once again; and only atheists were debarred from sitting in the House of Commons, after the emancipation of the Jews in 1858. Charity and compassion were accepted as the two essential principles of social and private virtue. Yet a section of educated Victorians, holding strongly to the moral standards of their day, found that, according to these moral standards, the Scriptures had become unacceptable.

This educated group was in a minority, but it was vocal and included many gifted people. Their arguments turned on the accuracy of the Scriptures and their sufficiency as a moral guide in the nineteenth century. Scientists, even before Darwin, were casting doubts on the literal truth of the Old Testament, and their conclusions were being reinforced, mainly by German scholars, in the fields of history and philology. These sophisticated ideas were not likely to go far beyond an educated élite in England, but the arguments of the moralists were more pervasive. J. A. Froude, F. W. Newman, A. H. Clough, George Eliot and others rejected orthodox Christianity because they found in the Scriptures ideas which were not compatible with an advanced nineteenth-century view of moral justice.[5] The God of the Old Testament was often arbitrary and unjust; He condoned slaughter and sacrifice; the Church taught that He condemned sinners to everlasting torments and that only the blood of the innocent Christ had mollified His wrath at the fall of man. Once these moral doubts had been experienced, it was easy to accept continental writings which taught that the Bible was a profane compilation like the sacred books of any other religion. George Eliot adopted the view that a stern sense of moral duty was higher than a mere unthinking acceptance of orthodox dogma. The philosophical school of Mill was also opposed to the Church. Froude and Clough, in particular, seemed to speak for a generation of young men who had experienced agonising religious doubts while at the university. Their numbers could not be estimated, but they were vocal enough to give the impression of being numerous and so aroused great fears within the Church. Frederic Harrison,

[5] For a fuller discussion of intellectual doubt see Willey, B. *Nineteenth Century Studies*. Penguin, 1964, and *More Nineteenth Century Studies*. Chatto & Windus, 1956.

the positivist, said with some satisfaction in 1861 that the universities were 'honeycombed with disbelief, running through every phase from mystical interpretation to utter atheism'.[6] Clough was not a popular poet, but his work expressed the uncertainty of some of his contemporaries.

> Eat, drink and die, for we are souls bereaved,
> Of all the creatures under this broad sky
> We are most hopeless, that had hoped most high,
> And most beliefless, that had most believed.
>
> (*Easter Day* 1849)

Parallel to the religious doubts expressed in intellectual circles was the militant unbelief of the secularist groups, who attributed social injustice to Christianity and tried to spread this belief among the working classes. Some of the former Chartists, especially Henry Hetherington, expressed social discontent in terms of atheism and maintained that the churches fostered class distinctions. G. J. Holyoake (1817–1906), also a former Chartist, began the London Secular Society in the early 1850s, and the secularists became even more notorious later in the century under the leadership of Charles Bradlaugh (1833–91). He organised the National Secular Society in 1866, and the secularists also ran a number of small and violent periodicals, notably Bradlaugh's *National Reformer*.[7]

Many churchmen came to believe that their first task was to defend the doctrines of their Church from the attacks of rationalists, and they began to look for an authority which should be strong enough to repulse all assaults. By the 1860s this search for authority in the Church had become a major preoccupation, and it was intensified because of fear, not only of rationalism, but of dissent. While the rationalists tried to undermine the Church's doctrine, the dissenters aimed at its temporal privileges. After gaining a voice in the administration of the country, the dissenters, especially the Congregationalists, became increasingly militant. They demanded that education should not be left entirely to the Church, they wanted university degrees, the right to perform legal marriage ceremonies, the use of churchyards for burials, and, in particular, exemption from paying rates in support of the established Church. The most active agitation began in 1844, when Edward Miall (1809–81), a Congregationalist minister and editor of the influential journal the *Nonconformist*, started the British Anti-State Church Association, which changed its name in 1853 to the Society for the Liberation of Religion from State Patronage and Control, more commonly

[6] Harrison, F. 'Neo Christianity', *Westminster Review*, No. 18, 1860, p. 331.

[7] See Sylvester Smith, W. *The London Heretics*. Constable, 1967, Ch. 2.

known as the Liberation Society. Miall himself became MP for Rochdale in 1851, and the Liberation Society, through publications, lecture tours, and petitions to Parliament, became the nucleus of discontent among dissenters.

Educated doubt and militant dissent were more vociferous than the indifferent masses, and the Church turned to face them. Orthodox church-men looked for more authority within the Church; less orthodox churchmen denied that such authority was necessary and adopted a policy of com-promise towards those who attacked the Church. These incompatible aims split the Church into warring parties, in an atmosphere of bitter and personal controversy. Militant dissent was partly a State problem and was resolved in spite of the Church, but doubt was the Church's responsibility.

Recent authors have seen this period as one of religious uncertainty, in which those who had abandoned orthodox religion were more confident of their position than those who tried to save it.[8] Yet it seems that the tragedy of the Church at this time was not its doubts but its certainties. Each group was utterly convinced of the truth of its position and was not prepared to admit differing viewpoints. Perhaps men like John Henry Newman had turned to the Church of Rome in an attempt to stifle all uncertainty, but those who remained were unshaken in their beliefs. The leaders of the three great divisions of High, Low and Broad Church showed no chinks in their armour; and whatever their differences of opinion, all rested on a dogmatic sense of certainty. Few showed tolerance. Tait reflected to himself: 'The great evil is — that the liberals are deficient in religion and the religious are deficient in liberality.'[9] Nor was Tait himself free from intolerance.

Church divisions were accentuated because they were always carried on under the public eye. The newspapers were willing to give plenty of atten-tion to ecclesiastical rifts and doctrinal problems, and helped to awaken the interest of the reading public in difficult points of theology, not always intelligently. As an article in the *Spectator* stated:

> Of all tastes common among the middle class, the taste for discuss-ing half-understood theology is perhaps the most pronounced. Every word of the arguments in the Gorham case, every quotation cited, every explanation offered, were perused by men usually content with police reports and the Debate....[10]

Even the remotest country clergyman was unable to remain unaware of controversies in Oxford or London; the newspapers and popular periodicals

---

[8] Cockshut, A. O. J. *Anglican Attitudes.* Collins, 1959, pp. 20–4.

[9] Lambeth, Tait MSS 75f, 154. Reflections at Llanfairfechan, 12 Sept. 1863.

[10] *Spectator*, 25 May 1861, p. 555.

brought him into contact with the thoughts of others, and he too was prompted to indulge in controversy. The privately-printed pamphlet was a recognised way for a clergyman to express his opinions, as may be seen by the innumerable examples of this type of literature which survive.

Church parties had always existed of course, but during the eighteenth century their hostility had been more political than doctrinal. The Church was stirred from its apathy towards the condition of the industrial towns by the advent of Methodism, and in the early years of the nineteenth century its spiritual life awakened and it involved itself more wholeheartedly in social action. This was the period of anti-slavery campaigns, societies for popular education and evangelisation, Sunday schools and missionary effort overseas. High and Low Churches had their differences, but these were not really in dispute until a great wedge was driven between them by the Oxford Movement and the publication of *Tract XC*. The Oxford Movement itself may be seen as a search for authority by men who feared the encroachments of rationalism, and who looked back to the days of a powerful and authoritarian medieval church, with final power to pronounce on all matters of doctrine. The Tractarian view of Church authority and the power of the priestly hierarchy gave comfort and hope to many, but to a large section of the Church it was 'popish' and untenable. Rifts appeared in the Church societies. The National Society split between High Churchmen and Evangelicals, and the latter left in 1851 to form a separate Church Education Society. The Church Pastoral Aid Society, begun in 1836 to provide more curates and lay workers, also split, and High Churchmen formed another group, the Additional Curates Society. Party differences were thus allowed to interfere with the essential work of the Church.

Yet both High and Low Churchmen were seeking for authority: the High Church within the Church itself, the Low Church in the sole authority of the Scriptures. The Broad Church brought further disruption by claiming that the only authority lay in private judgment and in the individual conscience, which could alone interpret the Scriptures. They hoped to bring peace by encouraging latitude of opinion, but succeeded only in stirring up more strife, for the orthodox of all parties could not conceive of a faith without complete certainty. In the course of the debate some Broad Churchmen became embittered and as dogmatic as their opponents, as will be seen in the case of Rowland Williams. The ecclesiastical courts were used as battlegrounds for party conflicts. The teaching of the Church of England, as set forth in the Articles and Prayer-Book, was difficult to interpret, but in the mid-nineteenth century the final power of interpretation was left to a court which many churchmen could not accept. In 1832 the power to judge ecclesiastical appeals was handed over from the unwieldy, slow and expensive Court of Delegates to the Judicial Committee of the Privy Council. Although this court included any bishops who happened to be members of the Privy Council, it also included laymen, and there was no provision that any member should be learned in ecclesiastical law.[11] Many churchmen were not satisfied with such a court, and believed that the Church itself should have sole right to judge matters of doctrine.

Between 1845 and 1865 the ecclesiastical courts were busy with doctrinal cases, and their decisions kept the Church in a continual state of anger and anxiety. During the 1870s the litigation continued with prosecution of ritualists. The two greatest commotions before 1860 were caused by State action in Church affairs. The first was Lord John Russell's appointment of Renn Dickson Hampden to the see of Hereford in 1847 in the teeth of opposition from many churchmen, for Hampden was suspected of unorthodox opinions. This was followed by a further shock in 1850 when the Judicial Committee accepted that the Calvinistic ideas of baptism taught by the Rev George Cornelius Gorham were not contrary to the doctrines of the Church, although Henry Phillpotts, Bishop of Exeter, and a majority of High Churchmen thought they were.[12] Both cases were attended by much publicity.

Apart from these there were several other scandals: ritualists were prosecuted, Pusey was suspended from preaching for two years, and anti-ritual riots occurred in London at St Barnabas's in Pimlico and St George's-in-the-East. In 1860 Lord Ebury (1801–93), a Liberal peer who was most interested in Church reform, informed the House of Lords indignantly that there had been at least sixteen expensive ecclesiastical cases in the previous eighteen years. 'It has been conjectured,' he said, 'that the total amount of money spent in these unseemly contentions would be sufficient, as far as money can do so, to provide the means of coping with all the spiritual destitution of the Metropolis.'[13]

In the 1860s matters reached a climax. In 1860 six clergymen and a layman published *Essays and Reviews*, which was an open statement of Broad Church opinions. The only two beneficed clergy of the group, Rowland Williams (1817–70) and Henry Bristow Wilson (1803–88), were tried for heresy, suspended from their livings for a year by the Court of Arches, and then had the sentence reversed on appeal to the Judicial Committee in 1864. The notoriety which this long case attracted was increased by the similar case of John William Colenso (1814–83), Bishop of Natal, who had questioned the literal accuracy of the Old Testament. Colenso was tried

[11] Kemp, E. W. *An Introduction to Canon Law in the Church of England*. Hodder & Stoughton, 1957, p. 74.

[12] For Hampden and Gorham see Chadwick, P. *The Victorian Church*. A. & C. Black, 1966, pp. 237ff., 250ff.

[13] *Hansard*, 1860, Vol. clviii, p. 846.

and deprived by the Bishop of Capetown in 1863, only to be acquitted by the Judicial Committee in 1865. As Colenso's 'heresies' and the results of his trial almost duplicated those of the essayists, they will not be discussed here except for occasional comparison, because there were other most complicated factors involving the legal relationship between the Church in England and in the colonies.[14] It must be remembered, however, that the closeness of these two trials helped to keep Church tempers inflamed for most of the decade. During the 1860s it was difficult for any clergyman to keep clear of party disputes, and a slight detail in his dress or his services might stamp him as a party man in the eyes of partisans, however mild his personal ideas. Even a bishop as moderate as Lonsdale of Lichfield could not escape calumny; when he attempted to found a theological college and to encourage the training of nurses for purely practical reasons, he was accused of supporting Jesuit seminaries and popish sisterhoods. Churchmen tended to see their differences in black and white; only the Broad Church maintained that shades of grey existed.

Although clergymen might lean towards one party or another, there were, of course, infinite gradations of opinion, while the extremists tended to be the most clamorous. As party groupings were so important to the Church at this time it will be necessary to consider them in some detail, and to mention the men who led them.

The Evangelicals, as the Low Churchmen were now called, had undergone great changes since the end of the eighteenth century. Traditionally they were men who put the teaching of the Scriptures before the organisation of the Church, and who insisted on the Protestant value of personal devotion rather than priestly mediation. In the eighteenth century a general reaction against 'enthusiasm' and fanaticism of any kind caused them to decline into a somewhat soporific state, and towards the end of the century the term Low Church denoted little more than a connection with political Whiggery against the combination of High Churchmanship and the power of the Crown. During this period, however, there was a revival of religious fervour among some Evangelicals which ran concurrent with, but independent of the Wesleyan movement.[15] The Evangelicals were accused of putting a somewhat narrow piety before learning, but allied themselves with many worthy social causes, notably the abolition of slavery, and worked to bring religion to the industrial cities and the mission fields.

By 1860 the Evangelicals were at the height of their influence in government and society, and were on the whole contented with the existing

[14] For a full discussion see Hinchliff, P. *John William Colenso*. Nelson, 1964.

[15] Walsh, J. D. 'The Origins of the Evangelical Revival', *Essays in Modern Church History in Memory of Norman Sykes*. Black, 1966.

relationship between Church and State. The Judicial Committee supported the evangelical Gorham, so before 1860 the Church's legal machinery did not disturb them as much as it did the High Church. They were no longer considered vulgar enthusiasts, were favoured by the Queen and Prince Albert, and received aristocratic support from Lord Shaftesbury, who had considerable influence with Palmerston in Church appointments. They preferred pastoral work to politics and were generally apathetic towards any Church organisation which was not for spreading the Gospel and aiding its ministers. Hence they were active in the mission societies but were not particularly interested in the revival of Convocation, diocesan synods or gatherings of bishops; indeed, as these things were favoured by the High Church, they usually distrusted them. Only in the 1860s, when their ideas seemed threatened by both ritualism and rationalism, did they start forming party organisations.

The political quietism of the Evangelicals appealed to ministers like Palmerston, who did not want any alteration in the relations between Church and State, so by 1860 there were sixteen bishops out of the twenty-seven who had fairly evangelical inclinations,[16] and this position was not altered much until Gladstone came to power. In spite of their old reputation for lack of learning, the Evangelicals had several weighty scholars amongst them, though none on the bench except Ellicott of Gloucester, who helped to produce a revised version of the Bible. His main defence against unbelief of any kind was that many passages of the Bible had been mis-translated in the Authorised Version, which had led to misconceptions. There were also William Goode, Dean of Ripon, who refuted ritualism with solid erudition, and Alexander M'Caul, Professor of Hebrew and Divinity at King's College, London, who defended Genesis from Darwin and *Essays and Reviews*. Of a lesser order, but still of some weight, was Edward Garbett (1817–87), who was at various times editor of the two major Evangelical newspapers, the *Record* and the *Christian Advocate*. He delivered the Boyle lectures in 1861, devoted to refuting *Essays and Reviews*. But on the whole the Evangelicals could produce few men who could pretend to deal with edu-cated critics on their own ground.

Evangelical publications, especially the *Record*, were often mere unin-formed vituperation, and none were as erudite as the High Church *Christian Remembrancer*. The Evangelical ideal was found less in learning than in the piety of families like the Bickersteths, who in two generations produced a famous Evangelical leader, two bishops and an archdeacon, all men of

---

[16] These were: the Sumner brothers, Baring, Bickersteth, Campbell, Davys, Graham, Hamp-den (who became an orthodox Low Church bishop), Jackson, Lee, Ollivant, Pelham, Phill-pott, Turton, Villiers and Wigram.

exemplary life but not writers or scholars. As individuals the Evangelicals undoubtedly did much good work, but as a party they were frequently narrow-minded and short-sighted. Because they depended on the Scriptures they tended to class all Bible critics together, whatever their motives, as enemies of religion and, in the cases of diocesan synods and theological colleges, they opposed a great deal of much-needed organisation in the Church through suspicion of the ritualists.

The High Church was equally insistent on the authority of Bible and Prayer Book, but relied on the authority of the Church to interpret them. The High Church had also undergone a revival of religious life earlier in the century, and escaped from the indignity of the term 'high and dry'. A group of High Churchmen, nicknamed the 'Clapton Sect', had set an example of charity and personal piety to the High Church, but a much greater revolution had come in the 1830s with the Oxford Movement. Newman attracted not only members of the High Church, but erstwhile Evangelicals who, like the future Bishop of Salisbury, Walter Hamilton, did not find Newman's insistence on personal devotion and austerity incompatible with their own beliefs, and accepted with this his ideas on Church authority. Both the old High Church and the Tractarians emphasised the authority of the Church, but whereas the old High Church tended to look no further back than the English Reformation, the Tractarians revived interest in the medieval Church. Both were more interested in Church organisation than the Evangelicals, who were more concerned with societies for practical social ends.

After some of the original Tractarians had left the Church of England for Rome, their ideas continued among a generation of young men whom they had influenced, and these were more easily identified as a 'ritualist' party because of their concern for more elaborate services and church ornaments. Such practices were of doubtful legality at the time. Old-fashioned High Churchmen did not suffer these innovations gladly, and both Archbishop Longley and Bishop Gilbert of Chester, who were High Churchmen of the old school, engaged in prosecutions against them. On the other hand there were peaceable High Church bishops like Jacobson of Chester who would not countenance ritual prosecutions though he disapproved strongly of ritualism. Perhaps the most famous of these old High Church bishops was Phillpotts of Exeter, a relic of a period which had not considered political and ambitious bishops unusual, though by 1860 his days of controversy were ended by the feebleness of age. The High Church had in the past produced many learned bishops, such as William Warburton of Gloucester, but by the 1860s, when learned bishops were less esteemed than practical ones, the bench had no great reputation for scholarship. High Church bishops like Jacobson and Browne of Ely tended to be more scholarly than the Evangelicals on the bench, but their duties gave them little time for study, as Browne's biographer remarked regretfully: 'the pen ever drops into the second place when the crosier comes into use'.[17]

In the universities also the old High Church still had its adherents. At Oxford there was Edward Hawkins (1789–1882), Provost of Oriel for forty-six years until his retirement in 1874. It was Hawkins's misfortune to have supremacy in the college over those who later became more famous than himself, and as he opposed all university reform he appears as a stiff, dry reactionary. He was a churchman on the eighteenth-century model, who disliked religious enthusiasm of any kind and therefore he quarrelled with Newman, Hurrell Froude and R. I. Wilberforce, who were the Fellows of Oriel. Hawkins was equally suspicious of ritualism and rationalism, but the long sermon and pamphlet warfare he waged against theological opponents did not lead him into personal rancour. With Newman and Keble he was on respectful terms, and he treated the doubts of the young Clough gently. Newman himself admitted that he owed a debt to Hawkins's meticulous criticism of details.[18] In personal life, too, Hawkins was representative of the Old High Churchmen of his day; in his youth he and his friends at Oriel had occasioned some surprise by breaking with the eighteenth-century boisterousness of college life. For him the Church was no longer a place for drinking and hunting parsons. This attitude, however, did not lead to rigid puritanism, and he was later reported to find the severe asceticism of the younger Oriel Fellows rather dull.

One of Hawkins's best-known pupils and admirers, who carried on his theological battles, was J. W. Burgon (1813–88), who became vicar of the university church of St Mary the Virgin in 1863. Burgon was as reactionary as Hawkins, though with more humour, and died as Dean of Chichester after publishing two volumes of laudatory biographies of men with similar views to his own; the tombstones, as it were, of the old High Church party.

In the eighteenth century the High Church had been the foremost 'Church and State' party, but their attitude gradually changed during the nineteenth century. After the Hampden affair and the Gorham case they grew steadily more suspicious of State interference in ecclesiastical affairs and realised that the State no longer reflected the interests of the Church now that other religious groups were represented in Parliament. Yet the High Churchmen did not want disestablishment, though some of them began to see it in the distance as the only hope of preserving the Church from secular interference. Instead, they tried to find a compromise in Convocation, diocesan synods and episcopal authority, because these things

[17] Kitchin, G. W. *Edward Harold Browne.* 1895, p. 243.

[18] Newman, J. H. *Apologia pro Vita Sua.* First published 1864; 3rd Fontana ed. 1965, p. 101. See also Burgon, J. W. *Lives of Twelve Good Men.* 1888, Vol. 1, Ch. 4.

might give the Church an independent voice to preserve the balance of power with the State. While they tried to develop these independent groups, they also defended the Church's temporal privileges to the last, and tried to save Church rates and the Irish Church for as long as possible. Their views were represented mainly in the *Guardian.*

The ritualists, attacked by High and Low parties, had little love for the Church as an establishment. They were in constant fear of specific legislation against their practices; a fear which was realised in the Public Worship Regulation Act of 1874. They looked back to a Church unhampered by State interference, and wished ecclesiastical law to be free of State control. The Judicial Committee was their special aversion, and its decisions on Gorham, *Essays and Reviews* and Colenso brought home to them forcefully that separation from the State might be necessary, even if it meant disendowment. Gladstone sympathised with their views, and he and his friend Hamilton, the first bishop with Tractarian tendencies, thought that disestablishment might become inevitable if the Church's integrity were to be preserved.[19] The great hostility which they aroused caused many ritualists to regard themselves as persecuted upholders of the unadulterated faith of the Church against Erastianism, and they did not believe that ideals should be compromised in order to conciliate public opinion, as an article in one of their periodicals, the *Literary Churchman*, reveals:

> What if an impetuous Member of Parliament lay the axe to the root of our continuance as a national establishment? That does not affect our vitality as a Church. What if our revenues are assailed? Nothing can deprive us of the Apostolic Succession, which is the key-stone of our ecclesiastical system, and worth more to us than the favour of princes, the suffrages of Parliament, and the impertinent patronage of the daily Press.[20]

The ritualists encouraged works of learning, especially with a view to proving the historical validity of their own ideas; Lathbury's *History of Convocation* (1842) is a fundamental example. By 1860, in spite of popular hostility after the revival of Roman Catholic sees in England, the ritualists were gaining ground. Their ideas were expressed in the *Christian Remembrancer*, a quarterly review which had begun in 1819 during the days of the Clapton Sect, and had later come under Tractarian influence. Many of its articles were of a high scholarly standard and appealed to many thoughtful churchmen, though it came to an end in 1868. Its passing was a victory,

---

[19] Addit. MSS 44, 183. (Gladstone Papers) f. 369. Hamilton to Gladstone, 25 Aug. 1868.

[20] *Literary Churchman*, 16 June 1860, p. 221.

Mark Pattison thought, for the more unenlightened section of ritualist opinion, which preferred the less erudite *Literary Churchman*.[21] There was also the monthly *Ecclesiastic* which ran from 1846 to 1868; a much less intelligent review of Church affairs and current literature which poured unreasoning contempt on both the 'puritan' (Evangelical) and 'rationalist' (Broad Church) sections of the clergy.

The ritualist party was more truly a 'party' in that a sense of persecution and self-justification gave it more solidarity than most other churchmen felt. It also had its honoured leaders. In 1860 Pusey and Keble were the venerated remnants of the original Tractarians: the former still an active controversialist though sixty years of age; the latter in seclusion at Hursley, but emerging occasionally to lend the prestige of his name to gatherings of the ritualists. Also in Oxford was Henry Parry Liddon, Pusey's admirer and later his biographer, who was Vice-Principal of St Edmund Hall from 1859 to 1864 after having been forced to resign his post at Cuddesdon College because of his views. He later received promotion through the offices of Hamilton and Gladstone, and was finally appointed to a canonry in St Paul's. Like Newman, he had a great influence over young men at Oxford.

Of widespread controversial fame was George Anthony Denison (1805–96), Archdeacon of Taunton, who was the most outspoken of the ritualists and their leader in the Lower House of the Convocation of Canterbury. Denison became something of a hero to ritualists after a long series of legal actions between 1854 and 1858, in which he defended the ritualist view of the Eucharist.* Though Denison had brought the suit on himself by his inflexible attitude and determination to vindicate his ideas legally, the series of trials from the Archbishop of Canterbury's diocesan court to the Court of Arches to the Judicial Committee, from which he at last escaped through a legal loophole, made him very popular among fellow-ritualists. He championed their views as often and as loudly as possible, in his charges, in pamphlets and in Convocation. He thought that the ritualists were the only true defenders of religion in England, and prophesied doom for Christianity if education ever fell into secular hands.[22] He directed a great deal of energy against the Broad Church, and he continually asserted

---

[21] Pattison, M. 'Learning in the Church of England', *Essays*, ed H. Nettleship. Oxford, 1889, Vol. 2, p. 278.

*Chadwick, *Victorian Church*, p. 491 ff. The ritualists asserted that the Eucharist contained an inward reality (real presence) which was received by all who partook of it, whatever their state of mind. To the orthodox, this sounded the same as the Romish doctrine of transubstantiation.

[22] Denison, G. A. *Notes of My Life*. Oxford, 1878, p. 134ff.

the Church's right to judge and excommunicate those who did not preach the literal accuracy of the Bible. It is easy to see him as his opponents among the liberal clergy did, as an inquisitor or witch-hunter, but he was always consistent and courageous in his views, a capable organiser, an emphatic and witty speaker, who commanded the attention of Convocation.

The stresses of the mid-century tended to throw party differences into sharper relief as men tried to define the boundaries of their beliefs. But within the Church parties there were many variations of opinion, and three of the most influential clergymen of the time fitted into no group, though they might receive support from a particular section of the clergy. The first, Connop Thirlwall, was Bishop of St David's from 1840 to 1875, and was an isolated figure, the only bishop of that period to conform to the eighteenth-century idea of a scholarly bishop. He did not care to parade his theological opinions, but politically he was a Liberal, and commanded the respect of liberal clergy.

The second, Samuel Wilberforce, Bishop of Oxford from 1845 to 1869 and then Bishop of Winchester, was Thirlwall's antithesis in that his life was devoted to diocesan organisation and Church leadership. Posterity has acclaimed the first object above the second, but in the 1860s he was the best known of all the defenders of orthodoxy. He began life in a famous Evangelical family, but his views changed later, and his contemporaries thought of him as a High Churchman or even a ritualist. In reality he belonged to no one group, although his sympathy with and refusal to prosecute ritualists caused him to be suspected by Evangelicals. But he had many of the qualities of the Evangelicals in his love of popular speeches and extempore preaching.[23] The High Church bishops followed him willingly. Nor did he really accept ritualist ideas, except in a very mild way, but because he was less a thinker than a man of action it is impossible to sift a coherent system of theology from his writings, except a conservative love for the Bible and Prayer Book and an intense feeling of personal devotion.

The third bishop, Archibald Campbell Tait, who was Bishop of London from 1856 to 1868 and then Archbishop of Canterbury, had been a Fellow of Balliol and a great headmaster of Rugby. His life, like that of Wilberforce, was devoted to practical rather than intellectual works. He and Wilberforce were the two most active parliamentary bishops, though they usually voted on opposite sides in Church affairs, and also in Convocation. Tait might have been classed with the Evangelicals because of his nonconformist Scottish background and his hatred of ritualism, but it was not so much the ornate services of the ritualists he disliked as the tendency many

---

[23] For full studies see Ashwell, A. R. and Wilberforce, R. G. *Life of Samuel Wilberforce*. 1880–2 and Newsome, D. *The Parting of Friends*. John Murray, 1966.

of them showed to try and set up a Church system with rigid doctrines, with all critics excluded.[24] Tait's ideal was comprehensiveness, and the narrow Biblical beliefs of the Evangelicals were as alien to him as the exclusive church practices of the ritualists. He wished the Church to remain the established Church so that it might be saved from narrowness of life and dogma, and he thought this could be achieved only by tolerance, compromise and greater administrative efficiency. For this reason he was not hostile, as Wilberforce was, to any clerics who ventured to criticise the Church's teachings; indeed he knew many of the critics personally, and in the 1860s he was under considerable strain as the claims of friendship conflicted with the pressure put upon him to condemn *Essays and Reviews*, which he himself thought had gone too far. His main weakness was his intolerance towards ritualism, and he was instrumental in the passing of the Public Worship Regulation Act. He was also one of the few bishops to approve of the Judicial Committee of the Privy Council as an ecclesiastical court, because he thought it saved the law of the Church from falling into the hands of any one Church faction, whereas Wilberforce desired a purely clerical court which would have the power to judge all matters of doctrine.

The group which aroused the fear and wrath of all orthodox clergy of many shades of opinion was commonly known as the Broad Church. This term is misleading, because it suggests an organised party, and because it also implies a group falling somewhere between High and Low. The Broad Church was not a party, but a set of individuals, many of whom disagreed with each other except in the idea that the authority of the Bible and the Church might be subjected to historical and scientific criticism. They also considered that certain parts of the Scriptures were not useful as a moral guide, but that the spirit of Christianity, and of the Church of England, was strong enough to withstand any such criticism, for only false or antiquated ideas would be in danger. The Broad Church was not a faction but a restless and critical attitude of mind, and Broad Churchmen were drawn together more by the hostility they provoked than by their common ideas. They became the focal point of heated arguments about how much liberty of opinion should be allowed to clergymen who had affirmed at their ordination that they believed wholeheartedly in all the doctrines contained in the Articles and Prayer Book. Lay critics who sympathised with the Broad Church, like Goldwin Smith, the Regius Professor of Modern History at Oxford, had no such pressure on them, and did not arouse quite the same fury as the clerical Broad Churchmen.

'Liberal Anglicanism' has also been used as a synonym for Broad

---

[24] For a full survey of Tait and ritualism see Marsh, P. T. *The Victorian Church in Decline.* Routledge, 1969, especially Ch. 7.

Church,[25] and describes more adequately their attitudes towards theology, but it does not mean that these men were necessarily political Liberals, or even particularly advanced in their views of society, for this was not always the case. As 'Broad Church' was the term which was used at the time,[26] it will be used here. Even though the Broad Churchmen did not think of themselves as members of a party, their contemporaries did, especially after the publication of *Essays and Reviews*, which seemed to show that the Broad Churchmen were gathering to overthrow orthodox religion.

The Broad Churchmen can be seen to fall roughly into two generations, of intellectual activity rather than of age, and the first had finished its work by 1855 when the work of the second was just beginning. The clerical members of the first generation included Thomas Arnold (1795–1842), Julius Charles Hare, Archdeacon of Lewes (1798–1855), and his brother Augustus William; Connop Thirlwall (1797–1875), Frederick Denison Maurice (1805–72), Richard Whately, Archbishop of Dublin (1787–1863), and Baden Powell (1796–1860). Charles Kingsley also had affinities with this group, though he was famous chiefly as a novelist and practical worker. Hampden was classed as a Broad Churchman because his Bampton Lectures of 1834 had expressed the opinion that many Scriptural ideas had been obscured by centuries of dogma, but he had little connection with the mainstream of Broad Church thought. His ideas were derived more from eighteenth-century English traditions than from the new philosophy of Germany, which was the major influence on the Broad Church. Hampden contributed nothing to the theology of his time and specifically rejected the Broad Church in the 1860s.[27] It should be noted, however, that several of the Broad Churchmen of the older generation who survived into the 1860s reacted like Hampden and disowned their successors. Whately and Thirlwall, who had also reached episcopal dignity, strongly rejected *Essays and Reviews*.

The second generation, whose work might be said to reach fruition in 1855 with the publication of Benjamin Jowett's commentaries of St Paul and Rowland Williams's *Rational Godliness*, reached the peak of its notoriety in the 1860s. It included the clerical authors of *Essays and Reviews*, who were Jowett (1817–93), Williams (1817–70), Frederick Temple (1821–1902), Mark Pattison (1813–84), and Henry Bristow Wilson (1803–88). (The two remaining essayists were Baden Powell, who died in the year the book was published, and a layman, C. W. Goodwin.) *Essays and Reviews* stirred up

[25] Notably by Forbes, D. *The Liberal Anglican Idea of History*. Cambridge University Press, 1952.

[26] For the origins of this term see Sanders, C. R. *Coleridge and the Broad Church Movement*. North Carolina, 1942, pp. 8–9.

[27] Chadwick, O. *The Victorian Church*. Black, 1966, p. 116.

much controversy, less because of the originality of its ideas than because six of its authors were clergymen, some well-known. It sold 15,000 copies in three months and 22,250 in a decade.[28]

Other Broad Churchmen of repute included Arthur Penrhyn Stanley (1815–81), the most devoted of Thomas Arnold's pupils, who became Dean of Westminster in 1863. Henry Hart Milman (1791–1868), Dean of St Paul's, was also generally considered a Broad Churchman, though his views were not as advanced as Stanley's. Stanley, who possessed rather more personal charm than most of the Broad Churchmen, achieved notoriety mainly through his claim that subscription to the Articles and Prayer Book was damaging to the intellectual level of the clergy because it repelled thoughtful men from the ministry. Milman and Stanley both published histories of the Jews which treated the Old Testament as the history of Bedouin tribes and minimised the miraculous elements. Milman also shared Stanley's views on subscription, but took little part in active controversy.

Several of the leading Broad Churchmen formed a tightly-knit circle, strengthened by some common ideas and by affinities of friendship and relationship. This encouraged the impression that they were a 'party'. Julius Hare and his brother had been friends with Thirlwall when they were all at Cambridge. Julius Hare became the tutor of F. D. Maurice at Cambridge, and he and Maurice subsequently married each others' sisters. Augustus Hare was connected by marriage with the Stanleys. A. P. Stanley was taught at school by Arnold and at Balliol by Tait; he was a close friend of Julius Hare, and also of Jowett and Temple, who had been Tait's pupils as well. These links tended to soften differences of opinion; Stanley, for instance, made himself unpopular in orthodox circles by a discussion of *Essays and Reviews* in the *Edinburgh Review*, which defended the essayists' right to their opinions, even though he did not agree with all of them.[29] He was also more complimentary to the essays of Temple and Jowett than to those of the others, who were not his personal friends.

The essayists were aware that educated men were turning away from the Church, and wished to prevent this, even if in the process some of the Church's traditional teachings had to be discarded in order to preserve its most important truths. Nor did they believe that doubt could be confined to the educated only; they maintained that all churchmen had the right to interpret Scripture for themselves, nor need they accept everything which they found in it. The essayists thought that if educated people were forced to conform to a literalist belief in the Bible they would abandon religion

[28] Williams, E. *Life and Letters of Rowland Williams.* 1874, Vol. 2, p. 36n.

[29] Stanley, A. P. '*Essays and Reviews*', *Edinburgh Review*, No. 113, 1861, pp. 472, 497.

altogether. This would have repercussions at all levels of society, as Jowett wrote:

> I cannot help anticipating that increased freedom of opinion may lead to a real amendment of life. Hitherto, religion seems to have become more and more powerless among the educated classes. Do we not want a Gospel for the educated ... not because it is more blessed to preach to the educated than to the poor, but because the faith of the educated is permanent, and ultimately affects the faith of the poor?[30]

The Broad Churchmen all loved and venerated the Scriptures, but most of them were prepared to accept Jowett's maxim that they should be read and criticised 'like any other book'. They were supremely confident, however, that the value of the Bible, especially the New Testament, as a moral guide and spiritual revelation would arise unspotted from all objections that could be fairly levelled at it. Conservative clergymen frequently believed that every word in the Bible had been divinely inspired and that it therefore could contain no error, whereas the Broad Church accepted that the writers of the Bible, although their moral message was from God, were liable to human errors in matters of fact.

Orthodox churchmen, on the other hand, although they sometimes sympathised with doubters, were uncompromisingly hostile towards doubt. They considered that doubt was a kind of disease — 'a moral sickness', Wilberforce called it — which was self-induced because man, in the pride of his intellect, attempted to judge the revelation which God had given him. Wilberforce was particularly aware of doubt among young men because of his connection with Oxford University, and in 1861, while the *Essays and Reviews* controversy was gaining momentum, he preached two sermons on the subject in the university pulpit. These two sermons show him at the height of his oratorical powers; in long, rolling sentences he declared that no Christian ethic could stand without the strength of divine revelation behind it. He described vividly the process of doubt in the mind, arising from the belief that unaided human intellect could judge the truth of certain portions of the Scriptures, and finally resulting in a rejection of the whole. He attacked the intellectual pretensions of Biblical critics:

> It is but the smallest part of the mysteries of the eternal world which can be grasped by our feeble faculties.... Once let the mind, instead of receiving humbly, begin to doubt, and doubt will be every-

---

[30] Abbott, E. and Campbell, L. *Life and Letters of Benjamin Jowett*. 1897, Vol. 1, p. 362. See also *Essays and Reviews*, 12th ed. 1869, p. 452.

where. The struggles of such a soul in the uncertainty around it are like the plunging of the maddened herd into the boundless morass. Every effort engulfs in the quagmire more of the surrounding sward, and sinks the powerless victims in ruin.[31]

The climax of the second sermon was a highly-coloured description of the death of a doubter in agonies of despair at his own uncertainty, followed by a solemn warning to teachers who had been responsible for planting the seeds of criticism in a young man's mind. His advice to his hearers was to fling away doubt 'as if it were a loaded shell shot into the fortress of the soul'. The sermon drew forth a strong protest from Goldwin Smith, who objected that the suppression of doubt resulted in superstition and hypocrisy, 'The inevitable effect of your language', he wrote to Wilberforce, 'as it appears to me, will be to taint with the deepest suspicion every article of our belief, into which you would scare us from enquiry.'[32]

Edward Garbett also inveighed against doubt, and recognised that it sprang from historical, philosophical and scientific roots, all of which he denounced as shallow and conceited, but said that the clergy should try and understand these things in order to combat them.[33] Neither Garbett nor Wilberforce maintained that all critical inquiry into the Scriptures ought to be stopped, but they thought it should be undertaken only in a reverent frame of mind which would predispose men to make the right judgments. Tait also took up the question in his episcopal charge of 1862. He realised that many young men had difficulty in accepting the Bible as literal truth, and recommended that ministers deal gently with them, but he could find no better solution than Wilberforce; if all critical inquiry were undertaken reverently, then the inquirer would not stray far from the paths of orthodoxy. He did not think, however, that prosecutions for heresy would have any effect in deterring such inquiry. Tait's old pupils were disappointed at his attitude, especially after he joined the other bishops in condemning *Essays and Reviews*. He received an angry letter from Temple, who considered that Tait had led his pupils into the inquiries he now condemned.

> To tell a man to study, and yet bind him under heavy penalties to come to the same conclusion with those who have not studied it is to mock him. If the conclusions are prescribed, the study is precluded.[34]

The Broad Churchmen were not, of course, the first clergymen to doubt

---

[31] Wilberforce, S. *The Revelation of God the Probation of Man*. Oxford, 1861. Sermon 2, pp. 32–3.

[32] A Layman (G. Smith). *The Suppression of Doubt is not Faith*. Oxford, 1861, p. 2.

[33] Garbett, E. *The Bible and its Critics*. 1861, pp. 347–8.

[34] Tait MSS 80, f 37. Temple to Tait, 21 Feb. 1861.

the Biblical revelation. In the previous century there had been many latitudinarians within the Church who had considered that it was not always consistent with reason, and had looked for a revelation instead in the orderly workings of the universe and the inherent sense of propriety in the mind of man. In its extreme form, latitudinarianism led to deism, which bypassed the Scriptures altogether, and accepted the universe as a sufficient revelation in itself. Yet the deists, except perhaps Hume, did not doubt the existence of God or the necessity of religion. Deists tried to make religion conform to their idea of reason, but they had no way of attacking the Scriptures except to show up internal inconsistencies, or to maintain that miracles had no part in an ordered Newtonian universe. This led them to seek for natural explanations for miraculous events in the Bible, especially by discrediting the authority of the Evangelists or maintaining that the Apostles had manufactured 'miracles' for their own ends. One of the most notorious works of this kind was Conyers Middleton's *A Free Enquiry into the Miraculous Powers* (1747), which tried to show that the witnesses of the miracles in the primitive Church could not be trusted.[35]

By the mid-nineteenth century, however, the whole basis of Biblical criticism had altered, and the Broad Church based their criticism, not on 'reason', which tried to discredit the Evangelists, but on new historical and scientific evidence which threw doubt on the date and authorship of many of the Scriptures. It is noteworthy that this type of criticism was in full swing long before the *Origin of Species* added the testimony of natural science against the literal accuracy of the Old Testament. Nor do the Broad Churchmen seem to have been particularly influenced by Darwin; there is only one mention of his work in *Essays and Reviews*, where Powell, himself a scientist, used it to buttress one of his own points.[36] Orthodox clergy, however, misunderstood the basis of Broad Church criticism and considered that they were merely refurbishing the ideas of the deists. Wilberforce and Garbett thought they saw deism reincarnate in *Essays and Reviews*, and Bishop Jackson of Lincoln maintained: 'the defunct deism of the eighteenth century has lent its blunted arms to be furbished up anew by the rationalistic scepticism of the nineteenth'.[37] This was a too-convenient dismissal of Broad Church theories. It was generally accepted in the Church that eighteenth-century deism had been routed by the works of divines like William Butler and William Paley, and Butler's stately prose and Paley's

---

[35] Eighteenth-century ideas are developed fully in Cragg, G. R. *Reason and Authority in the Eighteenth Century*. Cambridge, 1964, Creed, J. M. and Boys Smith, J. S. *Religious Thought in the Eighteenth Century*. Cambridge, 1934; and Stromberg, R. N. *Religious Liberalism in Eighteenth Century England*. Oxford, 1954.

[36] *Essays and Reviews*, pp. 166–7.

[37] Jackson, J. *Charge, Lincoln*. 1861, p. 46.

ingenious explanations were still extremely popular. The orthodox therefore relied on these champions to save them once again, without realising that the whole argument had changed.

By 1860 Broad Churchmen believed with some justification that they were suffering from ecclesiastical persecution. The men of the older school had incurred hostility for views which were not even directly expressed. Thirlwall never wrote his own manifesto, but was suspected because he and Julius Hare had translated some German works. He was fortunate to receive a bishopric, which was presented to him mainly because Melbourne had some difficulty in finding Whigs who were of the right calibre for the bench. Thomas Arnold, later acclaimed by all parties as one of the foremost churchmen of the nineteenth century, and probably the most famous of English headmasters, never received a bishopric because of his enthusiastic ideas for a comprehensive Church which would include Dissenters. Arnold was much more notorious than Thirlwall, and so Melbourne cautiously refused to promote him, though he finally gave him the Regius chair of modern history at Oxford in 1841. Julius Hare remained an archdeacon, engaged in vindicating himself and his friends from orthodox attacks. In 1853 Maurice was forced to resign his divinity chair at King's College, London, because he doubted whether the torments of the wicked would be everlasting. He, like Arnold, won fame through his practical works and was respected for these in spite of his theological opinions.

The younger generation of Broad Churchmen believed themselves especially aggrieved by the weight of orthodox authority. Stanley had no chance of a bishopric because of his views, although he was an eminent candidate. Jowett's commentary on St Paul's Epistles included a passage which denied that God was a wrathful figure who was only appeased by the sufferings of the innocent Christ, and for this the Vice-Chancellor of Oxford requested him to sign the Thirty-Nine Articles once again; a great humiliation. Pusey and his followers blocked all proposals to annex a Christ Church canonry to the Regius chair of Greek, which had a miserable salary, because they did not wish to endow a chair whose holder might not be an orthodox churchman. Nor did Jowett realise his ambition to become Master of Balliol until 1870. Mark Pattison suffered similar setbacks, and became an embittered man after he lost the election to the Rectorship of Lincoln College in 1851. This was mainly due to intrigue and divided loyalties among the Fellows, but Pattison was always aware of religious hostility.[38] Williams and Wilson were arraigned in the Church courts, and Williams especially suffered from a sense of persecution. Temple managed to rise above earlier attacks when Gladstone made him Bishop of Exeter in 1869, but his consecration aroused anger in many High Church clergy. Edward Hamilton rejoiced that his

[38] Pattison. M. *Memoirs.* 1885, pp. 302, 314.

brother, the late Bishop of Salisbury, had not lived to see the day, and
Burgon, who had been an old friend of Temple, wrote to Wilberforce:

> To forgive personal iniquities, is, I hope, easy; but just as an
> Ambassador *could* not condone an offence offered to his Sovereign, so I
> feel that I have no alternative but to remain in an attitude of sus-
> pended hostility. Never shall Temple preach in my pulpit — nor will
> I ever call him my friend again — nor cease to regard him as a
> dishonorable man. That he is a dangerous one, I know full well —
> and you will all know, to your cost, ere long! (We were *very* intimate
> once.)[39]

Although it might seem from this description that Broad Church ideas
were confined to the more intellectual members of the clergy, some cases
which found their way into the ecclesiastical courts show that humble men
adopted them as well. German theology and the intellectual equipment
needed for personal research into the Scriptures were not available to all,
but a sense of the moral issues at stake was more common. Broad Church
ideas could prove costly to the careers of ordinary clergy without influence,
as the example of three parish clergy will show.

A case in point was the Rev John MacNaught, vicar of St Chrysostom's
in Liverpool. MacNaught was inspired by Coleridge and had some knowledge of German ideas. At meetings of the Liverpool Clerical Society, which
was a society of local clergymen formed for the purpose of studying the
Scriptures, MacNaught voiced his opinion that not all parts of the Bible
were divinely inspired. In 1856 his shocked fellow-members expelled him
from the society, and he offended the orthodox even further by publishing a
short book explaining his ideas. These were not very different from those
found in *Essays and Reviews*, though MacNaught was more sceptical of the
truth of miracles than most of the essayists. He experienced further hostility
from his fellow-clergy and his doubts increased. In 1860 he resigned his
living and went to London, where he thought of becoming a lawyer or a
Dissenting minister, though he longed to return to the Church of England.
He wrote another work to explain that miracles were not the most important evidences of Christianity, which rested on the truth of its moral system.
Finally, in 1867, he set up a proprietory chapel in Bath; a place of worship
on the fringes of the Anglican communion, which catered for the spiritual
needs of a shifting holiday population.[40]

In February 1860 the Court of Arches sat to try Dunbar Isidore Heath,

[39] Wilberforce MSS dep. c. 201. Burgon to Wilberforce, ii Feb.? 1870.

[40] MacNaught's ideas are set out in *Free Discussion versus Intolerance*. 1856; *the Doctrine of Inspiration*. 1856; and *Christianity and its Evidences*. 1863.

vicar of Brading on the Isle of Wight, who had been arraigned by his bishop, Sumner of Winchester, for unorthodox ideas. His opinions were largely based on Maurice's, and were concerned with various moral aspects of Christian teaching. In particular he urged that 'justification' meant that God would do justice to the whole human race, and he rejected the idea that Christ's death had 'propitiated' God's wrath against man. Heath had convinced himself, by ingenious verbal manoeuvring, that he was not contravening the Thirty-Nine Articles, but after several hearings in both the Court of Arches and the Judicial Committee he was deprived of his living. Heath was perhaps not a normal example, being certainly an eccentric man, who had also constructed a fantastic theory of the future life, but his eccentricity was no greater than that of numerous respectable Evangelical clergy who uttered equally incredible prophecies on the basis of the Book of Revelation.

Another humble Broad Churchman who became notorious was Charles Voysey (1828–1912), a parish priest who was influenced by *Essays and Reviews* but who had worked out his opinions before the book appeared. He was convicted of heresy in the Chancery Court of York in 1869, appealed to the Judicial Committee, but lost, and was deprived of his living. His case appeared to point out the dangers of the Broad Church position.

The publication of *Essays and Reviews* itself was in some measure an attack on what its authors believed to be a system of ecclesiastical terrorism. Jowett, whose experience over his commentaries still rankled, wrote to Stanley urging him to contribute to the volume: 'We do not wish to do anything rash or irritating to the public or the University, but we are determined not to submit to this abominable system of terrorism, which prevents the statement of the plainest facts, and makes true theology or theological opinions impossible'.[41] Stanley did not wish to disturb the ecclesiastical peace at the time, but Mark Pattison reflected moodily on the atmosphere of hostility surrounding any clergyman with unorthodox ideas. 'Every clergyman', he wrote in 1863, 'is compelled, on pain of professional ruin, to maintain a fair repute as "orthodox". His orthodoxy is his point of honour, and like a woman, to be suspected is to be lost.'[42]

This atmosphere caused the Broad Churchmen to look back into history for their vindication. While the ritualists deplored the Reformation as the rent in the Church's seamless coat, the Broad Churchmen hailed it as the triumph of private judgment and individual inquiry over organised ecclesiastical tyranny. Pattison, with his usual acuteness, realised that current debates about the nature of the Reformation had special relevance to his

[41] Abbott and Campbell. *Life and Letters of Benjamin Jowett.* Vol. 1, p. 275.

[42] Pattison, M. *Essays*, Vol. 2, p. 296.

own time.[43] By 1860 many Broad Churchmen thought that a second Reformation was in the air, and they its harbingers. Williams, during his trial, wished to be a martyr like Latimer and Ridley. Stanley, who was more modest, wrote to a friend in 1865:

> I agree with you that the prophet of the second Reformation has not yet appeared. Perhaps he never will. But that a second Reformation is in store for us, and that the various tendencies of the age are preparing the way for it, I cannot doubt, unless Christianity is doomed to suffer a portentous eclipse.[44]

Perhaps Stanley was more of a prophet than he thought.

[43] Pattison, M. 'Philosophy at Oxford', *Mind*, No. 1. 1876, p. 86.

[44] Prothero, R. E. and Bradley, G. *Life and Correspondence of Arthur Penrhyn Stanley*. 1893, Vol. 2, p. 239. See also Abbott and Campbell. Vol. 1, p. 160.

JOSEF L. ALTHOLZ

CHAPTER 2

THE MIND OF VICTORIAN ORTHODOXY: ANGLICAN RESPONSES TO 'ESSAYS AND REVIEWS', 1860–1864

T HE composite volume entitled *Essays and Reviews*, published in 1860, became the center of one of the major religious controversies of Victorian England — a crisis of faith contemporary with that provoked by Darwin's *Origin of Species* but more central to the religious mind.[1] *Essays and Reviews* was at once the culmination and the final act of the Broad Church movement. The volume itself was modest in its pretensions and varied in the character and quality of its seven essays. The first, by Frederick Temple, was a warmed-over sermon urging the free study of the Bible. Rowland Williams wrote a provocative essay on Bunsen, denying the predictive character of Old Testament prophecies. Baden Powell flatly denied the possibility of miracles. H. B. Wilson gave the widest possible latitude to subscription to the Thirty-nine Articles and questioned the eternity of damnation. C. W. Goodwin (the only layman among the Essayists) wrote a critique of the attempted 'harmonies' between Genesis and geology. Mark Pattison wrote a learned and cold historical study of the evidential theologians of the eighteenth century (perhaps the only essay of lasting value). The volume was capped by Benjamin Jowett's tremendous though wayward essay 'On the Interpretation of Scripture,' in which he urged that the Bible be read 'like any other book' and made an impassioned plea for freedom of scholarship.[2] Little of all this was original, though it was new to most Englishmen. It was not the cutting edge of biblical scholarship; rather, it was the last gasp of an outmoded Coleridgianism, contributing little except a demand that somebody — somebody *else* — engage in serious biblical criticism. But this work touched off a controversy which lasted four

---

[1] *The Origin of Species* was published 24 November 1859; *Essays and Reviews* in February 1860. The debates overlapped, and the reproach of Darwinism was often hurled against the Essayists, but incidentally and in a manner which indicated that biblical criticism and not evolution was the main concern.

[2] Benjamin Jowett, 'On the Interpretation of Scripture,' *Essays and Reviews* (London, 1860), pp. 338, 377.

years and mobilized the resources of both church and state. Outwardly, the conflict ended inconclusively, with the acquittal of Williams and Wilson by the courts and the condemnation of the volume by the clergy in Convocation. At a deeper level, it marked the exhaustion both of the Broad Church and of Anglican orthodoxy and the commencement of an era of religious doubt.

Historians have tended to study this controversy from the standpoint of the Essayists. Beginning with Basil Willey's stimulating but wrongheaded essay in 1956, we have been told how these liberal victims of persecution were ultimately vindicated by the progress of theology.[3] It might be more useful now for historians to pay some attention to the case of the other side, those who denounced *Essays and Reviews* from the standpoint of orthodoxy within the Church of England. They may well have been less attractive; they may even have been wrong; but they were certainly more numerous and more representative of the mind of the church. This essay, then, is an inquiry into the mind of Victorian orthodoxy.

It is, indeed, a mind that we are dealing with. The orthodox opponents of *Essays and Reviews* may seem obscurantist in their resistance to the higher criticism of the Bible; but an analysis of their writings reveals an ultimate reliance on a rigidly rational line of argument, resting on eighteenth-century evidential apologetics. An Anglican scholasticism (as we may call it) had produced a consistent rationalistic case for the acceptance of the Christian revelation. It was only after this rationalism had laid the intellectual foundations for belief that Anglican orthodoxy invoked the distinctively Victorian demand for certainty of faith. This position was shared by both major parties in the Church of England — Evangelicals and Anglo-Catholics — who transcended their differences in denouncing the Broad Church minority. They were, after all, the products of a common university education, old-fashioned but not unsophisticated; and their argumentation revealed the strength and the weakness of this intellectual heritage.

What is most striking about the approximately 140 replies to *Essays and Reviews* is the consistency of their fundamental line of argument.[4] To be sure, there were areas of disagreement. High Churchmen blamed the heresy of the Essayists on a reaction against the excesses of Evangelical Calvinism; low Churchmen blamed it on a reaction against the Romanizing tendencies

---

[3] Basil Willey, 'Septem contra Christum,' in *More Nineteenth-Century Studies: A Group of Honest Doubters* (London, 1956). See also M. A. Crowther, *Church Embattled: Religious Controversy in Mid-Victorian England* (Newton Abbot, 1970), and A. O. J. Cockshut, *Anglican Attitudes: A Study of Victorian Religious Controversies* (London, 1959).

[4] Nearly one hundred responses are listed under *Essays and Reviews* in the British Museum *General Catalogue of Printed Books*, and another thirty under the several Essayists. A further dozen or so were added at the Bodleian Library and Pusey House, Oxford.

of the Oxford Movement.[5] The High Church party stressed ecclesiastical authority; Evangelicals emphasized the Atonement as the 'central doctrine' of Christianity.[6] There was no agreement on which of the various 'harmonies' between Genesis and geology should be accepted, and some writers felt free to interpret Genesis 1 poetically.[7] There was no agreed-upon definition of the nature and limits of the inspiration of the Bible, nor was there a consensus as to whether it should be believed literally. Notwithstanding all this, however, there was a clear pattern to the replies. Indeed, they were so consistent, that it is possible to draw up a composite reply to the Essays, leaving only a few blanks to be filled in for the individual idiosyncrasies or party biases of the authors. What follows is a sketch of this composite reply.

The reply would begin with an *ad hominem* argument against the Essayists personally, criticizing them in their capacity as clergymen who retained their positions in the established church while attacking its doctrines. Their work never would have achieved such notoriety had they not been clergymen. The 'false position' of the Essayists, the morality of their behavior, was perceived as more important than the substantial issues which they raised. 'The question before us concerns not the truth of the new doctrines but the honesty of the writers.'[8] They should have left the church if they could not accept its standards; and the church ought to

---

[5] Rev. Henry Arthur Woodgate, *'Essays and Reviews' Considered in relation to the current principles and fallacies of the day* (London, 1861), p. 17, provides an example of the High Church view. 'The upholders of ultra-Protestantism and the self-styled evangelical bishops and clergy ... must be content to bear no inconsiderable portion of the responsibility.' See also idem, *Catholicity and Reason* (London, 1861), p. 10.
   An example of the Low Church view comes from Rev. William Smith Burnside, *The Lex Evangelica* (Dublin, 1861), p. 17, blaming the union of 'Tractarianism and Rationalism (that two-headed hydra which of late years has crept forth from Oxford).' The author of *The Right Way, and a way which seemeth right*, Protestant Reformation Society Tract 15 (London, 1861), p. 17, noted that 'The Essayist Dr. Williams is the child of the Tractarian Dr. Newman.' Even Bishop John Jackson of Lincoln in his 1861 *Charge* (London, 1861), p. 42, blamed the High Church, which 'tended to substitute authority for evidence....'

[6] Rev. John Cumming, *Popular Lectures on 'The Essays and Reviews'* (London, 1861), p. 120.

[7] G. Rorison, 'The Creative Week,' in *Replies to 'Essays and Reviews' (Oxford, 1862), p. 324. Replies*, sponsored by Bishop Wilberforce, was the second most prestigious collection of responses; Rorison was a Scottish Episcopal priest. For a treatment of Genesis 1 as 'parable,' see Edgar Huxtable, 'The Sacred Record of Creation Vindicated and Explained,' in *Faith and Peace* (London, 1867), p. 74, a High Church collection of tracts organized by Archdeacon Denison, originally published in 1861.

[8] A Graduate of Oxford, *Subscription to Articles: Is it Truth, or a Mockery? Considered in Reference to Essays and Reviews* (London, 1861), p. 13, cited in James J. Livingston, *The Ethics of Belief: An Essay on the Victorian Religious Conscience* (Missoula, Mont., 1974), p. 4.

purge itself of complicity by condemning them. As Carlyle put it, the sentry who deserts his post should be shot.[9] Related to this was an implication of conspiracy, the assertion that all the Essayists were jointly responsible for the statements of every one of them.[10]

After thus demonstrating that the Essayists were not entitled to be heard, the replies then proceeded to argue against them. It was first pointed out that arguments of the Essayists were not new; they were warmed-over repetitions of German criticism, itself derived from the deism of the eighteenth century which had led to revolution and infidelity. The deists had been refuted in their own day by the great Anglican apologists led by Butler and Paley. The German critics were confused, unintelligible, and mutually contradictory; furthermore, the tide of German thought had shifted, and recent conservative scholars had refuted the critics. The name of Hengstenberg was cited as an example with such frequency that F. D. Maurice was driven to ask, 'Is Hengstenberg then infallible more than other German doctors?'[11] Since the German critics had been contradicted by other Germans, their arguments might be dismissed.

The replies to *Essays and Reviews* also emphasized the danger posed by biblical criticism. Questioning the accuracy of the Bible might lead to a weakening of faith, to doubt (which was regarded as a state of misery), to Socinianism, and finally to unbelief.[12] Atheists, it was pointed out, were overjoyed that some of the clergy had given such aid to their cause. There was a nervous insistence that the faith of the multitudes must not be shaken, that the raising of doubts would lead to dangerous social as well as spiritual consequences.

Only after such points had been made did the replies to *Essays and Reviews* turn to the actual substance of the work. Many of the replies dealt with the Essays seriatim, taking up each point raised (or each error made)

---

[9] Attributed in Evelyn Abbott and Lewis Campbell, *The Life and Letters of Benjamin Jowett*, 2 vols. (New York, 1897), 1: 294. The military metaphor was used by orthodox controversialists, for example, 'An Officer in the Army who should pursue a similar line of action, would be dismissed the Service, — or worse.' John William Burgon, *Inspiration and Interpretation* (Oxford, 1861), p. lxx. See also Cumming, *Popular Lectures*, p. 2.

[10] For the significance of joint responsibility, see Josef L. Altholz, 'Periodical Origins and Implications of *Essays and Reviews*,' *Victorian Periodicals Newsletter* 10 (September 1977): 140, 154.

[11] F. D. Maurice, *The Mote and the Beam*, Tracts for Priests and People, vol. 1, no. 2 (Cambridge, 1861), p. 61.

[12] 'You must either receive the Bible as the infallible Word of God, or you sink at once into infidelity.' Rev. Daniel Wilson, *The Inspired Scriptures, not man's 'verifying faculty,' the final ground of appeal in matters of faith* (London, 1861), p. 19.

by each Essayist. There was no point made by the Essayists to which there was not a reply, usually a standard reply; but such arguments are as impossible to summarize as they are tedious to read. Other replies concentrated on some leading thought seen as pervading the Essays as a whole. The two most common lines of argument should be examined.

The first concerned an idea common to most of the Essayists (and ultimately derived from Coleridge), that divine inspiration applied only to those parts of scripture which conveyed a religious message, and that there was — in Rowland Williams's words — a 'verifying faculty' in the mind which could distinguish this message from 'narratives inherently incredible, or precepts evidently wrong.'[13] His fellow Essayist Wilson phrased it more tersely. 'The Word of God is contained in Scripture, whence it does not follow that it is co-extensive with it.' The religious mind must discriminate 'the bright centre of spiritual truth' from the human elements in the Bible in which it is embedded, with the aid of scholarly criticism but ultimately relying on its innate 'verifying faculty.'[14] The opponents of *Essays and Reviews* were quick to perceive this denial of plenary inspiration as opening the door to unbridled speculation and the abandonment of all objective standards of doctrine. If the entire Bible was not equally inspired, where was one to stop in getting rid of its human elements? What would be left?

This was recognized as a central question and was addressed by nearly all of the anti-Essayists. But it was a difficult question to deal with in a clear and comprehensible manner, partly because of the diffuseness and vagueness of Essayists such as Williams and Wilson, and partly because the defenders of orthodoxy did not agree among themselves about the definition of inspiration — whether it was mechanical or dynamic, whether it was an inspiration of supervision only or an inspiration extending, in Dean Burgon's memorable phrase, to every word, every syllable, every letter, every jot, and every title.[15] It is a curious fact that the debate over *Essays and Reviews*, which ultimately revolved around the nature of the divine inspiration of the Bible, made no significant contribution toward the resolution of that question. Harold Browne, who wrote the most important reply dealing

[13] 'In short, whatever *finds* me, bears witness for itself that it has proceeded from a Holy Spirit.' 'I, who hold that the Bible contains the religion of Christians, but who dare not say that whatever is contained in the Bible is the Christian religion....' Samuel Taylor Coleridge, *Confessions of an Inquiring Spirit* (1840; rev. ed., London, 1890), pp. 295, 315, Rowland Williams, 'Bunsen's Biblical Researches,' *Essays and Reviews*, p. 83.

[14] Henry Bristow Wilson, 'Seances Historiques de Genève. The National Church,' *Essays and Reviews*, pp. 176, 177.

[15] Burgon, *Inspiration and Interpretation*, pp. 76, 94.

with this subject, thought that 'definite theories of inspiration' were positively 'dangerous.'[16]

The question of inspiration and the 'verifying faculty' thus failed to gain the centrality in the debate which it ought to have had until 1862, when Fitzjames Stephen, counsel for Williams and Wilson in their heresy trial, specifically upheld the idea that the Bible was not itself the Word of God, but that the Word of God was contained in the Bible.[17] This drew attention away from the dubious concept of inspiration and towards the phrase 'Word of God,' a phrase to which the clergy were devotedly attached and which was usually used as a synonym for 'the Bible.' A London Evangelical clergyman, Alexander McCaul, picked up this phrase and asserted that the central issue was upholding the Bible as being, not merely containing, the Word of God.[18] This was something ordinary clergy could understand; and this phraseology was inserted as one of the two main points of the Declaration signed in 1864 by a majority of the clergy.[19] Paul Tillich has remarked that 'if the Bible is called the Word of God, theological confusion is almost unavoidable.'[20] For the Anglican clergy of 1864, however, it provided a useful simplification of the theological issue, avoiding the difficulties of a definite concept of inspiration and providing a common ground on which to join in condemning the 'verifying faculty.'

The other leading argument of *Essays and Reviews* which its orthodox

[16] Harold Browne, 'Inspiration,' *Aids to Faith* (New York, 1862), p. 349. *Aids to Faith* was the most important and quasi-official of the composite replies. Samuel Wilberforce was similarly cautious. 'Holy scripture has never laid down any theory of inspiration; the Church has never propounded one; and we think sufficient reasons for this reticence.' 'Essays and Reviews,' *Quarterly Review* 109 (January 1861): 304. Nonetheless, many lesser figures provided or assumed definitions of inspiration, whether 'verbal' or merely 'Plenary.'

[17] James Fitzjames Stephen, *Defence of the Rev. Rowland Williams, D. D. in the Arches Court of Canterbury* (London, 1862). A similar point was made about the same time by Bishop Colenso, which added to the controversy.

[18] Alexander McCaul, *Testimonies to the Divine Authority and Inspiration of the Holy Scriptures, as taught by the Church of England, in reply to the statements of Mr. James Fitzjames Stephen* (London, 1862). McCaul had anticipated the issue earlier in *Rationalism and Deistic Infidelity* (London, 1861), pp. 20–21, originally published in the *Record*, 7 January 1861.

[19] 'We, the undersigned Presbyters and Deacons in Holy Orders of the Church of England and Ireland, hold it to be our bounden duty to the Church and to the souls of men, to declare our firm belief that the Church of England and Ireland, in common with the whole Catholic Church, maintains without reserve or qualification the plenary Inspiration and Authority of the whole Canonical Scriptures as the Word of God, and further teaches, in the words of our Blessed Lord, that the 'punishment' of the 'cursed,' as the 'life' of the 'righteous' lasts for ever.'

[20] Cited in H. D. McDonald, *Theories of Revelation: An Historical Study, 1860–1960* (London, 1963), p. 178.

opponents were unanimous in condemning was its attack on the accepted 'evidences' of Christianity. The eighteenth-century Anglican apologists, especially Bishop Butler and Archdeacon Paley, had constructed an evidential theology which rested the case for Christianity on the arguments from miracles, the fulfillment of prophecies, and the correspondence of types and antitypes in the Old and New Testaments.[21] The ablest orthodox controversialist of the 1860s, H. L. Mansel, thus summarized the evidences for or against the claims of the Christian faith:

> the genuineness and authenticity of the documents; the judgment and good faith of the writers; the testimony to the actual occurrence of prophecies and miracles, and their relation to the religious teaching with which they are connected; the character of the Teacher Himself ...; those rites and ceremonies of the elder Law, so significant as typical of Christ, and so strange and meaningless without Him; those predictions of the promised Messiah ...; this history of the rise and progress of Christianity, and its comparison with that of other religions; the ability or inability of human means to bring about the results which it actually accomplished; ... the character of those by whom it was promulgated and received; the sufferings which attested the sincerity of their convictions....[22]

These were the 'external evidences' which had been denigrated by the Broad Church since Coleridge and which were explicitly attacked in *Essays and Reviews*: Powell had denied miracles; Williams had denied that prophecy was predictive; Jowett undermined the use of types and antitypes; Pattison had put the evidential theologians in their historical place.[23]

There was a similar solidarity in defense of the evidential theology on the part of the anti-Essayists. Frequently it seemed that the greatest sin of the Essayists was not their questioning of the Bible or of doctrine but their

---

[21] Joseph Butler (1692–1752), bishop of Bristol (1738) and Durham (1750), was the author of *The Analogy of Religion* (1736). 'I can scarcely deem that man a Christian, who can remain insensible to the obligations under which the author of the *Analogy* has laid the world.' Rev. Arthur T. Russell, *A Letter to the Right Rev. the Lord Bishop of Oxford, upon the Defence of the 'Essays and Reviews' in the April Number of the 'Edinburgh Review,' 1861* (London, 1862), pp. 117–118.

William Paley (1743–1805), was archdeacon of Carlisle (1782), the author of *Evidences of Christianity* (1794) and *Natural Theology* (1802), and 'the man whose memory Cambridge reveres' (An M. A. of Cambridge, *A Reply to the 'Essays and Reviews'* [Cambridge, 1861], p. 28). Archbishop Whately of Dublin regarded *Essays and Reviews* as designed as an answer to his recent edition of Paley. Richard Whately, *Danger from Within* (London, 1861), p. 18.

[22] Henry L. Mansel, *The Limits of Religious Thought examined* (Boston, 1859), Lecture 8, p. 214.

[23] The centrality of the 'evidences' explains why Pattison's historical essay, which was not intrinsically controversial, was denounced with the others.

attack on this specific form of defense of Christianity. The anti-Essayists spoke of the 'evidences' as the 'foundations' of the faith, and used language which implied that, if these 'foundations' were shaken, the faith would be unable to stand.[24] The 'evidences' provided the clearest point of difference between the Essayists and their opponents. The evidential theology, asserted as necessary and sufficient, had become almost as much a part of orthodoxy as the articles of faith, employed so routinely as to constitute an Anglican scholasticism.

In some ways this fact is surprising. The evidential theology, very much the product of the eighteenth century, is strictly rational, indeed rationalistic — as rationalistic as the deism it was designed to combat. One might expect that it would be antithetical to the religious movements of the nineteenth century, whether Evangelical or Anglo-Catholic, which reasserted the nonrational forces motivating faith. Yet both parties accepted it. Indeed, the Evangelicals were particularly committed to the evidential apologetic, perhaps because they felt that their theology was otherwise dangerously subjective.

> It seemed ... to be required, in order that the evangelical revival of religious life might be gathered into the Church, and spread from her as a centre so as to have its permanency secured, that subjective faith should be showed to rest upon a morally certain basis of evidence, however incomprehensible to unrenewed reason the objects of faith themselves.[25]

Because they regarded the intellectual foundations of belief in revelation as secure, both Evangelicals and High Churchmen could venture into those more subjective regions in which they habitually disported themselves.

It is clear that a standard apologetic based on the eighteenth-century evidential theologians had been taught to aspiring clergy (and others) at the universities, where Butler and Paley were standard texts, and that it had been mastered and internalized by the students.[26] In the *Essays and Reviews* controversy, this apologetic proved itself invulnerable against a Broad Church critique which convinced only a minority of the clergy. Let

---

[24] 'Either the predictive character of Old Testament prophecy must be maintained or Christianity (as a Divine system) must be abandoned.' *'Another Gospel' Examined* (London, 1861), p. 22.

[25] Charles Gooch, *Remarks on the Grounds of Faith, suggested by Mr. Pattison's Essay on the Tendencies of Religious Thought* (Cambridge, 1862), p. 9.

[26] Paley's *Evidences* remained a required textbook at Cambridge until 1920. See D. L. LeMahieu, *The Mind of William Paley* (Lincoln, Neb., 1976), p. 153. Paley was cited more often by Cantabrigians, Butler by Oxonians.

me now attempt to state systematically this orthodox apologetic, this Anglican scholasticism, the mind of the Church of England in the 1860s.

The orthodox apologetic assumed the traditional natural theology, common to medieval scholastics and deists, which had received its most ample
formulation in Paley's *Natural Theology*. The existence of God was not the
subject of debate; rather, the argument revolved around the question of a
special revelation which went beyond natural theology. On this point
Butler had labored to demonstrate not so much that the Christian revelation was true but that it was credible — or rather, that it was not
antecedently incredible; that is, that the criticisms of such a revelation were
subject to the same objections as had been raised against the arguments in
favor of it. The sophisticated line of reasoning of Butler's *Analogy of Religion*,
with its reliance on probability rather than proof and on affirmation by
double negative (that is, revelation is no more improbable than the alternative), was matched in the nineteenth century only by Newman's *Grammar of
Assent*; and its double negatives were potentially doubled-edged. Nonetheless, Butler had shown that Christianity was not incredible. The next step
was to show that it was in fact true, a factual rather than a philosophical
argument, relying on evidence. The proper evidences of a religion such as
Christianity, Butler reasoned, were miracles and prophecies, which aut-
henticated the message by showing the divine approval of the messenger.
Although this was not a new approach, it was reserved for Paley's *Evidences
of Christianity* to work out in its fullest perfection a demonstration that the
miracles and prophecies cited in scripture were in fact historically true.
Paley's reasoning rested on certain assumptions about the value of human
testimony, under the conditions in which the Gospel witnesses operated, to
provide evidence which, once their truthfulness was established, could be
accepted as factually true. The Gospels being thus demonstrated to be
genuine records of authentic facts, and the facts of miracles and fulfilled
prophecies demonstrating the divine credentials of those who accomplished
them, the message which they delivered must obviously be a divine message
to be believed without further argument. The result of all this was a
tight, complete, self-sufficient scholastic argument for implicit belief in
the Bible. It is best summed up by a writer who may be selected for his
conventionality.

> Butler, by his analogical reasoning, proved there is nothing incredible
> in Christianity; Paley, by his historical demonstration, established the
> reality of its history; and these combined should command, by the
> fulness of their proof, the assent of every reasonable mind to the truth
> of revelation.[27]

[27] John Nash Griffin, *Seven Answers to the Seven Essays and Reviews* (London, 1862), p. 229.

'The assent of every reasonable mind': this was a strictly rational argument, with a logic unchallengeable within its premises, a defense of revelation by an appeal to reason. The opponents of *Essays and Reviews* were neither obscurantists nor fideists; they were conscious of a reliance on reason which, in this case, served the interests of religion. This explains why they so frequently criticized the Essayists for being not merely 'unscriptural' but also 'unphilosophical'.[28] But they carried this rational argument only up to a point, demonstrating that the message of the Bible was credible and valid. Once this was proven, they argued, reason had done its work; it had brought people to the portals of scripture, whose message was then simply to be accepted, without any further exercise of human reason.[29] 'Believing that the revelation which makes them known is from God, we receive them by faith, reason satisfying us of this, that there is nothing in them incredible.'[30]

Nothing is more striking than the way in which an argument hitherto strictly rational turns into an argument from faith. The orthodox apologetic defended the approaches to the Bible but did not enter within it.[31] The human mind, it was asserted, was capable of judging the credentials of a revelation but not of passing judgment on its contents.[32] The contents were simply to be accepted as data, to be believed, not judged. Hence scripture was sufficient to establish doctrine, with no external reference, whether to facts or to conscience. This fundamental concept was expressed most frankly by Mansel. 'If there is sufficient evidence ... to show that the Scripture, in which this doctrine is contained, is a Revelation from God, the doctrine

---

[28] Charles Forster, *Spinoza Redivivus* (London, 1861), p. 10; E. M. Goulburn, 'The Education of the World,' in *Replies to 'Essays and Reviews,'* p. 30.

[29] 'If, upon the acknowledged principles which guide human life in other matters, this evidence leaves no other alternative open besides the Divine origin of the revelation, then the human mind must submit to an authority the credentials of which have been thus recognized.' Rev. Edward Garbett, *The Bible and its Critics ... the Boyle Lectures for MDCCCLXI* (London, 1861), p. 369.

[30] Griffin, *Seven Answers*, p. 233.

[31] 'Reason leads us to the door of the Sanctuary. But let it not cross the threshold.' Christopher Wordsworth, *The Interpretation of the Bible* (London, 1861), p. 40.

[32] Reason 'is competent to deal with the question whether a religion is from God, but when once that question is settled in the affirmative, it is not competent to sit in judgment upon the doctrine which it teaches.' John Cumming and R. P. Blakeney, *Scripture Miracles Vindicated*, Protestant Reformation Society Tract 6 (London, 1861), p. 26. 'The intellect is qualified indeed to examine the grounds upon which a revelation purports to proceed from God but, the fact once being recognized, the intellect has only to accept the 'dicta' of that revelation with as blind a submission as childhood's own.' Rev. Archer Gurney, *The Faith against Free-Thinkers* (London, 1864), p. 23.

itself must be unconditionally received, not as reasonable, nor as unreasonable, but as scriptural.'[33]

Two assumptions underlying this argument should be noted. First, the orthodox apologetic treated the Bible as essentially a collection of data, a factually verified record of facts, disregarding (at least for controversial purposes) its spiritual quality or its effects upon the heart and conscience.[34] Victorians usually exalted the heart over the head; yet it was only the heretics of the Broad Church who dared to apply that approach to apologetic theology. Second, it was assumed that the only legitimate response to these facts was simple acceptance of them — in other words, faith. Indeed, the nature of faith itself was an underlying issue in this debate, though it was rarely made explicit. Perhaps the High Church leader Pusey was the only one to express this clearly. In an 1855 sermon on faith, he had said:

> Faith, whether in God or man, is an implicit, full, unswerving reliance on the Being Who is the object of faith. If it is not absolute or perfect, it is not Faith.... He who rejects any one revealed truth, does not hold whatever other truth he does not part with out of submission to the authority of God Who has revealed it, but because it approves itself in some way to his own natural mind and judgment. What he holds, he holds of himself, accounting it to be truth, not as Faith.

Pusey regarded faith as an act of the will rather than of the intellect, a total acceptance of revealed truth to which the intellect could only 'submit blindly.'[35] In these terms, indeed, the criticism of *Essays and Reviews* was literally 'soul-destroying,' destructive of that self-abasement of reason which was necessary to faith.[36]

The orthodox apologetic, having first validated scripture by reason and then having declared that it must be accepted by faith, further insisted that,

---

[33] Mansel, *The Limits of Religious Thought,* Lecture 6, p. 168. Mansel's epistemology, based on Sir William Hamilton, was accepted by few other orthodox spokesmen, but the passages selected for quotation are representative of their thought, if somewhat pithier.

[34] William Tait, *Inspiration and Justification* (London, 1861), p. 12, regarded the Bible as 'communications from the eternal throne.' Christianity is 'an historical religion — a religion made up of matters of fact, and propounded on the evidence of matters of fact.' William Fitzgerald (Bishop of Cork), 'On the Study of the Evidences of Christianity,' *Aids to Faith,* pp. 77–78.

[35] 'Real Faith Entire,' quoted in Henry Parry Liddon, *Life of Edward Bouverie Pusey,* 4 vols. (London, 1898), vol. 4, ed. J. O. Johnston, R. J. Wilson, and W. C. E. Newbolt, p. 7. Pusey is representative of orthodoxy in referring faith to the will rather than the intellect.

[36] Pusey to Lord Shaftesbury, 28 February 1864, ibid., p. 51, with reference to the judgment in favor of the Essayists.

since faith must be without reservation, the acceptance of the data of revelation must be total and uncritical. If the Bible is God's message, it is entirely so, and it must be accepted in its entirety. Even those who did not maintain the literal inspiration of the Bible insisted on its plenary inspiration. The question was usually put moralistically in terms of the truthfulness both of God as the author of the Bible and of Christ and his apostles, who appealed to the miracles, prophecies, and events recorded in scripture.[37] The corollary of this simplistic approach to the reliability of scripture as a moral rather than a factual question was the assertion that, if one statement in the Bible was shown to be false, the entire revelation was unreliable and must be rejected. It was common for orthodox writers to proclaim that they would give up their faith if one error could be found in the Bible. Bishop Lee of Manchester declared that 'the very foundation of our faith, the very basis of our hopes, the very nearest and dearest of our consolations are taken from us when one line in that Sacred Volume on which we base everything is declared to be unfaithful or untrustworthy'.[38] This is the famous either-or argument: either you believe everything in the Bible as the Word of God, or you must abandon, not merely some parts of the Bible, but all of Christianity.

The either-or argument had been employed by Newman on behalf of Roman Catholicism: either you must go all the way (to Rome) or you will lose all faith. Its application to biblical criticism is attributed by Owen Chadwick to Pusey's disciple Liddon in his 1866 Bampton lectures on *The Divinity of Our Lord*; but in fact it was a commonplace among orthodox writers throughout the debate over *Essays and Reviews*.[39] It represented a willingness to stake all of Christian faith on the text of the Bible and ultimately on a particular scholastic argument which justified that reliance.

---

[37] Thus Liddon could say as late as 1889, 'The trustworthiness of the Old Testament is, in fact, inseparable from the trustworthiness of our Lord Jesus Christ.' Quoted in S. L. Greenslade, ed., *The Cambridge History of the Bible: The West from the Reformation to the Present Day*, (Cambridge, 1963), p. 267. 'The question of the genuineness and authenticity of Daniel cannot ... be separated from that respecting the fallibility or infallibility of the Saviour.' McCaul, 'Prophecy,' *Aids to Faith*, p. 142. See also Rev. Charles Bullock, *'Essays and Reviews:' The False Position of the Authors* (London, 1861), p. 10.

[38] *The Guardian* (1863), quoted in Bernard Reardon, *From Coleridge to Gore* (London, 1971), p. 343, n. 1. 'The admission of one doubt undermines all certainty.' Archdeacon Henry Law, *Charge* (Weston-super-Mare, [1862]), p. 13.

[39] Owen Chadwick, *The Victorian Church*, 2 vols. (London, 1970), 2: 75. 'There is no middle course between the absolute acceptance, and the absolute rejection, of revelation.' Garbett, p. 390, see also p. 396. 'Our only alternative lies between faith and scepticism.' Rev. Sanderson Robins, *A Defence of the Faith* (London, 1862), p. 215. 'There is no standing-place between the faith of the Church and infidelity.' George Moberly, *Sermons on the Beatitudes* (Oxford 1860), p. lvii.

In one sense this may have been a sign of insecurity, in that it obviated analysis of specific biblical difficulties by an overriding appeal to faith; in another sense it was a supreme act of self-confidence, in that it was prepared to rest the case for Christianity on its most vulnerable point. In any case it was an act of hubris, a tremendous raising of the stakes. The either-or argument, argued so forcefully as to impress itself even on doubters, was responsible more than anything else for the peculiar dimensions and intensity of the Victorian crisis of faith. Either you accepted all of revelation and orthodox theology, or the whole edifice would fall if any of its elements were denied — so argued the 'defenders' of the faith. The argument was double-edged: if you could not accept any one point of revelation or doctrine, you must renounce, not only that point, but all of Christianity. In all previous controversies, the doubter had been given the alternative of heresy — wrong faith, but faith nonetheless. Now it was held that there was no alternative between orthodoxy and total 'infidelity.' The result was inevitable: England ceased to produce heretics and began to produce infidels.

For this, the mind of Victorian orthodoxy had prepared the way, not by its unreason, but by its reason, by that rationalistic Anglican scholasticism which had provided so apparently secure a foundation on which an edifice of faith could be constructed. The fatal combination of an eighteenth-century evidential theology and a nineteenth-century concept of faith had produced both a false certainty and a dangerous demand for certainty. There was a lack of flexibility in Victorian orthodoxy. It was due, not to the narrowness of their faith, but to the narrowness of the structure of reason on which they believed their faith to be founded.

D. N. HEMPTON

CHAPTER 3

BICKERSTETH, BISHOP OF RIPON: THE EPISCOPATE OF A MID-VICTORIAN EVANGELICAL[1]

O N Thursday 27 of November 1856 the Reverend Robert Bickersteth, M. A., Rector of St Giles in the Fields London, Canon
Residentiary of Salisbury Cathedral, received a letter from the
Prime Minister, Lord Viscount Palmerston offering him the Bishopric of
Ripon vacant by the translation of Bishop Longley to the See of Durham.[2]
Bickersteth is described in most textbooks as one of the Palmerston
bishops, since he was not, like Ellicot and Jacobson, distinguished in
scholarship and did not have the aristocratic family connexions of Villiers
and Baring. What recommended him most was that he came from the
Church of England's leading evangelical family when Shaftesbury was
acting as Palmerston's ecclesiastical adviser. Bickersteth was one of the
crop of Evangelicals appointed to sees in 1856–57 when Shaftesbury worked quickly because he felt the time of the Palmerstonian Cabinet was short.
Palmerston was happy with the Evangelicals because they were not as
detested as High Churchmen and were unlikely to stir up theological and
political controversy in high places. Chadwick has described the process
with customary panache.

> Cavalier Palmerston wanted simple non-theological bishops. Round-
> head Shaftesbury wanted evangelical bishops. Most evangelical
> clergymen were simple and godly.
>   The profession of evangelical opinion had until this moment
> erected a fence against preferment. In February 1855 the fence col-
> lapsed and reappeared as a ladder.[3]

Being neither an eminent theologian nor a Whig aristocrat, Bickersteth
has been passed over by historians, but that says more about past trends in
writing church history than anything else, for he took charge of one of

[1] I wish to thank Hilarie Keene for her help in researching this article, and Dr Sheridan Gilley
for his comments on the draft.

[2] MS entry in Archives of the See of Ripon housed at Bishop Mount, Ripon [hereafter RA].

[3] O. Chadwick, *The Victorian Church*, part 1 (1966), 471.

the biggest, most populous and most industrial dioceses in England when the Established Church was desperately worried about the results of the 1851 religious census, especially in the Northern manufacturing districts. Moreover, if Bickersteth did not outshine his episcopal colleagues, he certainly outlived them for he was in Ripon until 1884. The appointments of the mid-eighteen-fifties gave the Evangelical wing of the Church of England, for the first time, the episcopal representation warranted by its numerical strength, but they made Evangelicals if anything more unpopular. Charles Greville wrote that Bickersteth's appointment excited 'great astonishment' and the Queen advised Palmerston 'in the case of future appointments to remove any impression of the Church patronage running unduly toward party extremes'.[4] According to one Evangelical clergyman Bickersteth's preferment was received with 'great bitterness and wrath' at Cambridge, though this was partially defused by the Bishop's 1857 university sermon on the second coming.[5] This was certainly not the golden age of Evangelicalism, an opinion reflected in historical writing on Evangelical ecclesiastics, which often stops with Simeon and starts with Ryle. Nevertheless Bickersteth's episcopate is important not just because he was in pastoral charge of a million Englishmen but because of his views, which were faithfully passed on to his diocesan clergy, on the major mid-Victorian social, political and theological issues — the sanitary and spiritual condition of the working-classes, elementary education, the plight of Ireland and the progress of ritualism, scepticism and Biblical criticism.

Bickersteth's pastoral experience in St Giles from 1851 to 1857 gave him valuable insights into the social and religious conditions of the urban working-classes. Balleine describes St Giles as 'the largest and most degraded parish in London'.[6] Bickersteth's lecture to the Leeds Philosophical and Literary Society in 1860 on his time there illustrated the Evangelical frame of mind at its best. The Bishop described the types of relief on offer in St Giles but concluded regretfully 'that there still remained a dense mass of the population unreached, unbenefitted — a multitude of our fellow-parishioners, fellow immortals, upon whom all attempt for their social or moral amelioration was apparently so much wasted energy'. Bickersteth rightly argued that the physical condition of the people made it impossible for teachers, clergymen, or city missionaries to make the slightest impact on the more ill-defined moral and religious problems. He stated that mind and

[4] D. W. R. Bahlman, 'Politics and Church Patronage in the Victorian Age', *Victorian Studies*, XXII (no. 3) (1979), 270.

[5] M. C. Bickersteth, *A Sketch of the Life and Episcopate of the Right Reverend Robert Bickersteth, D. D.* (1887), p. 87 [hereafter *Life*].

[6] G. R. Balleine, *A History of the Evangelical Party in the Church of England* (1909), p. 268.

matter were closely linked and that 'we must cease to do evil that we may learn to do well'. He echoed with feeling Paul's judgement on the gentile population — 'they have no hope and are without God in the world'. If Bickersteth's diagnosis was accurate and his humanitarianism beyond dis-pute, his solutions were more debatable. Like all Evangelicals he deplored class conflict, believing that the God who created mountains and valleys 'ordained likewise the upland and the lowland of human society'.[7] These different regions should be linked by the rainbow of love, not sundered by the thunder clouds of social revolution. Bickersteth had scant regard for the colourlessness of working-class lives in condemning their expenditure on beer, tobacco, and spirits. His solutions were that familiar Victorian pack-age: collecting the facts, utilizing science, and passing legislation. It was the philosophy of an Evangelical paternalist in the mould of Shaftesbury.

Working in a London parish was good preparation for the equally demanding environs of the West Riding, and Bickersteth never lost his passionate commitment to the conversion of working-class people. The problem was how this was to be achieved, because the 1851 census revealed that even the more flexible Nonconformists had little impact on God's poor in Yorkshire (Appendix, Table 1). W. F. Hook and the Leeds ruri-decanal chapter drew up their reclamation programme in 1851 — short services for children, the celebration of Holy Communion at different hours, open-air services, greater pastoral commitment and the promotion of popular edu-cation.[8] The cornerstone of Bickersteth's strategy was preaching and church building. Inscribed on the front page of his Bible was a decree of the Council of Trent, *Praedicatio evangelii est praecipuum munus episcoporum*. In his first Charge to the clergy he spelt out clearly the value he placed on fervent preaching,[9] and he may have been unique among Anglican bishops in preaching more and more frequently during his episcopate. It is well known that within Wesleyan Methodism, for example, the amount of preaching was in inverse proportion to the ecclesiastical importance of the preacher. But Bickersteth was the old-style evangelist, an Anglican Ranter. He preached to colliers at the pit mouth, to navvies at the water works and to Leeds factory workers in their lunch hours. He threw himself into the city missions to Bradford, Huddersfield, and Leeds with customary vigour. In a letter on Bickersteth's preaching to Leeds factory workers, the Dean of Worcester wrote that he brought the Church to the masses by showing that 'religion was distinctly in its place in working days and scenes, a thought

[7] R. Bickersteth, *The Physical Condition of the People in its bearing upon their Social and Moral Welfare* (Leeds, 1860), pp. 3–11.

[8] N. Yates, *Leeds and the Oxford Movement*, Publications of the Thoresby Society, LV (1975), 16.

[9] R. Bickersteth, *A Charge to the Clergy of the Diocese of Ripon* (1858), pp. 26–31.

that seemed new to many'.[10] One of Bickersteth's most imprtant tasks as Bishop was to preside over the Church Congress at Leeds in October 1872. As the first speaker at the working men's meeting he criticized the lack of effective preaching and the system of pew monopolies.[11] When the cheers died down, he encouraged the working men to form themselves into small bands for evangelizing their parishes, but no cheers greeted this appeal to working-class responsibility.

Bickersteth was convinced that the Church needed to provide more churches for the mushrooming industrial parishes. In a confidential letter to 'the owners of wealth and the employers of labour in Leeds' he stated that the population of the city (214,143) was being served by thirty-six churches or one church per 6,000 people. That statistic concealed more appalling figures.

> For example, Hunslet with only two churches has a population of 24,000. Holbeck with church accommodation for only 2,500 has a population of above 15,000. In St Mary's district there is a population of 11,000 with only one church ... and there is a population of about 20,000 still ecclesiastically annexed to the Parish Church.[12]

Not a single new church was built in Leeds between 1855 and 1863, but in the next ten years eleven new churches were consecrated, primarily as a result of Bickersteth's appeal.[13] Although the Bishop was a tireless fund raiser, he realized that the sight of a new building and the sound of a church bell would not transform old habits. He advocated pioneer church planting and the erection of mission rooms in the centres of densest population.[14] In his twenty-eight year episcopate he consecrated 157 new or rebuilt churches[15] in the Ripon diocese, and this does not take account of the scores of temporary mission rooms. Whether these churches were ever filled is another matter, but the yearly confirmation statistics (Appendix, Tables 3 and 5) caused Bickersteth concern, not only because they were so low, but also because as time went on females came to outnumber males by two to one. He knew that lack of buildings did not cause that particular

---

[10] *Life*, p. 239.

[11] *The Authorised Report of the Church Congress* (Leeds, 1872), p. 347.

[12] RA, A typescript letter marked Private and Confidential, 13 Nov. 1863.

[13] RA, MS, R. Bickersteth, Nov. 1872 in a postscript to the above letter.

[14] Bickersteth, *A Charge to the Clergy of the Diocese of Ripon* (1870), p. 43.

[15] RA, there is a typed record of all churches consecrated between 1856 and 1884 giving details of places and dates.

problem; he attributed it to greater temptations for young men in the larger manufacturing towns.

Bickersteth, like Hook before him, looked on the Church's provision of popular education as potentially the most effective influence on working people. The Bishop's Charges, with their carefully presented statistics, are a mine of information on Church commitment to elementary education in a large manufacturing diocese before Forster's Act (Appendix, Table 4). At national level Bickersteth estimated that the number of scholars in Church of England elementary schools had risen from 1 in 36.7 of the population in 1840 to 1 in 13 in 1870, and that out of 14,709 parishes only 1,355 had no schools.[16] As one would expect in a large industrial diocese with a strong Nonconformist tradition, the figures for Ripon were below the national average. The real problem was not absolute growth in pupil numbers, which doubled in the period 1858 to 1879, but growth in relation to the total population. The Anglicans were clawing up an educational mountain which frustratingly became higher with the years. Bickersteth was acutely aware of the problem, and he understood the roots of it: lack of money and the failure to reach national agreement on the content of religious instruction. The heightened sectarianism of the eighteen-thirties and forties effectively ruined the attempts of successive governments to create a national system of education, and, without adequate State financial aid, the churches were left to provide as much schooling as they could.

The 'religious difficulty' that hindered governmental intervention in the earlier Victorian period entered in a new guise into the mid-Victorian educational disputes. Shaftesbury put it succinctly: 'I do not believe that the religious difficulty has ever had any existence whatever, except as a euphonious term for the assault and defence of the Established Church'.[17] The Nonconformists, except the Wesleyans, had made voluntaryism the catch-word for their assaults in the eighteen-forties, whereas by the eighteen-sixties even Baines was advocating State intervention.[18] The reason for this volte-face is simple. The notions behind voluntaryism were freedom, individual responsibility and ecclesiastical equality, but Baines, after his service on the Taunton Commission, became convinced that these were luxuries to the pauperized urban working classes. Individual responsibility for education without the money to implement it was in effect a philosophy of economic discrimination. Ironically, Baines's diluted voluntaryism and his sense of the need for limited State intervention thrust him straight into

[16] Bickersteth, *Charge* (1880), p. 17.

[17] F. W. Cornish, *The English Church in the Nineteenth Century* (1910), part 2, 283.

[18] See I. Sellers, *Nineteenth-Century Nonconformity* (1977), p. 79, and the helpful section by C. Binfield, *So Down to Prayers* (1977), pp. 80–91.

the anglican conservative camp. Meanwhile Nonconformist educational leadership passed into the more radical hands of the Birmingham Education League. The pressures from population increase, inadequate finance, militant Nonconformity, and, worst of all, secularism, made the educational dominance of the Established Church more fragile in the eighteen-sixties.

Bickersteth's educational philosophy, which he outlined in a speech to the working men of Huddersfield, was derived from his Evangelicalism. He saw education as neither the teaching of the three Rs nor the 'cramming of the mind with facts' but as the 'development of the faculties with which God had endowed them, with a view to their employment for the good of others, as well as for the glory of God, which was the highest object at which any human being could aim'.[19] For Bickersteth religious instruction was not simply part of the moral training of human beings, but the central purpose of education, to fit men for eternity. He felt this view to be threatened by the Newcastle Commission's recommendation that State financial aid should be contingent on examination results in reading, writing and arithmetic, but not religion. In his opinion the Revised Code would 'thrust the religious element into the background and ... secularize the system of national education'.[20]

The challenge posed by the Revised Code regulations was not as serious as the potential threat of the Birmingham Education League formed in 1869 under the leadership of George Dixon and Jesse Collings. Its aims were universal, unsectarian education funded by local rates and subject to government inspection. Two particular issues concerned Bickersteth and other Churchmen: what precisely was meant by unsectarian and what was to happen to the Church schools? The League addressed itself rather unwillingly to these difficulties in the first conference at Birmingham. Some League members, especially the working-class leaders and Miall's supporters, wanted elementary education to be purely secular, while the Nonconformist ministers in general and the Evangelicals in particular were stoutly against. Dixon propounded the old compromise that 'the word 'unsectarian' excluded all dogmatic and theological teaching, and all creeds and catechisms, and also that if the Bible were read it must be without note or comment'.[21] Francis Adams, the first secretary of the League and the historian of the elementary school contest, saw that this policy would not satisfy the secularists and would enrage the Church and the Tories. Warre Cornish later wrote that Dixon's definition of the word unsectarian 're-

---

[19] *Life*, pp. 231–32.

[20] Bickersteth, *Charge* (1861), p. 28.

[21] Francis Adams, *History of the Elementary School Contest in England*, ed. A. Briggs (1972), p. 202.

duced religious teaching to a caput mortuum' and that the 'Nonconformists, in opening the door to let out the parson, had let in the unbeliever'.[22] Bickersteth described the type of religious instruction urged by the League as 'colourless' and designed to eradicate 'dogma in order that it might disturb no prejudice and awaken no controversy'.[23] Bickersteth's definition of a colourful religious education would, of course, have included dogma, 'prejudice' and controversy! The other difficulty facing the League, what to do with Church schools, was decided by George Dawson at the conference in October 1869. He considered that the adoption of the League's plans would result in the demise of the existing system 'by a slow, sure, and, I hope painless extinction'.[24] The phrase was clever but too provocative to Church leaders who believed the survival of Church education to be one of the most important issues in England's history.

Forster's Elementary Education Bill introduced in February 1870 was precisely what he claimed it was not, a compromise. This was always likely in a society which was politically, religiously, and educationally pluralistic. England's educational evolution, like its constitutional development, has been low on ideology and high on pragmatism, or rather the latter defines the former. The resultant Education Act compelled local authorities to establish rate-aided elementary schools in areas without enough voluntary schools. Religious instruction in these board schools was not compulsory, and by the famous Cowper-Temple clause, it was to be non-denominational. Religious teaching in voluntary schools had to be at the beginning or end of the day to facilitate conscientious objectors. For the first time in English history State funds were made available for schools which could decide not to teach religion.

The extremism of the Birmingham Education League reduced Bickersteth's hostility to Forster's Act in spite of important objections to the religious provisions. Nothing was more likely to win his support for a measure than Chamberlain's opposition to it. In 1870 the Church of England got more than it expected from a minister of pronounced liberal views, and this dulled its perception of the likely long-term results. Bickersteth was not unduly disturbed about the government regulations for voluntary schools, but he was suspicious of religious instruction in Board schools, primarily because there was no principle of inspection. Acting on the basis that what the Church could control was bound to be better than what it could not, he advocated the foundation of 'Church Schools wherever the

[22] Cornish, *English Church*, p. 276.

[23] Bickersteth, *Charge* (1870), p. 15.

[24] A. Briggs, *Elementary School Contest*, p. xxi.

necessity is found to exist'.[25] As time went on Bickersteth's cautiously optimistic acceptance of Forster's Act changed to an anxious pessimism. By 1873 he was concerned about the intensity of the Birmingham League's opposition to a measure which he felt had already gone far enough. He concluded bitterly that the League's demands

> show the animus of our opponents, and testify, with a plainness not to be misunderstood, that hostility to the Church of England and jealousy of her influence are stronger feelings with them than either zeal for education, respect for liberty of conscience, or regard for the rights of parents in the matter of their children's education.[26]

By 1876 the Bishop realized more clearly that Forster's Act had loaded the educational dice in favour of Board schools because they were maintained by a compulsory rate. This was particularly galling, since the Birmingham School Board under R. W. Dale had temporarily abolished religious instruction. Drawing on the American model Bickersteth could visualize for the first time an educational system in which religious education was peripheral. Faced with this possibility, he stressed the new importance of Sunday schools to 'ward off the calamity of having a population around us bristling with intelligence, but destitute of piety'.[27] In the 1879 Charge, Bickersteth made an impassioned plea against sacrificing a single Church school because of financial difficulties. Nevertheless, it was clear by 1880 that in spite of prodigious efforts by Anglicans and the Roman Catholics, denominational education was at a serious disadvantage to the growing State system.

The period of Bickersteth's episcopate coincided with an important transitional phase in English education. The contenders for a purely secular education did not get their way in 1870, but Church control over the main portion of popular education was over. Henceforth spiritual well-being played second fiddle to the three Rs.

Bickersteth's desire to propagate the gospel extended to Ireland also, only there the problem was not popular infidelity but popular fidelity to the Church of Rome. The combined pressures of Catholic politicians after the Emancipation Act of 1829 and the hordes of Irish immigrants in the big English cities revived the latent anti-Catholicism of English Protestantism. Concessions to Irish Catholics by the Whigs in the eighteen-thirties and by the Tories in the eighteen-forties only fuelled the flames of religious sectar-

[25] Bickersteth, *Charge* (1870), p. 24.

[26] Bickersteth, *Charge* (1873), p. 28.

[27] Bickersteth, *Charge* (1876), pp. 22–23.

ianism. Bickersteth was the incumbent of St John's, Clapham Rise, in the years immediately after the Maynooth Act, and he openly preached 'an uncompromising hostility to what he thought the deadly errors of the Roman Church'.[28] Bickersteth succeeded his uncle Edward, rector of Watton, as honorary secretary of the Society for Irish Church Missions, one of those fanatically Evangelical associations of Victorian England that are still relatively neglected.[29] The Society was led by the Revd Alexander Dallas, 'a remarkable soldier-saint, a type of Protestant Loyola, or, as his Catholic critics might have complained, a latter-day Oliver Cromwell',[30] and its purpose was to convert 'starving Catholics while feeding them'.[31] The Society had impressive early successes in the West of Ireland where the Roman Catholic Church and the Church of Ireland had little popular influence. In his 1852 lecture to the Young Men's Christian Association at Exeter Hall Bickersteth was wildly enthusiastic about the new venture.

> Within four years of the commencement of the work, an impression
> has been made which has far exceeded the most sanguine expectations
> of the founders of the Association, aroused the attention of the empire,
> and wrung from the Romish hierarchy the unwilling admission that
> their power in Ireland is fast approaching destruction.[32]

This was the pugilistic optimism that had characterized the Methodist missionary crusade in Ireland fifty years before and the result was the same. The Catholic Church was remarkably resilient in the face of Evangelical storm-troops. Bickersteth's account of wandering through the desert wilds of Connemara breaking the chains of Romish bondage is at once admirable and bizarre. The Irish Church Missions achieved little lasting success, but the historian of the movement concluded that 'it is hard to overestimate the mischief caused by some members' in stirring up religious conflict in Ireland.[33]

The Papal Aggression crisis of 1850–51 coming hard on the heels of the

---

[28] *Life*, p. 48.

[29] See S. Gilley, 'Papists, Protestants and the Irish in London, 1835–70', in *Studies in Church History*, VIII (1972), 259–66.

[30] D. Bowen, *The Protestant Crusade in Ireland, 1800–70* (1978), p. 208.

[31] S. Gilley, 'Protestant London, No Popery and the Irish Poor: 2 (1850–60)', *Recusant History*, XI (1971–72), 21–46.

[32] R. Bickersteth, *Ireland:* A Lecture to the Y.M.C.A., on 6 Jan. 1852 (1852).

[33] D. Bowen, *Souperism: Myth or Reality* (1970). p. 131.

Tractarian hysteria of the eighteen-forties reinforced Bickersteth's anti-Catholicism and was the controversial back-cloth to his rectorship of St Giles, which was densely populated by the London Irish. He saw the 'inconsistency of working for the conversion of the Irish in Ireland while ignoring the Irish at his doors',[34] and he worked valiantly to bring the destitute Irish within the pale of his parish ministry. This was difficult in a parish the size of St Giles, but he persuaded Bishop Blomfield to grant temporary licences to a number of Irish-speaking Protestant preachers.[35] This expedient had limited success, for as Dr Sheridan Gilley has well pointed out, conversion to protestantism was more than a theological trans-action for Irish Catholics; it also involved the transformation of social habits and a change of political allegiance.[36] Undaunted, the rector of St Giles held weekly classes for 'inquiring Romanists' and reported in 1855 that

> the controversial class for Romanists continues to be well attended. Many cases of conversion have occurred in the course of the past year, in which there is reason to believe there has been not only a turning from the errors and superstitions of Romanism, but a real turning of the heart to God.[37]

However, it was the consistent experience of Evangelical city missionaries that the Irish forsook Catholicism more easily than they acquired Protestantism.

Throughout the eighteen-fifties Bickersteth frequently appeared on Exeter Hall platforms. The titles of his addresses to the Y.M.C.A. illustrate his interests; National Obligation to the Bible, Ireland, Romanism in its Relation to the Second Coming of Christ, and Social Effects of the Reformation. These preoccupations did not change much with Bickersteth's appointment to the bishopric of Ripon in 1856 but his aggressively anti-Roman optimism in the previous decade was gone for good. It turned to despair in 1869 when Gladstone disestablished the Irish Church. Bickersteth, who spoke rarely in the House of Lords and never on anything important, strongly opposed the second reading of Gladstone's Bill. It was not as good a performance as Bishop Magee's maiden speech but it remains a classic statement of nineteenth-century evangelical attitudes to Ireland.

> The primary objection which I entertain to it is, that it involves the assumption that it is no part of the duty of a Christian State to

---

[34] Gilley, *Recusant History*, XI, 23.

[35] Bowen, *Protestant Crusade*, p. 201.

[36] Gilley, *Recusant History*, XI, p. 32.

[37] *Life*, p. 72.

connect itself with the maintenance of Christian truth. Should this Bill become law, the State, as far as Ireland is concerned, will have disconnected itself altogether from religion. It will have virtually declared that all creeds are equally true or equally false.

Bickersteth denied that the type of ecclesiastical organization supported by the State should be determined by the beliefs of the majority of its citizens.

Truth was higher than democracy — this is the essential explanation of the apparently reactionary religious and political attitudes of the evangelicals. The Bishop also denied, accurately as it turned out, that the disestablishment of the Irish Church would pacify Ireland, because the land question was more important. He asserted that the main reason for disestablishment was the Church of Ireland's failure to become a majority communion.

> I must say here that the clergy of the Established Church in Ireland have ... been most unfairly dealt with. If they confine themselves to ministering to the Protestant parishioners of their respective parishes we are told that the Church has failed in discharging its missionary obligations; if they display any zeal in endeavouring to gain converts from among the Roman Catholics, they are immediately denounced as firebrands.[38]

This point was unanswerable in religious terms, but then the debate was about the politically expedient. According to the Evangelicals, this surrender of Protestant principle was the real apostasy. Bickersteth declared his belief in tolerance but not equality, and the speech ended with the familiar nineteenth-century religious cry 'that what is morally wrong can never be politically right'. Of course Irish Catholics could argue exactly the same way about a religious establishment which catered for less than 10 per cent of the population.

An interesting postscript to Bickersteth's involvement with Ireland was Hugh McNeile's appointment as Dean of Ripon in 1868. The big Irishman had whipped up no-popery enthusiasm in Liverpool in the eighteen-thirties and forties, and his preferment was even more controversial than Bickersteth's nomination, twenty-two years before. The combination of a doubled electorate and the threat to the Irish Church, convinced Disraeli that a few overtly Protestant appointments would improve Conservative prospects in the 1868 election.[39] His recommendation of McNeile to the Queen was unashamedly political. Disraeli's aim was to influence the two Lancashire constituencies by raising the old 'Church in danger' and 'no-popery' cries.

[38] *Hansard*, 3rd Ser, 1869, CXCVII, cols, 54, 56.

[39] See Bahlman, *Victorian Studies*, XXII, for a fuller discussion.

The Conservative leader could not spell McNeile's name, but he knew that the seventy-three year old Evangelical would suit his electoral schemes. If Bickersteth owed his appointment to pastoral concern for the London Irish, and to his family connexions, McNeile was indebted to his anti-Catholic oratory, and to Disraeli's ecclesiastical worldliness. Evangelicals did well to emphasize the mysteries of Providence.

Dean Wellesley's opinion that Disraeli's sop to 'millions of fanatics' would not gain him many votes was probably borne out in the 1868 election, in spite of Gladstone's defeat in South-west Lancashire. McNeile's appointment inflamed Church opposition to the Evangelicals without achieving its political objective. It was ironic that Bickersteth and McNeile, who had shared so many anti-Catholic platforms in Liverpool and Exeter Hall, should spend their last years in a sleepy Yorkshire market town. At least Ripon had an Irish community and, not surprisingly, a branch of the Irish Church Missions Society.[40]

Bickersteth's episcopate coincided with a period of conflict within the Church of England between Evangelicals and High Churchmen, and between Biblical critics and conservatives. The Ripon diocese is a convenient location for research into the first conflict because its Evangelical bishop always confronted a High Church vicar in its major city. From the appointment of W. F. Hook in March 1837, every vicar of Leeds was a High Churchman, and in such a large diocese, they enjoyed an almost sub-diocesan autonomy. The Tractarian domination of Leeds was probably more pronounced than that of any other large manufacturing city in England.[41] Hook, who had a life-long dislike of Evangelicalism, was an established, if controversial, figure when the younger Bickersteth bounded over him in the Anglican preferment league. Hook speculated satirically whether he could have 'filial feelings' towards a much younger man,[42] and there was an immediate conflict when Bickersteth was invited to preside over the annual meeting of the Bible Society in Leeds. Hook opposed the meeting, but the new Bishop held his ground, probably mindful that he had bowed the knee to the High Church Bishop Hamilton in 1855, over Bickersteth's association with Irish Church Missions. The Bishop of Ripon took the ecclesiastical discipline of Anglicanism seriously, whether as victim or inquisitor.

A second difficulty arose over that eloquent testimony to the pride, wealth and folly of the new commercial interests, the Leeds Town Hall.

---

[40] Its meetings were regularly reported in the *Ripon Gazette*.

[41] Yates, *Leeds Oxford Movement*, pp. 9–11, 65.

[42] An entrance by Hook in his journal for December 1856, reproduced by W. R. Stephens, *The Life and Letters of Walter Farquar Hook D. D.*, part 2 (1878), 336.

Hook, along with the choir of the Madrigal and Motet Society, had been involved in the carnival celebrations at the laying of the foundation stone in August 1853.[43] Five years later, and after twenty-one years' ministry in Leeds, Hook had to take a back seat as an Evangelical bishop of one year's standing was given the pre-eminent place in a day honoured by the Queen's visit. Hook's response was a mixture of gout and grace:

> Amidst it all I lacked my old enthusiasm, and suffered somewhat from rheumatism. I must own to a little mortification at first, at being entirely superseded on my own dunghill. The Bishop said the prayer and spoke at the banquet. But this nasty feeling soon gave way when I found him doing everything so much better than I could have done it myself.[44]

In spite of these interruptions, the relations between the two men were good, if brief, for Hook was installed Dean of Chichester in March 1859. Both had earned their early pastoral spurs in difficult industrial parishes, Hook in Coventry and Bickersteth in London. Both were passionately concerned to reclaim the urban working classes for the Church of England, and both were effective preachers with an interest in political and social affairs. They disliked indolent clergymen more than each other's theological opinions.

Nevertheless, Bickersteth spoke against High Church theology in his pastoral Charges to the clergy. Much of the 1867 Charge was devoted to a blistering attack on ritualism though the Bishop was careful not to denigrate the place of ritual in public worship. In his view 'the questions at issue in this whole Ritualistic revival are questions of doctrine and not of mere dress and ceremonial'. Although his central argument was a defence of the Protestant, and in his opinion the traditionally Anglican, understanding of the Lord's Supper, he did not think that the labouring population would be attracted by 'the extravagant decoration of churches, nor by gorgeous ceremonial, nor by startling appeals to the senses'.[45] According to Nigel Yates, Bickersteth was right, since his researches reveal the failure of ritualistic missions to the working classes in Leeds. Both St Saviour's and St Barnabas's relied heavily on middle-class worshippers from outside the parish to swell congregational numbers. Yates concludes that with some notable exceptions 'this was true in other cities as well, and that the popularity of ritualism in working-class parishes may have been largely

---

[43] See A. Briggs, *Victorian Cities* (1977), p. 166.

[44] Hook to a Friend, 7 Sept. 1858, reproduced by Stephens, *Life of Hook*, p. 337–38.

[45] Bickersteth, *Charge* (1867), pp. 38, 53.

misunderstood: 'the personality of parish priests was probably more important than their theological beliefs or liturgical practices'.[46] Chadwick's
conclusion, based on the London High Church parishes, is the same: 'the
movement nourished the devotional and aesthetic instinct of the educated
more than it attracted the interest of the uneducated'.[47]

Ritualism offended two of Bickersteth's life-long principles; his opposition to all things Roman, and his desire to take an unfettered gospel to the
industrial poor. This position did not lead to the harassment of his High
Church clergymen, even though Nicholas Greenwell's ministry at St Barnabas's helped it become 'the gathering place for the ritualistic societies in the
north-east of England'.[48] Bickersteth's Evangelicalism was of the principled
but not vindictive type, which was not all that common in mid-Victorian
England where the party lions had an excellent appetite. The Bishop
believed in a comprehensive Church within the limits defined 'by the
Articles and the Liturgy'.[49]

While Bickersteth was no intellectual, and published nothing of note
except sermons,[50] pastoral letters and occasional lectures, he took a keen
interest in all the theological disputes of the period. Usually he was less
concerned about the debates themselves (since his opinions were fixed)
than with their impact on the parish clergy and their congregations. His
response to *Essays and Reviews* shows how the Evangelicals were pushed into
a stronger emphasis on the fundamentals.

> You will find it common to all the writings to which I have referred to
> call in question the authority of the Bible as the inspired Word of
> God, to overlook the fundamental doctrine of the corruption of human
> nature, and to invalidate the doctrine of the Atonement of our blessed
> Lord and Saviour. Be it your constant endeavour, my Reverend
> Brethren, to set these doctrines plainly forth, and the rather because
> of the assault which has been directed against them.[51]

Three years later Colenso's peculiar mathematical challenges to Biblical
authority in the *Pentateuch* occasioned Bickersteth's fullest statement on

[46] Yates, *Leeds Oxford Movement*, p. 66.

[47] Chadwick, *Victorian Church*, 1, 317.

[48] Yates, *Leeds Oxford Movement*, p. 34.

[49] Bickersteth, *Charge* (1867), p. 54.

[50] See R. Bickersteth, *Sermons* (1866).

[51] Bickersteth, *Charge* (1861), pp. 42–43.

the distinctiveness of Evangelical theology. He claimed that the current crises in the Church of England were caused by leaning on mistaken authorities, the Church as an institution on the one hand and human reason on the other. He believed, not without foundation, that the one partially provoked the other, and that the basis of theological authority lay in the revealed Word: 'the fundamental truth of the supreme authority of revelation is practically obscured or denied, and we are in peril of being drifted into superstition . . . or swallowed up in the vortex of infidelity'. Bickersteth anticipated H. P. Liddon's Bampton lectures at Oxford in 1866 in basing his vindication of Old Testament authority on Christ's quotations from it, thereby making the issue as much christological as textual.[52] The Bishop's advice to his clergy was to maintain the authority of scripture, uphold the atonement and the everlasting punishment of the wicked, strive for personal holiness and devote themselves to winning souls. His response was fundamentalist, pietistic and evangelistically aggressive; therein lay the strength and weakness of Victorian Evangelicalism. Tractarianism and biblical criticism made evangelicals like Bickersteth suspicious of innovation in worship and wary about the place of the mind in Christian experience. Paradoxically, Bickersteth urged Irish Romanists to use their minds more[53] and English theologians to use theirs less.

Bickersteth argued against sceptical views because they hindered evangelism, and because the Church needed a far more sophisticated apologetic to preserve working-class minds from infection with unorthodox catch-phrases. Oxbridge theologians could afford to be more intellectually cryptic than a preaching prelate like Bickersteth. His constituency was the factories and the pits not the common room, and he noted with alarm the spread of 'blasphemous and infidel opinions' in the popular secularist newspapers in the eighteen-seventies.[54] In spite of these forebodings, Bickersteth only rarely gave vent to the prophetical speculations that were so much a part of early Victorian Evangelicalism and which contributed to its rejection by George Eliot and Francis Newman. The Bishop's commitment to evangelism usually saved him from looking for Christ in the clouds, though in 1876, after bemoaning the results of the Elementary Education Act, the work of the Liberation Society, and the growth of ritualism and

---

[52] Bickersteth, *Charge* (1864), pp. 31–35.

[53] In his lecture on Ireland to the Y.M.C.A. in 1852 Bickersteth stated that O'Connell and his political supporters 'were nursing a freedom of thought which, if once exercised in the province of religion, would operate to the breaking asunder of the fetters of spiritual tyranny', p. 15.

[54] See Bickersteth, *Charge* (1876) where he reproduces a quotation from the *Secular Chronicle*, IV, no. 23, 44–45. 'The God of the Bible is the product of an ignorant age, and would not command the devotion of any man of intelligence'.

scepticism, he concluded that 'it needed no prophetic insight to perceive tokens of a coming consummation'.[55]

Although Bickersteth was an Evangelical who wished a strong Yorkshire Nonconformity every success in stemming the tide of ignorance and infidelity,[56] he was also a strong Churchman. Nowhere is this better illustrated than in his treatment of Dr Blackwood, the vicar of Middleton Tyas, who invited the Revd Dr Steane, a well-known Baptist preacher, to use his pulpit. Both men were on their way to Scotland to create interest in the proposed general conference of Christians in New York and Blackwood defended his action on the basis of the soundness of Steane's doctrine. Bickersteth was unimpressed and warned Blackwood that he was legally guilty under the Act of Uniformity and the ecclesiastical Canons of 1604. The Bishop demanded and got contrition.[57]

Bickersteth, far from fomenting an Evangelical party within the Church, spoke against 'party spirit'[58] and its disharmony and pride. He played a full part in Church Congresses, though many Evangelicals preferred the security of their own gatherings. His son and biographer records that Bickersteth accepted the designation 'Evangelical' but not 'Low Churchman'.[59] Nevertheless, Bickersteth in his emphasis on lay co-operation, open-air preaching and simple services for the working-classes,[60] was a mid-Victorian imitator of that virginal Wesleyanism, which had by his day lost its virginity.[61]

In his private life, as in public, Bickersteth was unmistakably Evangelical. He read Macaulay and Scott but not much else of importance; he played draughts and chess but not late on Saturday night; he loved horses and nature but not with romantic abandon; he could be imaginative in his musings on Biblical prophecy, but he deplored a colourful Catholic carnival in Portugal;[62] he liked worship but not with too much ceremony; he loved working people but he lived in a beautiful rural palace; he loved Catholics

[55] Bickersteth, *Charge* (1876), p. 52.

[56] RA, R. Bickersteth to Christian Friends, 13 Nov. 1863.

[57] This whole debate was published in the press and the newspaper cuttings have been kept. See RA, Bickersteth to Blackwood, 23 Sept. 1870; Blackwood to Bickersteth, 30 Sept. 1870; Bickersteth to Blackwood, 21 Oct. 1870; Blackwood to Bickersteth, 22 Oct. 1870.

[58] Bickersteth, *Charge* (1876), p. 41.

[59] *Life*, p. 27.

[60] Bickersteth outlined his scheme for reclaiming the people in his 1870 *Charge*, pp. 34–52.

[61] A. D. Gilbert argues this point in more general terms in *Religion and Society in Industrial England* (1976), p. 137.

[62] *Life*, pp. 276–77.

but hated Roman Catholicism; above all he loved his Bible, his Church, his family and his God. He was diligent and pious, narrow minded yet surprisingly tolerant, politically aware but not a great strategic thinker. In his commitment to religious education, working-class evangelism, Protestant Ireland and an authoritative Bible, Bickersteth swam against the historical currents of his time. He was not moving the way the world was moving, and that made him defensive and anxious about the future. He viewed a changing England from the fixed star of Biblical revelation. This gave him strength and admirable consistency, but it limited his understanding of social and political forces. However, what he lost in mental power he gained in spirituality for Bickersteth was a man of compassion[63] and integrity. As a bishop he turned out to be a remarkably wise choice for the demands that Ripon made upon him, and at a time when the Church of England could ill afford anything else, Bickersteth was a working bishop, in spite of a playful letter to his son: 'I wonder what Palmerston can have been about to appoint such lazy drones. They ought to be made to work'.[64] Bickersteth's admonitions to his clergy about non-residence, insufficient services (especially for communion), educational apathy, and low baptism and communion figures, helped to produce a considerable improvement in the eighteen-seventies (Table 5). Without knowing how these results were achieved, it is difficult to assess their value and permanence. Outward conformity to Anglican practices did not necessarily mean more spiritual vigour in the individual or in the church.

Behind Bickersteth's pleas to the clergy lay the assumption that the Anglican product was good, but that its marketing was poor. This was partly true, but he failed to realize that many working-class people (especially men) were no longer interested in any religious product, for reasons only superficially connected to clerical indifference. John Kent reaches a similar conclusion in his recent study of Victorian revivalism.

> It is too simple to accuse Victorian Christianity of not making contact with the working class: it made contact and was rejected ... Rarely has so much effort been expended on the religious subjugation of a secular culture; but the effort was not a religious revival in itself and it failed to evoke one.[65]

---

[63] RA, see, for example, his printed circular on the destitution of the Lancashire cotton operatives as a result of the American Civil War.

[64] R. Bickersteth to his son, 28 Sept. 1861. 'Would my son like to know what the lazy, indolent, do-nothing Palmerstonian Bishop of Ripon has been doing during the last few days'. There followed a very full diary of sermons and engagements. *Life*, p. 131.

[65] J. Kent, *Holding the Fort: Studies in Victorian Revivalism* (1978), p. 33.

This 'effort' was the basis of Bickersteth's strategy. He believed in work for God, as he believed in God, and his indefatigable exertions played an important part in the limited and temporary restoration of Anglican fortunes in the third quarter of the nineteenth century.

APPENDIX

Table 1
Report of the Census of Religious Worship, 1851

| Denominations | Number of attendants at public worship in the West Riding | | | |
	Morning	Afternoon	Evening	Total
Church of England	113,683	87,712	36,387	239,792
Methodists (all types)	97,116	92,707	106,291	296,114
Others	75,743	51,694	37,383	164,820
Total	286,552	234,113	180,061	700,726

Population: 1,325,495
Number of individuals attending church on census Sunday based on Mann's calculation (i.e. Morning + ½ afternoon + ⅓ evening numbers): 463,628
Percentage of population: 35%
National Average: 40.5%

Notes:
A. The Diocese of Ripon included the major towns of the West Riding.
B. Church attendance was below the national average, and the Church of England was considerably less successful than the Dissenting denominations.
C. Mann was convinced, and this has not been challenged, that the missing multitudes belonged to the working classes.

Table 2
Professional clergy and Church sittings:
Ripon Diocese 1836–79

Year	Professional Clergy	Sittings*
1836	373	155,280
1870	661	231,558
1873	688	251,326
1876	708	256,824
1879	734	287,023

* Figures do not include chapels of ease and mission rooms.

Table 3
Baptism and Confirmation figures:
Ripon Diocese 1858–79

Triennial Periods	Baptisms	Confirmations
1858–60	—	12,702*
1861–63	70,065	12,788
1864–66	73,882	16,181
1867–69	70,347	17,035
1870–72	78,465	17,575
1873–75	83,866	19,207
1876–78	86,623	21,284

*Amended from the printed charge because Bickersteth made an arithmetical error.

Bickersteth also gives communicant figures, but, on his own admission, they are misleading, because they fail to account for the rapid increase in communion services.

Table 4
Pupil numbers in Church of England Schools:
Ripon Diocese 1858–79

Year	Week-day Schools	Sunday Schools	Adult Schools
1858	57,180	57,542	2,925
1861	—	—	—
1864	74,412	69,144	6,006
1867	78,434	73,490	—
1870	94,828	83,009	—
1873	98,851	—	3,770
1876	108,961	89,367	—
1879	112,084	99,031	5,117

Table 5
The Eighteen-seventies: numerical increases expressed
as a percentage of growth

Population (Yorkshire)	18.4%
Church sittings	24.0%
Confirmations	24.9%
Baptisms	23.1%
Sunday School pupils	19.3%
Day-school pupils	18.2%
Professional Clergy	11.0%

Freezing the historical continuum for such a short period is bound to bring distortion. However, the decade 1870–79 has been chosen for two reasons:

(i) It is the only decade for which full information is available.

(ii) It is in the middle of the Bickersteth episcopate. It is, therefore, difficult to attribute the trends to Bishop Longley, Bickersteth's predecessor.

Notes:

A. The population percentage has been computed on a county basis since the censuses of 1871 and 1881 took no account of diocesan boundaries. The figures for the Ripon Diocese (parts of the North and West Ridings) are unlikely to be substantially different from the county average.

B. The high figure for baptisms disguises a stagnation in the eighteen-sixties.

C. The low figure for professional clergy is partially due to a rapid increase in the period 1836–70.

RICHARD J. HELMSTADTER

CHAPTER 4

THE NONCONFORMIST CONSCIENCE

IN the nineteenth and early twentieth centuries religious Nonconformity played a prominent role in English public life. During that time religion was a generally more important feature of the social and political landscape than it became after the first World War, and those Protestants who dissented from the Church of England constituted an important interest group. Congregationalists, Baptists, Methodists, Presbyterians, Quakers, Unitarians, and members of a host of minor sects differed from each other in many respects, but they shared social situations, social values, and political goals sufficiently that they were conscious of forming a distinctive community within English society. As Matthew Arnold vigorously pointed out in *Culture and Anarchy*, Nonconformists also shared a tendency to emphasize rigid codes of personal behavior. They were the heirs of the Puritans, and their views of life were suffused with considerations of conscience. It is not surprising that the term 'Nonconformist conscience' came to be used as the name for Nonconformist opinion on public affairs.

The term, 'Nonconformist conscience,' did not, however, come into common use until the last decade of the nineteenth century, and it identified a configuration of views peculiar to that time. Nonconformity was then in the midst of a critical period in its history. It still enjoyed considerable strength, but it was beset with deep-seated confusion from which it never recovered. Earlier in the century the Nonconformist community possessed a relatively cohesive culture and a clear political orientation. It is the argument of this chapter that Nonconformist culture began to disintegrate in the late nineteenth century, and that the 'Nonconformist conscience,' when compared with the synthesis achieved earlier, sheds some light on the nature of that collapse.

On the surface there were few signs of weakness in the Nonconformist community toward the end of the nineteenth century. The only clear and readily visible evidence of declining vitality was the fact that Nonconformists constituted a smaller proportion of the whole population of England than they had in the middle of the century. At the time of the religious census in 1851, Nonconformists had accounted for about half the church-going public. There was never another national, official census of church attendance, but numerous local inquiries suggest that, at the turn of the century, rather more than half of those who normally attended church on Sunday were Nonconformists. Neither Nonconformity nor the Church of England, however, managed to increase their numbers sufficiently to keep pace with the growth of the population as a whole in the second half of the nineteenth century. On the political front, moreover, advancing democracy provides an additional reason for the decline in relative size and importance of the Nonconformist portion of the electorate. Reinforced by Victorian social convention, church-going was a normal and expected feature of upper and middle-class life. This was emphatically not the case among the working classes, the majority of whom had little or no connection with any church. Therefore the Reform Acts of 1867 and 1884, by extending the franchise further among the working classes, increased the number of voters who lived outside the range of the pulpit, and, presumably, beyond the reach of the religious press.

Nonetheless, Nonconformity toward the end of the century could still hope to wield considerable political power. With the exception of the Wesleyan Methodists, the large denominations, the Congregationalists, the Baptists, and the various schismatical Methodist bodies, were traditionally supporters of the Liberal party. From the middle of the century, the Wesleyans had been moving in a leftward direction, and by the 1890s they too, for the most part, had joined the Liberal camp. When they spoke with a united voice, Nonconformists were able to make their influence clearly felt in the Liberal party, and, when opinion among them was aroused and organized, they were able to have some impact on national affairs.

The machinery for organizing Nonconformist opinion, moreover, became much stronger and more efficient in the last two decades of the century. In most of the denominations central organization was improved, and the movement for reunion among the Wesleyans and the other Methodist groups was growing. The desirability of more cooperation among the de-nominations was clearly perceived in the 1880s, and in a number of towns free church councils were created to coordinate Nonconformist activity. This movement produced several national free church congresses in the 1890s, and eventually, in 1896, the National Council of Evangelical Free Churches was established. By 1901 the National Council had gone some way toward establishing machinery for unity among the free churches. Almost every eminent free church leader supported the movement, and seven hundred local councils and thirty-six district federations helped orga-nize the rank and file.

Developments in religious journalism also helped to make more possible the organization of Nonconformist opinion in the twenty-five or thirty years before the war. Throughout the century there was an enormous number of religious magazines and newspapers, and a great many ordinary secular newspapers adopted an editorial position which actively supported either the Church of England or Nonconformity. Some of those periodicals and newspapers were ably conducted, of high quality and great influence. One thinks of the *Eclectic Review*, the *British Quarterly Review*, and, on a less exalted literary level, the *Methodist Magazine*. Among newspapers, the *Leeds Mercury* under the Baines family from the beginning of the century, the *Patriot* under Josiah Conder in the thirties and forties, and the *Nonconformist* vigorously edited by Edward Miall from its foundation in 1841 until his death in 1881, were outstanding leaders of Nonconformist opinion. In the 1800s, Nonconformist journalism was able to draw on the techniques that were being developed to encourage massive increases in circulation for secular newspapers. At the height of its influence in the 1870s, the *Nonconformist*, a paper produced in the old-fashioned, staid, high-toned style, did not achieve a circulation above 15,000. In the early 1880s, the *Christian World*, more brightly written, less rigorously political, more chatty and with features for the ladies, edged toward a circulation of 150,000. Two newspapers which emerged in the eighties quickly became recognized as authoritative voices within the Nonconformist community. With their very large readership, they helped shape Nonconformist views on public affairs more effectively than had previously been possible. The *Methodist Times* was founded in 1885 by Hugh Price Hughes, and edited by him in order to propagate the generally progressive views which constituted what he called the Forward Movement. The *British Weekly* was established in 1886 as the successor to the *British Quarterly Review*. That canny man of letters, William Robertson Nicoll, edited it until his death in 1923. He made it the preeminent newspaper of Nonconformity. Less adventurous than Hughes, and more concerned with the economic implications of a large circulation, Nicoll succeeded in making the *British Weekly* the principal voice of moderate free church opinion.

Nonconformists had traditionally put great stress on conscience. They were, notoriously, men easily roused to militant defense of those principles which they considered rooted in conscience. Their great struggle, indeed, had been for freedom to worship as they pleased, for freedom of conscience. John Stuart Mill accorded religious Dissenters an honored place in the story of the progress of liberty. John Morley echoed a widely held view when he said of Nonconformity in 1873: 'Its creeds may be narrow, its spirit contentious, its discipline unscriptural, its ritual bleak, its votaries plebeian ... Dissent is not picturesque, but it possesses a heroic political record.'[1] Ironically, the late Victorian improvement in the organization of Nonconformity, and the appearance in general usage of the expression 'Nonconformist conscience,' occurred when the heroic days of politics and conscience were over for religious dissenters. Their leaders at the turn of the century seemed frequently concerned with problems too petty to warrant the energy and grand language expended on them, and the Nonconformist

---

[1] *Fortnightly Review*, August and September, 1873.

conscience seemed too often to draw on what was narrow rather than on what was heroic in the Nonconformist tradition.

The term 'Nonconformist conscience' was first used, as far as I can discover, in the correspondence columns of *The Times* in late November, 1890. Parnell, the leader of the Irish Party, had been named a correspondent in a divorce action brought by Captain O'Shea against his wife. No defense was offered, and when the judgment was handed down on 17 November, it touched off a wave of scandalized indignation in England that eventually drove Parnell from public life. *The Times*, inspired with its own grievance against Parnell, played a leading role in rousing public opinion to righteousness, as did a number of other newspapers. But the most unbridled denunciations of Parnell, from the beginning until the end, came from Nonconformist ministers, especially, perhaps, from Hugh Price Hughes, the militant Methodist who liked to compare himself with Savonarola. On 19 November in the *Pall Mall Gazette*, John Clifford, the most eminent among a new wave of progressive Baptists, put the Nonconformist position on Parnell clearly and carefully: 'He must go. British politicians are not what they were. Men legally convicted of immorality will not be permitted to lead in the legislature.' Hughes was less restrained. 'Parnell must go,' he told his family. 'If necessary everything must go. What are parties and causes compared to an issue like this — the establishing of Christ's kingdom?'[2] And on the Sunday after the judgment, Hughes pressed on his congregation at St James's Hall the rather strained argument that to permit Parnell to remain leader of the Irish Party would be 'to sacrifice our religion.'[3] More to the point, Hughes urged Gladstone to consider that, unless he got rid of Parnell, he might be sacrificing the support of Nonconformist voters, for 'there is no subject on which the Free Churches of the country feel so deeply as on social purity.'[4] On 28 November 'A Wesleyan Minister,' possibly Hughes himself, demanded in a letter to *The Times* 'unconditional abdication' from Parnell: 'Nothing less will satisfy the Nonconformist conscience now.' Thus the term emerged, and over the next twenty-five years it was frequently heard.

The Parnell affair helps to illuminate the nature of the Nonconformist conscience. It is true that the Nonconformist community in the late nineteenth and early twentieth centuries was corporately concerned with a wide range of political and social issues. The central organizations of the various denominations, and the National Free Church Council, felt increas-

[2] Dorothea Price Hughes, *The Life of Hugh Price Hughes*, 4th ed. (1905), p. 348.

[3] *Ibid.*, p. 353.

[4] *Methodist Times*, 20 November 1890.

ing pressure during this period to speak out on problems of poverty and the slums, on the significance of socialism, on war in general and the Boer War in particular, on old age pensions, the place of the Lords in the constitution, and other important questions of the age. The more influential newspapers and the leading ministers encouraged the community to take up all these concerns and more. But special emphasis was concentrated on a narrow set of problems that related personal sin and social or political behavior. Parnell's scandal is a case in point. Along with improper sex, gambling and drink made up a trio of sins that the Nonconformist conscience found peculiarly irritating — a trio that Nonconformist leaders tried, sometimes successfully, to raise to the level of important public issues. 'The three deadly enemies of England' were identified by Hugh Price Hughes in the *Methodist Times* (6 June 1895) as 'drink, impurity and gambling.'

Was the Nonconformist conscience rooted in a coherent view or philosophy of society and politics? Clearly the answer must be negative. While there was a definite drift among Nonconformist ministers in the generation before the war toward greater sympathy with the problems of the poor, there was no distinctively Nonconformist solution to the problem of poverty and, indeed, no consensus within the free church community as to what should be done. There was clearly an increasing disposition on the part of many Nonconformists to encourage the state to play a more active role in maintaining social welfare, but there was no consensus on specific measures. Paradoxically, at a time when the community and its organs of opinion were better organized than ever before, a systematically organized Nonconformist vision of the state and the means of social progress did not exist. There was a striking unity of free church opinion on 'the deadly enemies of England,' but this agreement on the evils of sex, gambling and drink represented an unstable amalgam of half-rejected tradition and current fashion. The Nonconformist conscience did not bring about a consensus of distinctive free church opinion on more important issues.

There is a parallel here, of course, between the Nonconformist conscience and the so-called New Liberalism of the same period. Nor is the parallel merely a matter of accident. Perhaps those who claimed that Nonconformity was the backbone of the Liberal party claimed too much, but there can be no doubt that the Liberals, at least from the beginning of Gladstone's leadership in the mid 1860s, owed a great deal to the organized support of Nonconformity. Near the end of the nineteenth century a number of leading Liberals lost confidence in what one might call the Gladstonian synthesis which dominated the party in the previous generation. This happened at the same time that a number of leading Nonconformists were rejecting the coherent mid-Victorian synthesis which had prevailed among religious Dissenters. Both the leaders of the Liberal party and the leaders of Nonconformity were responding to similar problems, and neither the politicians nor the religious chieftains succeeded in reshaping their traditions sufficiently to meet adequately the demands of the twentieth century. Both groups of leaders treated their traditions with profound ambivalence. Both rejected much that was considered fundamentally important by their predecessors. Neither group succeeded in creating a satisfactory new synthesis.

In sharp contrast to the weakness and tendency toward triviality of the Nonconformist conscience at the turn of the century, was the synthesis Dissenters achieved in the early and middle portions of Victoria's reign. For fifty years, from the 1830s to the 1880s, Nonconformists shared a comparatively well-integrated and coherent view of society, social progress, the state, and conscience. During this period, before the creation of the National Free Church Council and before the appearance of dissenting newspapers with circulations as large as that of the *British Weekly*, Nonconformists did not possess the organizational machinery that became available a little later on, but their community was probably more solidly united by widely held social and religious attitudes that interlocked and therefore reinforced each other. Central to these interrelated attitudes and ideas was the theology of evangelicalism.

By the middle of the 1830s all the Dissenting denominations had felt the force of the great Evangelical revival of the eighteenth century. Even that intellectual elite among the Nonconformists, the Unitarians, had felt the emotional attraction of religion of the heart, but the Unitarians never fully entered the Evangelical fold. As their social position declined in the later nineteenth century, Unitarians found themselves increasingly on the fringe of the Dissenting world, or beyond. The National Council of Evangelical Free Churches did not admit Unitarians. All the larger denominations, however, and a considerable portion of the Church of England, warmly embraced the central tenets of Evangelical truth by the 1830s. Evangelical theology was by no means as systematic and logically precise as the theology of Calvinism or the medieval schoolmen. Nor was it as intellectually demanding. But evangelicalism did contain a sufficient number of interrelated and widely shared theological positions that it is possible to describe it systematically.

Evangelicals all placed primary emphasis on the salvation of individual souls. In this, as in all its essentials, evangelicalism reflected the theological position developed in Wesleyan Methodism in the second half of the eighteenth century. Emphasis on individual salvation was a part of the Arminian theology advocated by John Wesley, but such emphasis was familiar among the Calvinists too. It was easily accepted within those Evangelical denominations such as the Congregationalists and Particular Baptists whose theological traditions were Calvinist. In the sixteenth and seventeenth centuries Calvinists had placed much more emphasis on the community of the saved, the visible and corporate elite that constituted their churches. Evangelicals did not stress the select community of the saved because, following the Arminian position and rejecting the Calvinist, they avoided the question of predestination and preached that all men might be saved. That Christ died to save all men was universally believed among evangelicals, and this more than anything else distinguished them from Calvinists. Nevertheless, confusingly and illogically, most Congregationalists and Particular Baptists, reluctant to admit a clear break with their theological past, continued to call themselves Calvinist as late as the 1880s. While most accepted the label 'modified Calvinist,' some insisted on being called 'strict' or even 'hyper-Calvinist' while preaching the possibility of salvation for all. Salvation, for most Evangelicals, meant going to heaven after death. Those poor souls who were not saved were thought to suffer never-ending pain in hell. More sophisticated versions of salvation were available, but they were exceptions to the general rule.

A standardized version of the process of salvation was accepted throughout the Evangelical community. It was preached from countless pulpits; it was taught in the denominational seminaries where ministers were trained; it was published in manuals intended to help sinners along their own roads to glory. John Angell James, the Congregationalist pastor of Carrs Lane Chapel in Birmingham, published the most successful of the manuals in 1834. The angel James, as he was sometimes called, designed *The Anxious Inquirer After Salvation* for those who asked, 'with some degree of anxiety, what shall I do to be saved?' He took his readers step by step through the process which culminated in conversion, that religious experience which Evangelicals frequently confounded with salvation and confidently regarded as the most important step preliminary to permanent residence in heaven. *The Anxious Inquirer* subsequently appeared in many further editions and was very widely distributed by the nondenominational Religious Tract Society. 'Millions in heaven are already saved,' James assured his readers, 'and myriads more are on the road to salvation. God is still willing, and Christ is still as able to save you as he was them.'[5] That was the central Evangelical message.

In keeping with their very strong tendency to treat men as individuals rather than as members of a larger corporation such as the church or the state, Evangelicals accorded to each individual a heavy weight of responsibility for his own salvation. This belief in the ability of individual men to shape their own destinies ran directly counter to the older Calvinist belief in divine predestination. Almost certainly, the Evangelical commitment to the idea of freedom of choice and the significance of individuals reflects the dramatic opening of new ranges of opportunity for individuals in England

[5] John Angell James, *The Anxious Inquirer* (1836 edition), p. 5.

during the time of the Industrial Revolution. 'You are invited' proclaimed the *Anxious Inquirer*. 'If you neglect the invitation you will find at last that you were lost, not in consequence of any purpose of God determining you to be lost, but in consequence of your own unbelief.'[6]

Each individual's active responsibility for the ultimate destiny of his soul began with the awakening of his conscience. The conscience was, indeed, fundamentally important in the Evangelical scheme of salvation, and conscience pervaded the Evangelical view of the world. Conscience, for Evangelicals, was the principal guide to action. Conscience was essential to salvation, and the key to individual improvement and social progress. Without conscience, all would be lost. Every man's concern for salvation began with his conscience, with his awareness of sin in general and recognition of his own sinful condition in particular. Once aware of the depth of his own depravity and frightened, perhaps terrorized, by the prospect of eternal damnation, the sinner was ripe for reformation. Thus did conscience, or awareness of sin, lie at the base of his subsequent pilgrimage of grace.

The next step on the road to conversion for the sinful Evangelical was recognition that he could not overcome his sinfulness entirely by his own efforts. Striving to increase anxiety at this stage, James admonished his anxious inquirers: 'You have not only sin enough in yourselves to deserve the bottomless pit, and to sink you to it unless it be pardoned; but sin enough, if it could be divided and distributed to others, to doom multitudes to perdition.'[7] At this point the sinner was caught in painful tension between his own responsibility and his apparent helplessness. Resolution lay in the Evangelical view of the Atonement.

Aided by the Holy Spirit, the successful inquirer learned to accept as if it were part of his own experience that Christ died on the cross to cleanse every man of sin, to take upon Himself the guilt of every man so that every man might be saved. He who truly believed in Christ and His atoning sacrifice was thereby enabled to cast himself on His mercy and rise above the intolerable burden of his sinful humanity. The feeling that this had really happened, the feeling that one had accepted Christ and the Atonement in a way that was profoundly vital and meaningful, the feeling that Christ had at that very moment welcomed oneself into a new and better life, all this is what evangelicals called conversion. Conversion was an experience, not an intellectual conviction. Evangelical theology was rooted more in feeling and practical experience than in thought. Central to the experience of conversion was a starkly simple theological version of the Atonement. The Atonement was, therefore, the central theological doctrine

[6] *Ibid.*, p. 114.

[7] *Ibid.*, p. 37.

of evangelicalism. That is why Evangelicals could advertise their orthodoxy by claiming loyalty to 'Christ and Him crucified,' a phrase with implications commonly understood throughout the evangelical world.

Until late in the nineteenth century, in order to become a fully joined, communicating member of most evangelical Nonconformist chapels, an applicant was required to testify that he had experienced conversion. Because conversion was a formal requirement, the testimonies of many must have been mere formalities. Applicants of good character, or good reputation at least, were never turned down. Nevertheless, the sense of having been born anew was clearly real for some, and the insistent emphasis upon conversion in Victorian chapel life, along with the increased status enjoyed by the converted in the chapel community, encouraged most Nonconformists to treat conversion very seriously. Certainly the rhetoric in which the experience was discussed — and it was discussed frequently — helped to reinforce the view that an individual's personal relationship with God was much more important than corporate worship. Also the idea that each individual was master of his fate was strengthened by the Evangelical preacher's perpetual plea to the unconverted to decide for Christ before death made decision impossible.

Underlying the simple evangelical interpretation of the Atonement was a simple view of the Bible. Almost all Evangelical Nonconformists, until Biblical scholarship and Biblical Criticism began to make headway among them in the 1880s, considered that the Bible was God's revelation written down by men acting under the direct guidance of divine inspiration. They accepted the Bible as true in a straightforward literal sense, and they made frequent reference to proof texts to support their central message about sin, salvation, and the Atonement. When the nature of Biblical inspiration began to be questioned in the late nineteenth century, and when evangelical Nonconformists felt the force of scholarly criticism which called into question the authority of the Bible as a repository of true statements, Evangelical theology began to crumble.

Evangelical Nonconformity produced no great scholars in the nineteenth century. The general drift of evangelicalism, which stressed feeling and experience more than systematic thinking, was toward practical rather than intellectual concerns. The Dissenting Academies which had been progressive centers of learning in the eighteenth century became, for the most part, seminaries for training ministers in the nineteenth. Ministers, moreover, concentrated on expository preaching aimed at encouraging conversions rather than on communal worship or on systematically raising the level of religious knowledge among their congregations. The thrust of evangelicalism toward the practical tended to de-emphasize the distinction between the ministry and the laity; and, in spite of the great attention given to the fate of the soul after death, the Evangelical orientation toward usefulness tended to encourage activity in this world. In practical philanthropy and practical politics Victorian Nonconformists were very active indeed, and in both spheres they developed policies and ideas that stressed the conscience and were in harmony with their theology of individualism.

The basic political posture of nineteenth-century Nonconformity derived from the traditional struggle of Dissenters for liberty of conscience, for greater freedom to decide for themselves in matters of worship and ultimate truth. After the Glorious Revolution of 1688, which resulted in toleration for Protestant Dissent, the political attention of Dissenters centered on achieving relief from the civil disabilities which their Nonconformity still entailed.

Heading the list of Dissenters' grievances were the Test and Corporation Acts. The Test Act (1673) made it illegal for any persons not receiving communion in the Church of England to hold office under the Crown, and the Corporation Act (1661) did the same for offices in municipal corporations. Conscientious Dissenters were thereby barred from many public offices, and Dissenters held up the Test and Corporation Acts as the principal symbols of their inferior status as citizens of the realm. Wealthy Dissenters in the City of London created an association, the Dissenting Deputies, in 1732 to press for repeal of the Test and Corporation Acts.

The Deputies soon became a sophisticated pressure group, working behind the scenes to protect the interests of Dissenters. In the late eighteenth century the Deputies helped organize a campaign for repeal that came close to success, and, finally, with the dissipation of the conservative reaction associated with the wars with France, the Deputies played a major role in pressing liberal Whigs to force through repeal in 1828. The Deputies, who continue to exist, have never abandoned the political style they developed in the eighteenth century. Consequently, when the techniques of pressure politics changed soon after 1828, the Deputies lost their role as the principal political voice of Nonconformity. More thrusting and vigorously optimistic leaders, including a number of newly powerful men from the self-confident industrial towns in the Midlands and the North, attracted Nonconformists toward associations designed to organize public opinion and exert pressure on Parliament from without.

Repeal of the Test and Corporation Acts was an event of high symbolic significance, for it conferred constitutional confirmation upon the movement toward religious pluralism in English society. But repeal was not the end of the Dissenters' battle for liberty. After repeal, Nonconformists continued to call for increased toleration and soon began to demand full equality with the Church of England. Their continued failure to achieve equality, along with their more successful but very long and drawn out struggle against legally imposed religious discrimination, encouraged Victorian Nonconformists to distrust the state. That the state should intervene as little as possible with the lives of its citizens was an axiom among Nonconformists. Furthermore, because they tended to confound conscience and religion and because they adamantly opposed any formal or legal connection between religion and the state, many Victorian Nonconformists assumed that there should be no connection between conscience and the state.

For a few years after repeal of the Test and Corporation Acts, Nonconformists hoped they had entered a new era in which the burden of discrimination under which they lived would be lifted. Their expectations were further raised by the passing of the Reform Act of 1832, but by the end of that decade they had achieved less than they had hoped for. A conservative reaction was making further progress difficult. Immediately following repeal of the Test and Corporation Acts, Nonconformists turned their attention to what they considered legal discrimination in five areas: church rates, marriages, civil registration of births and deaths, the ancient universities, and burials. They fought for reform in all five areas during the 1830s.

Church rates were taxes levied at the local parish level for the upkeep and repair of the parish church building. Anglicans and non-Anglicans alike were liable for these taxes which were based on the assumption, clearly false by the 1830s, that all the ratepayers would be worshippers in the Church of England. Nonconformists naturally found church rates oppressive, and in the 1830s they began to mount a campaign against the rates. In some parishes some Nonconformists refused to pay the church rates on the ground that conscience prevented their paying for support of a church whose association with the state they deplored. Some of those who refused to pay the church rate had their household goods seized and sold, and some went to prison. The battle against church rates was fought hard for more than thirty years. Beginning in the later fifties, the Liberation Society (see below) began to coordinate the thousands of local skirmishes and to carry the campaign into Parliament. The struggle, in which the language of conscience was freely employed, did not end until Gladstone secured statutory abolition of compulsory church rates in 1868.

The marriage question was more quickly settled by legislation passed in 1837. Before then Dissenters could not be married in their own chapels by their own ministers, but only in the Established Church by Anglican priests. The settlement of 1837 was not entirely satisfactory for it left lingering minor irritants, but the basic problem was solved. The Whig government dealt with the question by instituting civil marriage. Marriages could now be performed by the civil registrar of births, deaths, and marriages, or by Nonconformist ministers in chapels licensed for marriages so long as the civil registrar was present.

Civil registration of births, deaths, and marriages was itself introduced in 1837 to improve record keeping, and it incidentally met another Nonconformist complaint. Before 1837, the only official record of births, deaths, and marriages was the parish register, kept by the priest in each of the nearly 15,000 parishes. The record of births, moreover, was a record of baptism only, presumed in those days of precarious infant lives to have taken place soon after birth. Nonconformists, therefore, were compelled to have their children baptized in an Anglican ceremony by the parish priest if they wished to be able to establish a legally valid record of their birth dates. Civil registration resolved this difficulty entirely. It was, moreover, one more step toward further separation of the functions of the Church and the state, a step in the direction that Nonconformists approved.

Nonconformists were effectively excluded from taking degrees at the two ancient universities by the requirement of submission to the thirty-nine articles, the doctrinal code of the Church of England. At Oxford submission was required upon matriculation, at Cambridge upon taking a degree. Wealthy Nonconformists were, therefore, able to send their sons to Cambridge, where if they were conscientious about their Nonconformity they were unable to receive degrees. Oxford and Cambridge further irritated Dissenters by opposing in the early 1830s the granting of a charter to the new London University. London received its charter in 1837. Oxford ceased to require submission to the thirty-nine articles upon matriculation after the mid-1850s. But Nonconformists had to await Gladstone's first administration before, in 1871, they obtained full access to the degrees and most of the fellowships at Oxford and Cambridge

Burials proved a much more difficult and troubling issue than marriages, perhaps because the solution to the problem involved interfering with the control of the Church of England over its own property. The burial question added heat to the Nonconformist contention that the property of the Established Church was in fact the property of the nation at large, that it ought to be removed from the control of the Church and devoted to national and nondenominational uses. In the nineteenth century most urban Dissenting chapels, and the poorer rural chapels, had no ground in which to bury their dead. They were compelled to use the churchyards of the Established Church, where they might meet with several sorts of trouble. The parish priest might simply refuse permission to use his churchyard; he might dictate what should appear on the tombstone and disallow the title 'Reverend' for a departed Nonconformist minister; he would almost certainly deny Nonconformist ministers permission to conduct services in his churchyard. Not until the Burials Act of 1880 did Nonconformists win significant rights of entry into parochial churchyards. The Burials Act opened the churchyards to any Christian and orderly form of service, and the major Nonconformist complaint was answered. In the meantime, however, the creation of public cemeteries in densely populated areas helped make burials, next to church rates, the most acutely distressing and widespread Nonconformist grievance in the mid-Victorian period. The legislation of 1855 creating public cemeteries provided that each cemetery be divided into ground consecrated by an Anglican bishop and intended for Anglican burials, and unconsecrated ground intended for the rest. Endless trouble ensued, about the lower social status of unconsecrated ground, or about the character of the wall dividing the two areas. Nonconformists favored inconspicuous walls; the notorious Bishop Phillpotts of Exeter insisted on solid masonry at least three feet high; Dissenters, quite rightly, interpreted this as insulting. Time, and diminished antagonism between Dissent and the Established Church, gradually resolved these difficulties. They were never of great consequence, perhaps, but they distressed many families at times of personal grief and made the conflict between Church and Dissent seem deeply meaningful to a great many ordinary people.

Nonconformists, then, distrusted the state in the early and mid-Victorian periods because it dealt so slowly with their grievances. The state took more than fifty years to do what they hoped, just after the great reforms of 1828 and 1832, would be done in less than five. Furthermore, the state created new grievances as it moved into new, and religiously sensitive, areas of national life. Chief among these new areas was primary education for the poor. Among churchmen and Dissenters both in the 1830s there were many who recognized that a substantial amount of public money would be required every year in order to support an adequate number of primary schools for the great majority of English children who were unable to pay the cost of their education. At this time character building and improved morality were considered important goals in primary education. The state, indeed, was pressed to support education in order to create a more moral and therefore more peaceable, less potentially rebellious, citizenry. Partly as a consequence of the stress on morality in education, religion and education were closely intertwined.

Both churchmen and Nonconformists, therefore, watched closely lest the state act in a way which would give an advantage to their ecclesiastical rivals. Governments proceeded cautiously, anxious not to become the victims of sectarian feuding. The state began to give annual grants for primary education in 1833, distributing the money through two educational societies, the National Society for Educating the Poor in the Principles of the Established Church, and the dissenting British and Foreign School Society. All went fairly smoothly for ten years. The basis of a department of education was established at the national level in 1839, a system of school inspectors was created, and the parliamentary grants grew larger each year.

Suddenly, in 1843, there exploded a major controversy which had a significant impact on the general Nonconformist view of the state. In that year the home secretary, Sir James Graham, introduced a bill for the better regulation of labor in factories. The bill contained clauses setting up a system of primary schools associated with the factories and effectively under the control of the Church of England priests in whose parishes the schools would be located. Nonconformists reacted violently to these educational clauses. Even the Wesleyan Methodists, the most conservative of the denominations and the least active politically, joined their more militant fellow Nonconformists in denouncing the clauses. Petitions and demonstrations helped organize the anger of the Nonconformist community, and the government hastily withdrew the clauses that were attracting the clamor. At no other time over the course of the century did the Nonconformist community act with such unity and such determination. As time went by, Nonconformists looked back with nostalgia on the events of 1843. They drew from their victory the assurance that they could prevent the state from enlarging the sphere of the Established Church if they kept a jealous eye on all the activities of the state. Their predilection to distrust the state, to think of the state as a dangerous potential obstacle to social progress, was confirmed and heightened by the educational clauses of Sir James Graham's factory bill.

As a direct result of the controversy of 1843, Edward Baines the younger, editor of the powerful *Leeds Mercury* and a prominent Congregationalist, mounted an attack on all state intervention in the realm of education. He convinced Congregationalists to set up a system of voluntary schools which refused all assistance from the state. For many years he campaigned for what he called the Voluntary Principle, a version of *laissez faire* with religion and education at its heart, couched in the language of political liberty. He insisted that Nonconformists, rejecting state support for religion in the name of liberty, must logically also reject state support for religious education. And he broadened his opposition to state interference to include most areas of life: 'Governmental interference often retards advancement and shackles freedom. In support of my views, I appeal to the free press, the free literature, the free science, and the free education of England, in opposition to countries where all these things are taken under the care of Government.'[8]

Strict voluntaryism in education proved impossible; it was beyond the resources of the voluntaries. Most Nonconformist schools continued to accept state grants after 1843 because they could not raise enough money from other sources. By the late 1860s even Baines recognized that private money would never come forward in amounts large enough to support a comprehensive system of primary education. W. E. Forster's important

---

[8] Edward Baines, 'On the Progress and Efficiency of Voluntary Education in England,' in *Crosby Hall Lectures on Education* (1848), p. 8.

Education Act of 1870 created a system of nondenominational school boards, funded by local rates, to complement the work of the Anglican and Nonconformist education societies. A new phase of the volatile education controversy had begun.

The passionate vigor of the Nonconformist reaction to Sir James Graham's education clauses in 1843 had an impact well beyond the field of education. The church rate martyrs of the late 1830s had impelled Edward Miall to leave his pastorate of a Leicester Congregational chapel and establish the *Nonconformist* as the leading national organ of militantly radical Dissenters. Nonconformist anger at the educational clauses in 1843 encouraged Miall to organize the Anti-State Church Association in 1844. The association was renamed the Liberation Society on the advice of the more moderate Edward Baines in 1853. From shortly after its foundation until Miall's death in 1881, the Liberation Society was the most important political organization of the Nonconformist community. It took over the role once filled by the more old-fashioned and cautious Dissenting Deputies. It was more stridently militant, and it drew much more support from the industrial provinces. Whereas the Deputies had worked behind the political scenes to influence established political leaders, the Liberation Society appealed to public opinion and tried, with considerable success, to make Nonconformist views heard directly from Nonconformists in the House of Commons. Miall himself sat as MP for Rochdale, 1852–57, and for Bradford, 1869–74. He became a respected figure in political circles, widely recognized as the leading spokesman on political issues for liberal Nonconformity.

Miall and the Liberation Society helped organize the campaign against church rates, against religious discrimination in public cemeteries, against the religious exclusiveness of the ancient universities, and they kept a close eye on legislation in order to prevent new forms of religious inequality from emerging. But the society was committed to the belief that religious equality could not be finally achieved until the Church of England was disestablished and disendowed. Miall was riding the rising tide of democratic sentiment that increasingly threatened the Victorian social hierarchy. He sympathized with the Chartists and supported the Complete Suffrage Movement in the 1840s. He persistently attacked the aristocracy and the social order associated with it. He coupled religious equality with social equality, and he regarded the establishment of the Church of England as an important barrier in the way of general social progress. Not only did the establishment generate legal disabilities against Dissenters that had to be fought one by one, but it also encouraged a climate of snobbery in which Nonconformists suffered. 'The upper ten thousand,' he wrote, 'with very few exceptions regard connection with the authorized ecclesiastical institution of the kingdom as inseparable from their elevated position. Until comparatively recent times, both Houses of Parliament were closed against Nonconformists. To this day, the great national universities are governed with a view to the interests of the State-Church. Is it surprising that, under such conditions, the higher professions gravitate towards it? To belong to the church is to side with respectability; to dissent from it is to cast in your lot with the vulgar. Accordingly, Dissenters, simply as such, are esteemed inferior.'[9]

By the late 1850s the Liberation Society had become politically sophisticated. It served as a clearinghouse for information on Dissenters' legal and political concerns. It lobbied for Dissenters' interests in parliament. It sponsored traveling lecturers. Most important of all, perhaps, it began to organize politically aware Nonconformists at the constituency level in order to fight elections. During the decade of the sixties, the Liberation Society controlled what was probably the most effectively organized network of constituency associations in the kingdom. For some time Miall and the society had been moving toward a closer association with established politicians on the left, and as the Liberal Party emerged as a clearcut successor to the Whigs in the sixties Liberationists tended to put their trust in Liberals. Gladstone, officially a Liberal from 1859, was especially attractive to Nonconformists. His obvious religiosity and his deeply serious moral sense appealed to Dissenters. Gladstone, moreover, was sensitive to Nonconformist fears and ambitions. Aware of Nonconformist power in many constituencies, he was determined at least to appear conciliatory. He introduced the legislation which abolished compulsory church rates, and his first administration disestablished the Church of Ireland, opened the universities more freely to Dissenters, and tried to settle the education question. It is not surprising, then, that Miall's campaign for disestablishment of the Church of England reached its climax during that administration. In both 1871 and 1872 Miall introduced disestablishment motions in the House of Commons, and each time his motions were seriously debated. They were rejected. Never again did disestablishment of the Church of England receive such serious political consideration. Ten years later, at the time of Miall's death, disestablishment had ceased to be an issue that interested politically sophisticated men.

The liberalism of Nonconformity in the mid-Victorian period was much more than a matter of political tactics and the personal attractiveness of Gladstone. The political tradition of Dissent was dominated by the call for liberty, and Dissenters had traditionally relied upon the political friendship of leading Whigs who liked to present their party as a bulwark of civil and religious liberty. Very different, of course, was the political tradition of Wesleyan Methodism. John Wesley himself had been a staunch Tory,

---

[9] Edward Miall, *The Social Influences of the State Church* (1867), pp. 10–11.

concerned more with the preservation of good order than with the progress of liberty. His successor as the dominant figure in the Wesleyan Conference was Jabez Bunting, just as conservative as Wesley and no less willing to impose his will on the denomination. Until his death in 1858 the Wesleyan Methodists officially stood apart from most of the political activity of Dissent. But Wesleyan Methodists represented roughly the same groups in society as did the Congregationalists and the Baptists. It is not surprising, therefore, that over the course of the second half of the nineteenth century, Wesleyans moved into the Liberal camp along with the older Dissenting denominations. In the generation of Baines and Miall, the vision of society prevalent among Nonconformists, their schemes for social reform and their view of what constituted social progress all harmonized with positions taken up by Gladstone and the Liberal party.

Victorian Nonconformity was dominated by families belonging to the urban middle classes. Among the denominations, the Unitarians and the Quakers, both relatively small bodies, probably contained the largest proportion of wealthy families. Unitarians prided themselves on being the best educated and most open minded group among Dissenters. Quakers were probably the most socially exclusive. Congregationalists, New Connexion Methodists, and Wesleyan Methodists came next on a very rough general scale of wealth and social prestige. Baptists, Bible Christians, and other groups of Methodists followed closely behind. Of the major denominations, the least wealthy were the Primitive Methodists, an exception to the general middle-class rule that prevailed among all the other large Nonconformist churches.

It must not be thought that most Nonconformist congregations consisted of eminent merchants and manufacturers, bankers, or professional men. In all the large denominations there were many individual chapels that consisted almost entirely of working-class people. Even in the major urban chapels, such as Carrs Lane in Birmingham or East Parade in Leeds where the Baines family went, the majority of the congregation was drawn from social levels beneath what one usually considers middle class. Skilled artisans, shop keepers, clerks, domestic servants, and unskilled workers undoubtedly made up the majority of Nonconformists. The social mix varied from chapel to chapel, and town to town, but a general pattern seems clear. Most important chapels were dominated by a middle-class elite which provided most of the money and almost all the leadership. The politics of Nonconformity reflected the interests of that elite. The Nonconformist vision of society was essentially a middle-class vision. Writing in 1848, Algernon Wells, secretary of the Congregational Union, considered it a matter for regret that 'our churches — everything about them — preaching, buildings, ministers, manners, notions, and practices — all have on them the air and impress of English middle-class life. Our churches,' he continued, 'have more and more worked themselves into this mould, as time and change have proceeded. They are at this time more exclusively of that class than was the case a century ago.'[10] The political and social attitudes of Nonconformists were influenced by class as well as religion, but the influences of class were so much in harmony with those of religion that it is difficult to distinguish the two in the mid-Victorian period.

Early in the nineteenth century progressives of very different sorts, those men who generally approved the social and economic changes which were transforming English life, tended to select certain central features of the old social order as those most worthy of condemnation. They attacked privilege, patronage, and dependency as sources of corruption. They attacked paternalism as an enemy of liberty and manly independence. They attacked the aristocracy as the symbol and embodiment of privilege, patronage and paternalism. Nonconformists joined in this attack, impelled by the general considerations of their social class and encouraged by the individualism of their evangelical theology, by their traditional concern for liberty, and by their powerful commitment to an independent ecclesiology. With the Methodists excepted, the large Nonconformist denominations were made up of independent congregations that were proudly aware of their power to govern themselves. Each chapel financed its own operations, hired and fired its ministers, and established its own rules and regulations. As they became more deeply involved in missionary activity, both overseas and at home, the denominations developed more elaborate institutions for central organization. But the ideal of independence remained strong; perhaps the ideal grew even stronger as the reality faded.

This concern for local self-government fitted in particularly well with the concern for municipal self-government demonstrated by middle-class Nonconformists in the provincial towns. Nonconformists joined enthusiastically in the attack on privilege and corruption in the old order of society by supporting the campaign for parliamentary reform in 1830, 1831, and 1832. Elie Halevy, the great French historian of nineteenth-century England, wrote that immediately after the Reform of 1832, 'in every borough, the Nonconformists formed the backbone of the majority. In every constituency they were probably the majority of the Liberal party, and in some places perhaps the majority of the electorate.'[11] Yet Halevy could find only eight Nonconformists in the first reformed parliament: five Unitarians, a Quaker, a Congregationlist, and a Methodist. Nonconformity clearly did not include a significant number of men who were sufficiently rich and well established to leave their businesses in other hands and spend a large part of the year

[10] Algernon Wells, 'Thoughts on the Need for Increased Efforts to Promote the Religious Welfare of the Working Classes in England.' *Congregational Year Book* (1848), p. 88.

[11] Elie Halevy, *The Triumph of Reform* (1950), p. 62.

in London. But when municipal government was reformed in 1835, Dissenters flooded into town councils throughout the country. Strong at the local level, sparsely represented at the national, Nonconformists and men of their class naturally tended to distrust the central state which was still in aristocratic hands. Naturally, as well, they came to idealize the virtues of decentralized, local government which they could influence or control.

The progressive vision of society which Nonconformists shared with other liberals, a vision in which privilege and patronage were to be replaced with equality and individual independence, was embodied in the movement for free trade. Evangelical stress on individualism and personal responsibility supported the idea of a free market in labor. The idealized localism of provincial businessmen supported the call for an end to state interference in business affairs. Because the Corn Laws benefitted the landowning aristocracy by artificially maintaining the price of grain with tariffs, the campaign against the Corn Laws in the 1830s and 1840s attracted very strong Nonconformist support. Many chapels held anti-Corn Law tea meetings. The Anti-Corn Law League was able in 1841 to organize a meeting of nearly seven hundred Nonconformist ministers to demand repeal of the Corn Laws. After repeal the league organized an essay contest on the effects of free trade and a Baptist minister, Henry Dunckley, won first prize. Nonconformists raised free trade to the level of moral principle, and they saw its introduction as a critical turning point between the old order of society and the new. The Reverend F. A. Cox told his brother ministers in 1841 that, if the free trade movement failed, 'despotism was likely to restore the darkness of the middle ages — that society would be on the eve of retrogression, and the bright era of the nineteenth century likely to suffer an eclipse.'[12] The *British Quarterly Review*, edited by the Congregationalist historian Robert Vaughan, noted 'the parallelism or coincidence of economical truth with practical Christianity'[13] in an article on the free-trade movement. Henry Dunckley wrote boldly that 'Free Trade is but a part of the unrestricted development of the national mind; it implies the doing universally what is just.'[14] The society of the future, as Nonconformists saw it at the middle of the century, was a middle-class millennium in which the corrupt power of the aristocracy was eliminated, the Church of England was merely another denomination like the rest, and every individual proved his own worth before God and his fellow men.

At this time Nonconformists had a clear view of the meaning of poverty, and there was little disagreement among them on the general question of

[12] *Report of the Conference of Ministers of Religion on the Corn Laws* (1841), p. 110.

[13] *British Quarterly Review* (1845), p. 561.

[14] Henry Dunckley, *The Charter of the Nations* (1854), p. 404.

how the condition of the poor might be improved. They considered poverty the result of two very different causes. Aristocratic oppression was one, and Nonconformists believed that the power of the aristocracy to oppress the poor either directly through taxation, or indirectly through destroying their ambition with paternalistic social arrangements, was rapidly fading away. The other cause of poverty, and the more important one, lay in the individual moral weakness of each poor person. Men were poor because they did not work hard enough, or because they were not thrifty enough, or because they were not independent enough to search out opportunities for self-improvement, or because they drank too much. Charles Haddon Spurgeon, the great Baptist preacher, wrote two series of tracts offering practical advice to the people: *John Ploughman's Talk* (1869) and *John Ploughman's Pictures* (1880). These tracts epitomize the attitudes toward poverty and the condition of the working classes which were widely held by Nonconformists of Spurgeon's generation. Individual self-help is the main theme of the tracts. Sobriety, persistence, work, and the force of independent willpower were pictured as the keys to personal success. 'Stick to it and do it,' Spurgeon had John Ploughman say. 'Set a stout heart to a stiff hill, and the waggon will get to the top of it. There's nothing so hard but a harder thing will get through it; a strong job can be managed by a strong resolution. Have at it and have it. Stick to it and succeed.'[15]

Until close to the end of the century, the Nonconformist explanation of poverty was optimistic. Aristocratic power was declining. And Nonconformists were committed to the idea that individuals really could change the course of their own lives so long as they lived in a condition of liberty. Conversion was a central and essential event in the lives of Evangelical Nonconformists. That men and women might be essentially changed, born again into a new way of life, was a principal article of belief among Evangelicals. Conversion from laziness to hard work and conversion from sin to righteousness did not seem far removed from each other, moreover, and evangelicals tended to confound them. The Religious Tract Society, the single greatest force in Evangelical publishing in the Victorian period, issued denunciations of dirt and waste and drink as well as pleas for the unconverted to throw down the burden of original sin and seek repose in Christ. Both social progress and eternal salvation seemed matters which individuals could determine. The choice was theirs. It was the duty of preachers and philanthropists both to make sure that the choice was governed by conscience. 'Before you begin a thing,' warned Spurgeon, 'make sure it is the right thing to do: ask Mr. Conscience about it.'[16]

Nonconformist ideas about poverty did not differ a great deal from the

---

[15] Charles Haddon Spurgeon, *John Ploughman's Pictures* (1880), p. 123.

[16] *Ibid.*, p. 126.

prevailing liberal view of the problem during the half century after the New Poor Law was passed in 1834. The more secular and scientific treatment of the poor, however, relied more heavily on pressure than on conversion. The theory behind the New Poor Law was that by making tax-supported welfare arrangements very uncomfortable, only those who absolutely needed such aid would seek it. The Charity Organization Society, founded in 1869, attempted to organize private charity along the same lines so that private generosity did not make unemployment so attractive that men and women would be discouraged from working. While they put much more stress on reformation of character, Nonconformist philanthropists shared with the secular social engineers the assumption that individuals controlled their own social destinies.

Perhaps the most characteristic Nonconformist effort at social reform in the early and mid-Victorian periods was the temperance movement. Drunkenness went out of fashion among the upper and middle classes early in the nineteenth century, and, at the same time, it began to be considered a serious social problem affecting the poor. It was easy to see drink as an obstacle to individual improvement and social progress. Drink inhibited work, destroyed ambition, and ruined health. Drink was a form of waste. Drunkards were dirty. Drink interrupted the orderly rhythm of effort which modern industrial life required. Drink diminished self-control. Drink anaesthetized the conscience. It is not surprising that Nonconformists who valued sturdy independence, thrift, self-motivated effort, and success should come to regard drink as a device of the devil. The temperance movement began in the 1830s, and from that time most of the temperance leaders were Nonconformists. Temperance, which gradually came to mean total abstinence for many, became a feature of Victorian chapel life. Temperance societies were organized in many chapels to help provide a wholesome social life for adults, and Bands of Hope were established to set children on the right path. In keeping with the general Nonconformist approach to social reform, the temperance movement did not at first appeal to the state for legislation. Instead, the temperance reformers used the techniques of religious evangelism and appealed to the conscience of individual drinkers. Temperance meetings resembled religious revivals, as speakers, some of them converted drunkards, called upon the unreformed to cast aside their evil ways and enter upon righteous and sober lives.

But progress was disappointingly slow. As time went by, Nonconformists tended to elevate the importance of the drink question. Samuel Morley, an enormously wealthy Congregationalist hosiery manufacturer and an important figure in political and philanthropic circles, said in the early 1860s that 'the Temperance cause lay at the root of all social and political progress in the country.'[17] Many others must have agreed with Morley, for over the

---

[17] Edwin Hodder, *The Life of Samuel Morley*, 2nd ed. (1887), p. 153.

preceding ten years a prohibitionist movement had been developing to complement and support the call for personal reformation. Organized in Manchester in 1853, the United Kingdom Alliance called for law to make the task of conscience easier through legislation that would limit the sale of drink. The policy of the United Kingdom Alliance became, over the next half-century, the central policy of the temperance movement as a whole. Because it appealed to the state rather than the individual conscience, the UKA did not recieve the support of the entire Nonconformist community, even at the end of the century. On the whole, however, Nonconformists were much more ready to appeal to the state at the end of the century than at the middle. The evolution of policy within the temperance movement foreshadowed a general shift in the entire range of Nonconformist attitudes toward social reform.

The synthesis of religious, political, and social attitudes which dominated Nonconformity between the early 1830s and the mid-1880s was suffused with individualism. During these fifty years the prevailing emphasis in Nonconformist theology, the dissenting political tradition, the social situation of the Nonconformist elite, dissenting doctrines of church organization, and Nonconformist attitudes toward social reform all complemented and reinforced each other. In all these areas of Nonconformist life, the individual conscience was given a place of high importance. Evangelical Nonconformists rejected the Calvinist doctrine of spiritual predestination just as they rejected theories of social determinism. Each man, they thought, was truly free and master of his fate. Each man could choose to follow Christ and escape eternal damnation. Each man could choose to work hard and escape the poverty and drunken degradation of the slums. Each man ought to shape his life according to the guidance of his conscience. Liberals generally during this period set themselves against aristocratic privilege and state interference in the free working of the economy. Nonconformists attacked the state church as a form of antiquated privilege, they fought for their own civil liberties in the face of legal discrimination, and, on the whole, they set themselves against state interference in the free working of society. Conscience, for them at that time, was properly located in free individuals, not in the community and not in the state.

In the decade of the 1880s the mid-Victorian Nonconformist synthesis began to crumble. No single cause for this can be assigned. Just as the synthesis itself was the product of a number of related intellectual and social factors, its collapse was brought about by changes in a number of areas of Nonconformist life. Major reorientations in theology, important developments in the social situation of Nonconformists, and new approaches to social problems reacted upon each other in such a way that Nonconformity began to lose its cohesive culture. None of these changes was sudden; their destructive effect was felt over the span of at least one, possibly two, generations. Contemporaries recognized in the 1880s that traditional Nonconformity was giving way to something new. On the eve of the first World War there were definite signs of weakness in the Nonconformist community. After the war, Nonconformity was no longer a major force in English public life. Margot Asquith, herself intimately familiar with the parallel decline of liberalism, acidly pronounced its epitaph: 'At one time the Nonconformist Conscience was the backbone of the country,' she said in 1922, 'but the men I know who claim to have it today are maidenly, mulish, and misled.'[18]

The progressive democracy and assertive individualism of Evangelical theology had been central to the Nonconformist synthesis. During the last twenty years of the nineteenth century that theology came to seem old-fashioned and outworn among the rising generation of leading Nonconformist ministers. They changed it in several important ways. The new leaders of Nonconformity wished neither to cut their own ties with their religious traditions nor to offend that great majority in their congregations who were suspicious of anything new in their religious lives. Even very advanced men continued, therefore, to proclaim in a general way their loyalty to Evangelical truth. At the same time, they reoriented their theological emphases so radically that they effectively rejected their Evangelical inheritance.

Three powerful currents of change swept through the old Evangelical theological positions, each reflecting a loss of confidence in old truths. Men began to doubt that an all-merciful God would consign a portion of mankind to everlasting pain and torture. Men began to doubt the supreme significance of the cross, and to place more importance on Christ's life than on his atoning death. And the growing respectability of Biblical Criticism encouraged men to doubt the simple Biblical base of the old Evangelical message.

Evangelicalism, over the first three quarters of the nineteenth century, was an essentially optimistic religious mode. Evangelicals believed that progress was possible for both men and nations. They were oriented toward success both in this world and the world to come. The reformed drunkard and the converted sinner were archetypal figures among them. Sermons and tracts made much of hell and damnation, but always in order to persuade the unconverted to seek salvation while there was still time. The fate of the damned, the misery of the poor, were never matters for dwelling upon in lamentation. Evangelicals were not much interested in failure except as a practical example to encourage those who might succeed. By the 1880s, however, many Nonconformists began to take failure more seriously and to contemplate with sympathy the fate of the damned.

Sympathy for the damned was not altogether a new phenomenon in the

---

[18] Stephen Koss, *Nonconformity in Modern British Politics* (1975), p. 167.

1880s. Frederick Denison Maurice, a liberal Anglican theologian and early Christian Socialist, had been dismissed from his post at King's College, London, in 1853 for daring to deny that eternal damnation really meant everlasting torment. But among Nonconformists concern for the damned themselves became widespread only in the 1880s.

This new fascination with failure is difficult to explain. Perhaps it was associated with anxiety about Britain's prestige as her power and commercial supremacy were clearly challenged in Europe and America. Perhaps it was connected with increasing appreciation for how little progress had been made toward solving the social problems of urban poverty. In any event, a significant number of Nonconformist ministers in the 1880s began to soften their views of damnation, to suggest that their faith in God's mercy prevented their interpreting eternal damnation literally as meaning torture that would go on forever. As early as 1874, R. W. Dale of Birmingham, an eminent Congregationalist and respected theologian, committed himself to the notion that the wicked were annihilated, not everlastingly punished. By the late 1880s, W. R. Nicoll, the astute editor of the *British Weekly*, thought that the increasing rejection of the doctrine of eternal punishment was the most significant development in the theology of contemporary Nonconformity.[19]

Closely associated with the new emphasis on God's mercy toward the unrepentant was the stress on the Fatherhood of God which began to be fashionable in the 1880s. God as a slightly indulgent Father began to replace God the judge who demanded the atonement of Christ and required faith and moral effort on the part of man. The Fatherhood of God became an immensely popular sermon subject, attractive partly because it permitted preachers to speak loosely and enthusiastically about the brotherhood of man. As president of the Congregational Union in 1906, John Henry Jowett complained of the vague effeminate softness of the popular stress on Fatherhood. Four years later in his presidential address to the National Council of Free Churches, Jowett argued that the dominance of the Fatherhood theme in fashionable Nonconformist theology was enfeebling: 'a skimmed theology will not produce a more intimate philanthropy.'[20]

The Atonement, the central religious doctrine of the old Evangelicalism, was pushed toward the sidelines in the last twenty years of the nineteenth century. The cross lost its supremacy. Christ's death ceased to be considered the most important event in Christian history. Christ's life took its place, and the Incarnation received the attention formerly given to the

---

[19] W. B. Glover, *Evangelical Nonconformists and Higher Criticism in the Nineteenth Century* (1954), p. 92.

[20] Arthur Porritt, *John Henry Jowett* (1924), pp. 98, 104.

Atonement. Christ as a model for men, Christ as a teacher of ethics, replaced Christ as the way toward salvation. Just as the humanity of Christ was given greater importance, so was the idea that God dwelt in every man. Divine immanence, the place of Christ in every man, was used to justify pleas for increased benevolence toward those who were failing in life. The old Evangelicalism, a religion of stength, encouraged democracy in the form of equality of opportunity. Incarnationism, a religion of weakness, encouraged democracy in the form of increased welfare for those who were not successful. 'Every kindness that you show to the drunkards of the Regent Street slums,' said Hugh Price Hughes, 'to the harlots of Piccadilly, and to the starving poor everywhere, is a kindness shown to Jesus Christ.'[21] Or again: 'A harlot is dying in a back slum. You say: 'What is that to me? She suffers for her own sin.' When you spurn that harlot you spurn Christ.'[22]

The emphasis on the Incarnation was not a natural development of earlier tendencies in the theology of Evangelical Nonconformity. Nor was Incarnationism peculiarly the property of the free churches. It flourished among Anglicans as well, and its most famous expression was probably a collection of essays, *Lux Mundi* (1889), published by a group of Anglo-Catholics including Charles Gore, the well-known Christian Socialist. The impact of Incarnationism upon Evangelicalism was entirely destructive. Its logical end, to which very few Nonconformists were willing to travel, was the so-called New Theology announced by R. J. Campbell of the Congregationalist Church, the City Temple, in 1907. Campbell argued that man and God were two expressions of divinity, that sin was not so much wickedness as error. Christ's purpose was not to save man from his evil nature, but to show him how to construct God's kingdom on earth. Campbell's humanitarian theology created a public sensation for a time, but it received little official support. Eventually Campbell recanted, left Nonconformity and joined the Established Church. The New Theology, however, epitomized in unacceptably extreme form an important and widely shared tendency in free church religious thought.

The third, and probably least corrosive, force that weakened Evangelical theology in the late nineteenth century was Biblical Criticism. Nonconformists, in common with most other Englishmen, until the last third of the century, held a simple view of the Bible as God's revealed word. They were able comfortably to refer to a number of Biblical passages which they took as proof of the importance of the Atonement and as guarantees of the Evangelical scheme of conversion and salvation. From the middle of the century there were Nonconformist scholars who were aware of the develop-

---

[21] Hugh Price Hughes, *Social Christianity* (1889), p. 88.

[22] *Ibid.*, p. 61.

ment of Biblical studies in Germany, but not until the 1880s did the genera-
lity of educated Nonconformists and their ministers begin to take Biblical
Criticism seriously. Even then it was not entirely safe to argue publically
that the authors of the Bible were other than inspired scribes who wrote
down the words that God dictated to them. Robert Forman Horton, former
Oxford don and pastor of Lyndhurst Road Congregational Church in
London, conservatively reported the findings of recent Biblical scholarship
in *Inspiration and the Bible* (1888). But his rejection of the old idea of verbal
inspiration lost him some members at Lyndhurst Road, and he had difficulty finding a publisher among the firms that specialized in Nonconformist works. By the turn of the century, however, Biblical Criticism as a
whole was no longer an issue among educated free churchmen. Almost all
ministers accepted the validity of using the latest and most scientific techniques of historical and literary analysis in order better to understand the
Bible. No sophisticated Nonconformist searched the Bible anymore for texts
that would prove Christ died for all men and that all who truly believed in
Him would win everlasting peace. Biblical Criticism was, in fact, accepted
among free churchmen with very little struggle. There were no great
contests to set beside the legal trials and public uproar that accompanied
the Anglican battles over Biblical Criticism in the 1860s. The easy progress
of Biblical Criticism among Nonconformist ministers at the end of the
century was partly due to those Anglican battles having been already
fought, partly to the growing number of obviously devout English Biblical
scholars, and partly to the fact that Evangelical theology was being abandoned anyway and for other reasons.

No serious, organized efforts were made to stem the tide of fashionable
new ideas which swept away the old Evangelical verities. The most percep-
tive among free churchmen recognized the intellectual weakness and
inchoate condition of post-Evangelical theology. R. W. Dale commented as
early as 1877 on the general decline of interest in theology and the disap-
pearance of a distinct theological literature in the Nonconformist community.[23] A generation later, on the eve of the first World War, no principle
of authority had emerged in free church thought. Dale's successor at
Carrs Lane, Birmingham, spoke in 1910 of 'the impoverishment of our
thought.'[24] Yet there was no effectively organized resistance to new currents
of thought. Charles Spurgeon, the great Baptist preacher, remained insis-
tently an Evangelical of the old school until the end of his life in 1892. He
attempted in 1887 to use his enormous prestige to stop the erosion of
old-fashioned truth within his own denomination. But his articles accusing
the Baptists of being on the downgrade, sliding into a confused morass of

[23] *Congregationalist* (1877), pp. 3–5.

[24] Arthur Porritt, *John Henry Jowett* (1924), p. 105.

modern thought, did not receive a cooperative response from the leaders of the Baptist Union. Spurgeon, feeling rebuffed, withdrew from the union. The Baptists were the most conservative, old-fashioned denomination among the major free churches. The 'downgrade controversy,' as it came to be called, demonstrated clearly how widespread was the loss of confidence in the old-style evangelicalism among Nonconformists by the later 1880s.

Insofar as evangelicalism was associated with a distinctive Nonconformist culture, changes in the social aspirations of Nonconformity in the late nineteenth century encouraged leading free churchmen to be open minded toward modifications in their theology. From the 1880s, or a little earlier, Nonconformists began to reject their distinctive culture as provincial and narrow. Their leaders drew them toward assimilation into the mainstream of English society, and they began to grow uneasy about their humble heritage. Wealth and education were the two forces behind the growing anxiety about provincialism. As more Nonconformist families grew more wealthy, they played a greater role in the government of their towns and they sent more members to Parliament. They also, naturally, tended to emulate the manners of their more socially prestigious Anglican neighbors. Peculiarities of chapel culture became embarrassments. Quakers gradually gave up using 'thee' and 'thou.' Nonconformists from wealthy families began reading novels, going to concerts, and finally, in significant numbers in the 1880s, going to the theater. Even ministers began going to the theater in the 1880s, to Spurgeon another sign of the downgrade, and ministers began to write novels as well as read them. The more successful free church ministers by the end of the century modeled their behavior generally on that of the upper middle classes. They delighted in club life; the National Liberal Club was their favorite. Even Spurgeon took his holidays on the Riviera and kept a carriage and pair. And they gloried in golf.

Assimilation was encouraged by education. Nonconformists went to Oxford and Cambridge in increasing numbers after religious tests were abolished in 1871. Wealthy Dissenters sent their sons to the famous public schools or to denominational schools created in the image of Winchester, Rugby or Eton. The Congregationalists even established a theological seminary, Mansfield College, in Oxford in the mid-1880s in order to have an official presence in the heartland of established English culture. At the opening of the college in 1889, A. M. Fairbairn, the first principal, spoke emotionally of the departure of Dissent from the University in the seventeenth century, and the new spirit of assimilation: 'Now it is a matter of supreme importance that the old estrangement should cease and the new reconciliation be complete, ... that our much divided people come to feel a single people once more.'[25]

---

[25] W. B. Selbie, *The Life of Andrew Martin Fairbairn* (1914), p. 178.

Calls for reunion among the Protestant churches were frequently heard toward the end of the century. The fire had gone out of the disestablishment movement. The Liberation society had difficulty raising money after Miall's death in 1881. After the Burials Act of 1880 opened the churchyards to Nonconformists the Society had no major grievances to fight against. Nonconformists were not prepared to wage a major campaign for disestablishment now that the privileges of the Church of England did not seem as significant or as discriminatory as they once did. During the eighties the Liberation Society ceased to be the effective political arm of Nonconformity. Its place was taken, at the turn of the century, by the National Council of Free Churches. Growing numbers of men and women hostile or indifferent to organized religion caused both churchmen and Nonconformists to discuss the possibility of reunion. The National Free Church Council was itself the product of the need men felt for better organization of Christian forces in an increasingly secular society. Although the possibility was raised, no serious effort was made to merge Nonconformity in the Church of England. But many men called for more cooperation between Anglicans and free churchmen. W. R. Nicoll, with a good journalist's talent for reflecting the temper of his time, told a group of Anglican clergy in 1899 that Nonconformists were puzzled: 'They cannot understand why there should be a Nonconformist conscience. They think there should be a Christian conscience, and that there should be an organization of all Christians strong enough to make that conscience prevail in the land.'[26]

But assimilation exacted a heavy toll from sensitive and conscientious free churchmen. Ambivalence toward their past was painful. They became restless and uncertain about their identity. They lost the clear and unquestioned sense of purpose from which their fathers and grandfathers had drawn strength. R. F. Horton is a case in point. He had been up at Oxford in the 1870s, and he kept in his study the sixth thwart of the New College boat that he had helped move from the bottom to the top of the river in a single season. Well known as the minister of Lyndhurst Road Congregational Church, he liked to call himself a nonconforming member of the Church of England. Albert Peel, a distinguished historian of Dissent, wrote that Horton, famous and successful, was in 1900 'the outstanding representative of Nonconformity, one whose status, culture, and ability were everywhere acknowledged and respected.'[27] Yet Horton was never sure of his role. He never championed a major cause for long or led an important movement. He spent his talent in a vast amount of ephemeral writing for magazines, in restless traveling and speaking. He wrote fifty-four books, but

[26] W. R. Nicoll, *The Lamp of Sacrifice* (1906), p. 327.

[27] Albert Peel and J. A. R. Marriott, *Robert Forman Horton* (1937), p. 15.

not one of genuine importance. And he filled his diaries with gloom, despair, and sentimental introspection.

At the time that they were abandoning their old theology and softening their attitudes toward privileged groups in the upper reaches of English society, the leaders of late Victorian Nonconformity changed radically their vision of society and social reform. No longer did they see society as merely a collection of individuals; no longer did they preach the reform of individual character as the principal mode of social reform. They developed a stronger sense of English society as a community with a corporate life, and they turned more and more to the state as the agency best able to bring about social improvement. Hugh Price Hughes, probably the most influential spokesman for the emerging Nonconformist conscience in the late 1880s, made his commitment to an organic view of society entirely clear. He credited T. H. Green and the Positivists with teaching him that no individual can realize his own ideal until his social environment is favorable; they emancipated him from 'the selfish individualism and parochialism which have so often disfigured conventional Christian thinkers.'[28] He repeated with approval Bishop Westcott's reflection that 'We are suffering on all sides from a tyrannical individualism.'[29] And he preached numerous variations on the theme that corporate society was divinely sanctioned: 'Jesus Christ legislated for *man* — not for individuals only, not for Christian churches only, but for man in all his relations, and in all his circumstances. He legislated for *States*.'[30]

In his stress on the social conscience of the well-to-do and powerful, in his emphasis on the social responsibilities of the state, in his warm sympathy toward the poor and least successful, Hughes was by no means alone. The same general views were preached from all the leading free church pulpits and advocated in the most important Nonconformist journals. Sturdy individualism, highly valued among Nonconformists a short time previously, came to be castigated as a social vice. The mission of Christianity, wrote Silvester Horne, minister of Whitefield's Tabernacle in London and a Member of Parliament after 1910, is 'to reconstruct society on the basis of brotherhood, and substitute cooperation for competition, and federalism for selfish individualism.'[31] John Clifford, after Spurgeon's death in 1892 the most respected and best-known Baptist minister in London, was for a time an active Fabian socialist. S. E. Keeble, a Methodist minister

[28] Hugh Price Hughes, *Essential Christianity* (1894), pp. 32–33.

[29] Hugh Price Hughes, *Social Christianity* (1889), p. xii.

[30] Hugh Price Hughes, *Philanthropy of God* (1892), p. 51.

[31] C. S. Horne, *Pulpit, Platform and Parliament* (1913), p. 3.

who worked for Hughes on the *Methodist Times* until the end of the century, became a socialist, and so did R. J. Campbell at the time of the 'new theology' uproar.

While most free church ministers did not become socialists in any strict sense, the majority of the leading men certainly did follow the prevailing fashion of humanitarian concern for the poor. In an article commissioned and published by the National Council of Free Churches, J. Scott Lidgett in 1910 summed up the view of social problems that was approved by the leaders of Nonconformity at that time. Lidgett saw slum dwellers as the embodiment of the most important social problem of his age. They were reduced to their state of misery, Lidgett thought, by low wages and unstable employment. Their difficulties could be softened by trades unions, old-age pensions, and housing reforms, but the state ought to approach their problem as an organic whole and aim at 'the complete abolition of demoralizing and degrading poverty.' Lidgett, a Methodist minister, was not without experience of practical affairs. He had been active in London politics for many years, and from 1908 he was the leader of the Progressive party in the London County Council. He assured his readers in 1910 that the social problem was soluble, but the solution he proposed was strikingly moralistic and without practical point. The answer did not lie in state socialism or any economic doctrine: 'The social consciousness must become sovereign in its authority over the national life, subordinating, until it utterly expels, selfish individualism, class jealousies and timid dislike of necessary change.'[32] Lidgett did not think that the problem of the slums lay in the unreformed characters of slum dwellers. Therefore he directed his appeal to the conscience of the successful, and ultimately to the conscience of the state.

The shift of emphasis away from individuals toward the conscience of the community was clearly under way in the early 1880s. The London Congregational Union sponsored an investigation into slum life and published its findings in 1883 as *The Bitter Cry of Outcast London*. The report, put into final form by Andrew Mearns, the secretary of the Union and former pastor of a chapel in Chelsea, created a sensation and reached an audience well beyond the boundaries of Nonconformity because it presented a vividly detailed picture of physical misery and moral degeneration in London's east end. *The Bitter Cry* absolved the slum dwellers themselves of responsibility for their plight. It found in the slums some morally upright, hard-working men and women who were locked into miserable poverty by circumstances beyond their control. It argued that the sloth and moral laxity of the

---

[32] J. Scott Lidgett, 'The Modern Social Problem,' in *Christ and Civilization* (1910), edited for the National Council of Free Churches by the Rev. John Brown Paton, Sir Percy Bunting, and the Rev. Alfred Garvie.

majority of the very poor were products of their evil environment, and not the other way around. Samuel Morley, approaching eighty years old and a voice from the past, reacted to *The Bitter Cry* with the comment that most of the misery of London was self-inflicted. But this view was in rapid retreat. The emerging Nonconformist conscience saw in the slums a moral challenge to the community at large.

How was that challenge to be met? On the philanthropic level, Nonconformists accomplished a great deal that was practical and beneficial to the poor. They participated in the settlement movement, establishing outposts of civilization in the slums. These were designed to be both social centers for the poor in the surrounding neighborhoods and places where well-to-do young men might live for a time in the midst of poverty, gathering experience that would help them lead the kingdom toward a better future. Beginning in the early eighties, Nonconformists also built a number of mission halls in the poor districts of large cities. These missions concentrated on social services and recreational facilities; formal religious worship was not stressed. Many city center churches were abandoned by their middle-class congregations who moved to the suburbs at this time, and these buildings were frequently turned into social centers for the poor.

The so-called institutional church had its roots in the eighties. Institutional churches supported in addition to their obviously religious activities a broad array of social clubs, athletic societies, hobby groups, study groups, and welfare services. These philanthropic activities, however, useful as they were, did not come close to satisfying the consciences of those men who felt impelled to attack the social problem at its heart. Silvester Horne, for example, was minister during the Edwardian years at Whitefield's Tabernacle in London, probably the most active institutional church in the kingdom. In 1910 Horne went into Parliament because he thought that fundamental social reform could be achieved only on the political level.

On the political level effective sustained action in support of social reforms proved impossible. On the political level the Nonconformist conscience proved a decidedly inadequate guide. There were two basic reasons for this. In the first place, over the thirty years before the war there was a decided gap between the progressive views of the leading ministers and the attitudes of their more conservative congregations. This was true both in theology and politics. J. D. Jones of Bournemouth, for example, felt that he had to keep from his congregation his advanced position on Biblical Criticism. And R. F. Horton of Lyndhurst Road said 'every time I pleaded the cause of the people the wealthy employers and successful professional men charged me with introducing politics into the pulpit.'[33] On political issues which united the lower and middle classes — opposition to aristocratic

[33] R. F. Horton, *An Autobiography* (1917), p. 83.

privilege, parliamentary reform, free trade — Nonconformity had been able
to take up a clear and strong position. On issues which divided the lower
and middle classes — the legal position of trades unions in the nineties, the
possibility of a minimum wage — Nonconformity was ineffectual. No
matter how strong the drive of their humanitarianism, most Nonconformist ministers could not take the side of labor in a politics of class. The
powerful, middle-class members of their congregations would not allow it.

The second reason why the Nonconformist conscience could not support
a coherent program of basic social reform was that it provided no principles
for determining what that program should be. The theology of Fatherhood
and Incarnationism stressed the importance of humanitarian activity, but it
provided no political blueprint for establishing the Kingdom of God on this
earth. Nothing in their new theology helped late Victorian Nonconformists
shape a new political program. This helps to explain why they were driven,
like J. Scott Lidgett in 1910, to vague moralism when they described the
need for fundamental social change. Their vague theology encouraged
vague humanitarianism. A united position on a specific practical question
was extremely difficult to achieve. This was true even of major issues
toward which Nonconformity had established a traditional posture. War is
an example. Dissenters had given support to the peace movement from the
middle of the century, and opposition to war was referred to in the 1890s as
one of the principles of the Nonconformist conscience. Hugh Price Hughes
denounced war with almost as much passion as he spent in attacking
prostitution. But the Boer War at the turn of the century split the free
church community, and only a small remnant continued to stand up for
peace as war fever swept through the nation. Even Hughes supported the
war. In public affairs a simple desire to act rightly and benefit mankind is
not adequate. A method is required to distinguish right action. Evangelicalism had provided guidelines that worked for a time. But the men who
professed to act on the Nonconformist conscience at the end of the century
had no clear guide on many issues, and so they swayed uneasily in the
breeze of public opinion. The Nonconformist community was unable to
take a clear stand on what free churchmen themselves considered the major
problems of their time — poverty, slum life, and the relations between
capital and labor.

Free church leaders, however, set a high value on united stands. They
were most anxious to create a spirit of consensus within the Nonconformist
community so that the community might be strengthened through a broad
base of voluntary participation in its activities. Therefore they tried to focus
the Nonconformist conscience on issues that would unite as many free
churchmen as possible. This generation of late Victorians was enchanted by
the idea that in a democratic age success could be measured in numbers.
They were obsessed with size, and they counted incessantly. How many in

the Sunday school? The congregation? The men's meeting? Will a gymnasium attract more young people to church? Or a cycle club? Or a boys' brigade? Or a football team? What is the circulation of this newspaper or that magazine? The *British Weekly*, so that it might start with a bang, included a religious census of London in its first number in 1886. The *Daily News* tried to increase circulation with another count of church attendance in London in 1902. A decline in the relative size of the church going public was clearly indicated in the surveys, with Nonconformists holding their own a little better than Anglicans. Leading free churchmen saw this decline as a challenge to their ability to hold their community together while they tried to encourage its growth. They were, in consequence, attracted to popular issues which could be easily understood by the unsophisticated masses. 'The real Christ,' Hugh Price Hughes once remarked, 'is the one who, when seen, attracts the crowd everywhere.'[34]

The issues that attracted the conscience of the Nonconformist crowd during the twenty-five years before the war were rooted in the Nonconformist synthesis of the previous period. They were traditional Nonconformist concerns, and they reflect the inability of late Victorian free churchmen to create a new basis for consensus within their community. In the first place, there were those matters of social reform which involved personal sin, a category dominated by that evil trinity — sex, gambling, and drink. Here the conscience lighted the way clearly, and no shadows darkened the path. From early in their pastorates Hughes, John Clifford, Silvester Horne, Robert Horton, and an additional host of ministers of this generation were involved in the campaign against prostitution. Several established homes for abandoned girls, several were associated with Josephine Butler and her drive for social purity, and Hughes and Clifford gave strong support to W. T. Stead when he was in trouble for the sensational adventure he reported in *The Maiden Tribute of Modern Babylon*. Fierce defenders of the sanctity of the family, Nonconformists staunchly opposed any relaxation in the divorce laws. Gambling, encouraged by the growth of yellow journalism and the development of Association Football, was becoming much more popular among the working classes toward the end of the century, and, like prostitution, it roused the wrath of organized Nonconformity.

But gambling was never considered as important as sex, and Rosebery remained leader of the Liberal party despite the Nonconformist noise about his celebrated activities on the turf. Organized opposition to drink had a long history, and Nonconformity had been the backbone of the temperance movement from its beginning. But not until the last two decades of the century did the temperance movement achieve universal acceptance among Nonconformists. Not until then were ministers expected to set a teetotal

[34] Hugh Price Hughes, *Social Christianity* (1889), p. 4.

example. By that time Nonconformist opinion on drink had hardened into political effectiveness, and it is probably on the drink question that the Nonconformist conscience had its most persistent impact in Parliament.

Drink, intemperate gambling among the working classes, and prostitution were all genuine social problems at the turn of the century. Therefore they appealed to the social conscience of progressive men like John Clifford and Hugh Price Hughes. Because they could be understood in terms of personal morality, these problems appealed to the majority of Nonconformists who traditionally conceived social reform as the reform of individual character. Because Nonconformists could speak out with a fairly unified voice against intemperance, gambling, and illicit sex, these issues came to dominate the Nonconformist conscience. Free churchmen tended to overstress the general social significance of these partly ethical problems. The tendency to exaggeration was natural, especially because Nonconformists had traditionally treated the conscience as something for rousing, not for searching. Nonconformist leaders were men of action rather than discrimination, fighters rather than thinkers. They were most at home with practical problems and they understood practical solutions. What Hugh Price Hughes called 'the three deadly enemies of England' had the great practical merit of rousing the Nonconformist conscience. England's more important social problems did not have that advantage.

Among the traditional political concerns of Nonconformity, education remained after 1880 the last major issue that involved the interests of free churchmen as a body. In 1902 the Conservative Government passed an education act that elicited the fury of Dissent. Free churchmen reacted more explosively and with more unity than they had mustered since Sir James Graham's education proposals of 1843. The Act of 1902 angered Nonconformists because it made denominational schools, of which the majority were Anglican with the Roman Catholics next, eligible for direct support from local rates. In the late 1860s Dissenters, with the exception of the Wesleyan Methodists, had given up hope of supporting their own primary schools and had taken the position that the state should provide a system of nondenominational schools. An uneasy compromise was achieved in 1870, when Forster's Education Act established a dual system: nondenominational board schools financed by local rates, and denominational schools aided by parliamentary grants. The Act of 1902 seemed a distinctly retrogressive step to most Nonconformists. Drawing on the tradition of the church rate martyrs of the 1830s, free churchmen, with John Clifford at the fore, organized a campaign of passive resistance, refusing to pay that portion of the education rate that would go to support distinctive denominational teaching. The campaign was enormously successful in generating enthusiastic support and a sense of unity among Nonconformists. The outraged Nonconformist conscience may well have contributed substantially to the Liberal party's triumph in the general election of 1906. But the Liberals, in power with a too-comfortable majority, disappointed their free church supporters. There were, according to the Nonconformist newspapers, over two hundred free church MPs in the new Parliament, but less than half of those were reliable friends of Nonconformity.[35] The Liberal majority was so large that militant Nonconformists did not have to be kept in a good humor. After the first years of enthusiasm, the passive resistance movement lost much of its popular support. The Liberals made a series of only half-hearted attempts to deal with the education issue. From the Nonconformist point of view, the problem was never satisfactorily solved. The Education Act of 1902 awakened, for a time, an echo of the once-powerful political will of Nonconformity. But the echo died away, and as early as 1906 Lloyd George dared to poke gentle fun at militant Nonconformity. At Clifford's seventieth birthday celebration he said: 'When Dr Clifford wants a rest cure he sits down, takes up a pen and says "Whom can I go for?"'[36] In 1922 Clifford received his fifty-seventh summons for non-payment of the education rate. By then, of course, his protest had lost political meaning. It was Clifford's way of keeping faith with his past.

In the late nineteenth century and early in the twentieth, English Nonconformity began to lose its cultural identity. Its libertarian political heritage had been developed under a burden of discrimination that was now so light as to be almost without significance. Its vigorous individualism, coinciding in time with the great days of Gladstonian liberalism, was now rejected by its progressive leaders. Evangelical theology, which had previously reinforced both the political and social ideas of Nonconformity, was now transformed in all but name. Fashionable new emphases on Incarnationism and the Fatherhood of God did not constitute an adequate intellectual base upon which free churchmen might fashion a new view of themselves and their distinctive mission in English society. Free churchmen, in spite of their active press and increasingly efficient central organization, gradually faded into a religiously indifferent social landscape. The Nonconformist conscience, to some at the time an indication of strength, is more accurately viewed as evidence of weakness. Free churchmen were unable to develop a new synthesis of religious, political, and social attitudes. The Nonconformist conscience had no future, but it did, for a time, enable men and women dedicated to the spirit and heritage of Dissent to keep faith with their past.

---

[35] Stephen Koss, *Nonconformity in Modern British Politics* (1975), p. 78.

[36] James Marchant, *Dr John Clifford, C. H.* (1924), p. 196.

W. R. LAMBERT

CHAPTER 5

SOME WORKING-CLASS ATTITUDES TOWARDS ORGANIZED RELIGION IN NINETEENTH-CENTURY WALES

T he religious historiography of nineteenth-century Britain has hitherto concerned itself primarily with exchanges of letters between church leaders, with denominational histories, and with analysing the attitudes of religious leaders to problems of poverty. Too rarely is religion studied in action at the community level; too rarely is the religious organization seen as a small 'society' with internal strains and recurring organizational problems. Sectarianism, schism, revivalism and secularism preoccupy sociologists of religion but are only beginning to interest historians of religious institutions in nineteenth-century Britain.

As Dr Pelling has noticed, it is particularly disappointing how little we yet know about the relationship between organized religion and the nineteenth-century working class. The difficulty has been that historians both of church and of chapel have concentrated on the story of the foundation and early growth of their respective denominational institutions, and on explaining their subsequent development, from the point of view of the loyal believer. Doctrinal changes and disagreements are usually well treated, but comparatively little attention has been paid to the composition of the lay membership and its occupational and class characteristics, the degree and intensity of its religious commitment, and its numerical relationship to the total population of the country. Wearmouth's work on Methodism and the British working class consists largely in listing those trade union leaders who received a Methodist upbringing, without making any systematic attempt to distinguish the reasons for the extent and limits of Methodist influence, or the local and occupational pattern of the various sects concerned.[1] More recently, however, more valuable attempts have been made to emphasise the importance of working-class religious commitment in Britain in the nineteenth century, notably by Inglis, Currie, Pell-

---

[1] R. F. Wearmouth, **Methodism and the Struggle of the Working Classes, 1850–1900** (Leicester, 1952) and **Methodism and the Trade Unions** (1959).

ing, Kent, Mole, Thomis and Soloway in England, and by E. T. Davies and Professor Ieuan Jones for Wales.[2]

It is a commonplace of course that in its religious adherence nineteenth-century Wales was predominantly nonconformist with, broadly speaking, Calvinistic Methodism holding sway in north Wales and Independency and the Baptists predominating in south Wales.[3] The strength of nonconformity was revealed statistically in 1851: two in every three of the people who had attended religious services on census Sunday were nonconformists; over half of the population of Wales attended a place of worship compared with only a third in England.[4] Of the working population which attended, 22 per cent are said to have attended the services of the Established Church and 78 per cent are said to have attended nonconformist chapels. By 1866 it was claimed with justice that 'in Wales, nonconformity is — speaking broadly — the national creed and the national practice'.[5]

However, the disabilities of nonconformity disqualified many people from becoming effective members of the social order long after the repeal of the Test and Corporation Acts. Little wonder that a Merthyr nonconformist could write in 1885 that 'the history of Nonconformity is that of one long continuous fight of right against might and of the oppressed against the oppressor'.[6] The sense of deprivation was caught in some of the hymns of the period: **Alone on the raft, Throw out the lifeline, Hold the fort,**

[2] K. S. Inglis, **The Churches and the Working Classes in Victorian England** (1963); R. Currie, **Methodism Divided. A Study in the Sociology of Ecumenicalism** (1968); H. Pelling, 'Popular Attitudes to Religion', in his **Popular Politics and Society in late Victorian Britain** (1968); J. H. S. Kent, 'Feelings and Festivals. An interpretation of some working-class religious attitudes', H. J. Dyos and M. Wolff (eds.), **The Victorian City,** vol. 2 (1973); D. E. H. Mole, 'The Challenge to the Church', ibid; M. I. Thomis, **The Town Labourer and the Industrial Revolution** (1974), Chapter 6; R. A. Soloway, **Prelates and People: Ecclesiastical Social Thought in England, 1783–1852** (1969): E. T. Davies, **Religion in the Industrial Revolution in South Wales** (Cardiff, 1965).

[3] See **Minutes of the Committee of Council on Education, 1839–40,** 1974, 176–7; Cardiff Central Library, M.S. 2.329. A Cambrian Literary Gentleman, **The Social, Industrial and Literary State of the Cambrian Nation,** (1880) pp. 5–7. For this pattern in Glamorgan in the early 1830's see Cardiff Central Library. MS 5.153. Return of Nonconformists in Glamorgan in 1836.

[4] For comment on and criticism of the census see E. T. Davies, op. ct., pp. 32–42, and the articles by: K. S. Inglis in **Journal of Ecclesiastical History,** XI (1960), 74ff: W. S. F. Pickering in **British Journal of Sociology,** XVIII(1967), 382ff; D. M. Thompson in **Victorian Studies,** XI (1967), 87ff.

[5] **Welsh Nonconformity and the Welsh Representation. Papers and speeches read and delivered at the conferences held, September and October 1866** (The Liberation Society, 1866), p. 1.

[6] **Merthyr Express,** 20 June 1885.

The Heavy Cross. Voluntary introversion played a part. The Revd. J. Idrisyn Jones of Brecon maintained in 1881 that it was the interpretation of the New Testament that separated nonconformists from churchmen, and this 'led the earlier Nonconformists to endure their terrible persecutions and sufferings, and leads modern Nonconformists to incur the loss of social prestige, and often times the frown of their neighbours and losses in business'.[7] As Professor Gwyn Williams has remarked: 'A religion of manners and morals characterized this socially-isolated group whose exclusion from power and prestige served only to emphasise its ingrown and inward-looking satisfaction with itself and its values'.[8] Dr Kent has argued that for Britain as a whole such deprivation bred social aggression and that beneath the surface, the 'nonconformist conscience' was chiefly a way of fighting for social objectives — 'a form of social aggression rather than of outraged morality'. He sees the nonconformity of the second half of the nineteenth century as having been engaged in an attempt to impose its own standards on the rest of British society, and explains this as a reaction to the fact that although it was strong and self-confident it nevertheless felt itself to be socially rejected.[9] But 'social aggression' was not the only motivation, for many nonconformists took account of the seriousness of the social problems which they sought to mitigate by crusading zeal and by legislation.

In 1867 it was estimated that there were 3,107 nonconformist chapels in Wales, together with a further 120 Welsh chapels in England.[10] Many complaints were made of over-building, and it is likely that the number of chapels was no test of the religious condition of Wales.[11] Many chapels were built under the influence of sectarian zeal or personal ambition, without due regard to the heavy debts left upon them.[12] But the chapel —

---

[7] Rev. J. Idrisyn Jones, **Why are we Nonconformists?** (Newport, 1881), p. 6.

[8] G. A. Williams, 'Hugh Owen (1804–1881)'. **Pioneers of Welsh Education** (Swansea, 1962), p. 59.

[9] G. V. Bennett and J. D. Walsh (eds), **Essays in Modern Church History in Memory of Norman Sykes** (1966), p. 191.

[10] Henry Richard, **Letters on the social and political condition of the Principality of Wales** (1867), p. 19.

[11] For example, see **Y Diwygiwr,** January 1852, p. 13; **Y Drysorfa,** October 1852, p. 353.

[12] See **Church Quarterly Review,** vol. 15, no. 29, October 1882, p. 68. For example, 73 of the 997 Independent chapels in Wales in 1875 had been established between 1839 and 1842. Most of them were 'Chartist churches', having been established by members of already existing Independent chapels, who disagreed with their fellow worshippers on the question of the Charter. See Thomas Rees and John Thomas, **Hanes Eglwysi Annibynol Cymru** (Liverpool, 1875), vol. 1, pp. 21, 118, 189; vol. 2, pp. 15, 88, 184–5.

that self-governing ecclesiastical republic — was, as we know, a very important institution in Welsh communities for it provided offices of real responsibility which made status aspiration possible in a society in which status positions for deprived nonconformists were scarce.[13] As a recent historian of Methodism has claimed: 'This vast officialdom created an interior social mobility, within the chapel community, far more important than that exterior mobility, from rags to riches, of which Methodist histor-iography is so proud'.[14] For many people the chapel became the major centre of cultural activity in their community. In many chapels five services were held on Sunday, with further services on three or four week nights. **Y Drysorfa** noted: 'The chapel .... is the social centre around which its adherents gather; it is school, lyceum, club, church, all in one .... It is round the chapel that not only the associations common to all form's of Christian faith are wont to gather, but those which spring from the use of a peculiar and ancestral tongue'.[15] The writer in **Y Traethodydd** in April 1852 was not perhaps over-exaggerating when he stated that the Welshman went to chapel 'to seek for that which the Englishman goes to the playhouse to look for'.[16] Hagen has argued that creativity often occurs in a group which has suffered a depletion in social status. After a time, alternative means are found to regain the status which has been lost.[17] The nonconfor-mist culture and way of life may have been the result of such creativity.

From the early nineteenth century, noncomformity in industrial south Wales was essentially working class in character. The great Liberationist, Edward Miall, remarked in 1849 that the religiosity of the working population of Wales stood out as 'a cheering exception' to working-class apathy in religious matters which afflicted the rest of Britain.[18] The Revd. Thomas Rees of Beaufort, however, claimed far too much for Welsh non-conformity when he maintained that nine-tenths of the middle- and working-classes in Wales were 'either professors of religion or constant

---

[13] On this, see Thomas Darlington, 'The Church in Wales an alien Church'. **Contemporary Review,** LXIII, June 1893, p. 819; C. C. Harris, 'Church, Chapel and the Welsh'. **New Society,** no. 21, 21 February 1963, p. 18; Inglis, **Churches and the Working Classes,** p. 62.

[14] R. Currie, op. cit. p. 46. See also T. J. Morgan, 'The Peasant Culture of the Swansea Valley'. S. Williams (ed.), **Glamorgan Historian,** vol. 9 (Barry, 1973), p. 110.

[15] **The Treasury,** 18, 1881, p. 239.

[16] **Y Traethodydd,** April 1852, p. 454.

[17] See E. E. Hagen, **On the theory of social change,** cited in R. W. Ram. 'Dissent in Urban Yorkshire. 1800–1850'. **The Baptist Quarterly,** 22, no. 1 (January 1967), p. 17.

[18] E. Miall, **The British Churches in relation to the British People** (1849), p. 221.

attenders on the means of grace'.[19] He said that nonconformity in Wales
had captured 90 per cent of the working class and even 75 per cent of the
Welsh-speaking population in anglicized areas, whereas these classes in
England were irreligious, or at least indifferent.[20] Rees claimed that the
success of evangelistic work among the working population of Wales was
attributable to the fact that nonconformist chapels kept clear of the 'sin' of
making any distinction between one class and another. 'We readily recognize the usual distinction of classes in our daily intercourse and secular
transactions, but the moment we cross the threshold of the sanctuary, or
meet to hold a religious service anywhere, our social distinctions are entirely forgotten'.[21] Later in the century, as we shall see, after the growth of a
heightened class consciousness, this class attitude of the churches was an
extremely potent factor in driving men from the churches.

It should be recognized of course that only a certain type of working man
attended religious services. Some workers were regarded as being beyond
redemption; others, from the respectable, law-abiding part of the working-
class community, formed the members and adherents of nonconformity in
Wales. In 1885 a Nantyglo collier — obviously belonging to the latter
group — differentiated strikingly between the various sections of the
working population in a letter published in the **Merthyr Express** on 5
September.

'In the first place there is what we may term the residuum of our
working classes, sunk so low in the cesspool of moral degradation that
any effort made to extricate them is hopeless. This section always
maintains a state of apathy and indifference. They heed not who or
what is in power or place — the low pothouse and the brothel are the
haunts they frequent. Another section are those that advocate an
extreme measure of reform — the uprooters of constitutional form and
order — they belong to the mad communists of France and continental Europe; they are the pothouse politicians of our working class;
they ensconce themselves in our snug public-house parlour and boast
of a certain amount of social refinement and political knowledge all
self-acquired but as superficial and thin as the ice of a November
frost. But there is another section of our working class. You will find
them occupying positions of trust in our collieries and iron and
tinplate works; superintendents and officials in our Sunday Schools
and Nonconformist churches, presidents of our Temperance Societies

[19] Thomas Rees, **Miscellaneous Papers on subjects relating to Wales** (1867), p. 96.

[20] Ibid., pp. 24–9.

[21] Ibid., p. 28.

and Bands of Hope; leading men in our gigantic Friendly Society organization, and, led by those champions of civil and religious liberty, the Nonconformist ministry, this section of our working class are exerting an influence upon working class political thought that no-one knows but those that mingle with them. From the ranks of this section the aristocracy of the working class will spring, those that will rouse their fellows from their graves of moral degradation and intellectual death.'

It is generally true that those who are stable or downward mobile in society will report a much greater interest in religion than those who are upward mobile, if only because the chapel played an important part in the movements encouraging social mobility upwards in the nineteenth century.[22] We know that most of the great numbers of immigrants from mid- and west Wales who came into the south Wales coalfield during the first half of the century brought their religion with them in the form of a letter of recommendation — **llythyr canmoliaeth** — which handed the person over to the care and supervision of another chapel in the district in which he was settling.[23] Thus in 1840, 75 per cent of the community which grew around the Varteg Iron Works attended a church or a chapel regularly or occasionally.[24] Indeed, working-class religious commitment in early and mid-nineteenth century Wales seems to have been most complete in isolated single-occupation districts, where a sect or denomination could acquire a high degree of identity with the entire community, and some of the community's natural leaders could serve as its evangelists. Copper miners formed the backbone of nonconformity at Amlwch. In the 1820's and '30's prayer meetings were held for the workmen at the Parys Mountain copper mines near Amlwch. Two services a day were held, at 6 a.m. and at 10 p.m., so that every miner had an opportunity to attend at least once a day. The miners were convinced that it was because they were believers in God that accidents at the mines were not more frequent.[25] Many witnesses testified that for most of the nineteenth century the 'princely givers' to nonconformity were not the rich, but miners, servants, seam-

[22] See G. E. Lenski, 'Social Correlates of Religious Interests', **American Sociological Review,** 18, (1953), pp. 533–44.

[23] **Y Diwygiwr,** 1852, p. 117.

[24] **Report of the Privy Council on Education** (1840), p. 172; G. S. Kenrick, **The Population of Pontypool and the Parish of Trevethin** (1840), passim.

[25] J. Rowlands, 'A study of some of the social and economic changes in the town and parish of Amlwch, 1750–1850' (University of Wales M.A. thesis, 1960), pp. 353–4.

stresses, and farm labourers.[26] Furthermore, nonconformity and the vast majority of working men were at one in their opposition to the truck system. By paying the men in kind and not in money, the system deprived them of the power to contribute those voluntary subscriptions that were essential for the support of ecclesiastical institutions maintained by means other than state aid.

Ministers and church officers were elected from the ranks of the predominantly working-class congregations and thus, during the early and mid-nineteenth century they were socially at one with their congregations.[27] The occupations of the appointed trustees of Carmel Baptist chapel, Sirhowy, in 1847 were stone-cutter, weigher, collier and miner.[28] William Taylor, a puddler who later became a publican, was the 'original seed' from which Caersalem Welsh Baptist chapel, Dowlais, grew.[29] Those deacons of Caersalem (1820–90) whose occupations are recorded were mostly working class until about the 1880's: 3 colliers, 3 carpenters, 2 masons, 2 weighers, 2 publicans, and one each of yeoman, puddler, clerk, bootmaker, miner, shopkeeper, milk vendor, refuse collector, roller and overman.[30] In the mid 1860's the membership of Zoar Independent chapel, Tredegar, was composed mainly of miners, colliers and fireman;[31] and in the 1870's the social composition of the **set fawr** at Brynhyfryd chapel, Rhymney, was cobbler, storekeeper, grocer and draper, a notable increase here in middle-class representation.[32]

What attracted the working population to nonconformity? Chapel influence helped them become more integrated. There seems little doubt that several of the Nantyglo collier's 'residuum' came under the influence of nonconformity. It might be suggested that miners who drowned their hardships in drink, who lacked education and a sense of their individual worth, who might be in turn meek and compliant, and then desperate and violent, who lacked purpose and vision and lived only for the interminable rhythm of their oppressive labour, could not expect to rise above the level

[26] For example, see James Owen. **The Free Churches and the People** (Cardiff, 1890), p. 22.

[27] See **The Treasury,** 18, 1881, p. 239; **Morning Chronicle,** 15 April 1850.

[28] Evan Powell, **History of Carmel Baptist Chapel, Sirhowy** (Cardiff, 1933), p. 29.

[29] J. R. Williams and G. Williams, **History of Caersalem Welsh Baptist Chapel, Dowlais** (Llandysul, 1967), p. 89.

[30] Ibid., pp. 89–92.

[31] John Thomas, **Sunshine on the 'Hills', being a narrative of a revival of the Lord's work at Tredegar during the visitation of the cholera in the year 1866** (n.d.), p. 1.

[32] Thomas Jones, **Rhymney Memories** (Newtown, 1938), p. 139.

their birth assigned them. Nonconformity took hold and shaped some of these men because the sins it inveighed against were the source of their impotence and the virtues it extolled were the means of their resurrection. Nonconformity offered an equality of opportunity for salvation. As a rough generalization it may be said that a church is likely to be the more puritanical the closer it is to the masses of uneducated population, because the need to give some order and discipline to lives which are not otherwise organized by convention is so great.[33] The inflexibility of the nonconformist code regarding drinking and all forms of pleasure may not have offered much scope for personal enjoyment, but it was the means by which many men found an objective and secured recognition as well as their self-respect. Of course, the chapels produced many narrow, bigoted and hypocritical creatures, but what is more important is that a new standard of personal dignity and self-reliance was presented, and the rigidity of the discipline had the effect of making men into more independent and fairly intelligent beings. For above all, nonconformity taught the value of the individual soul in the face of his God. The chapel, a 'moral property' in Thomas and Znaniecki's excellent phrase, was a very emblem of the community's collective existence. It attracted men because it gave them something to do; its democratic structure offered scope for the participation and originality of its members; for some, its friendships were the chief source of prosperity in business; it gave the individual duties and obligations and a feeling that he had a share in the consummation of functions. Chapels and Sunday Schools taught the elements of reading and writing. Class meetings were sometimes held in order to discuss the contents of the Bible and their application to the problems of daily life. Such meetings crystallized out the canons of moral behaviour. Through the medium of the chapel men learned the art of speaking and organizing. A nonconformist could participate in administering the affairs of his own religious communion; he was, perhaps, able to understand its circumstances, needs and controversies; through its meetings he became acquainted with the conduct of public business; and he was a member of a majority or a minority which tried to make its own opinions prevail. These features helped to make up a political education: the nonconformist was able to look at public affairs with his own eyes; the value of the individual contribution to the collective enterprise was recognised.

What role did the Established Church play in the life of the working man at this time? We know that one of the greatest weaknesses of the church was its failure to provide any means whereby men of humble origin could play an active part in its religious life or for that matter in its social work. Moreover, the movement for reform in the Church of England failed

---

[33] See D. Jenkins, **Congregationalism: a restatement** (n.d.), p. 113.

to bring the church nearer the urban working-class population largely because the clergy shared the attitudes and anxieties of upper-class society. The middle-class idea of 'religion' was denominational allegiance and regular Sunday worship, together with financial support of a minister and buildings. 'Religion' here denoted a religion of 'mere creeds, rites and church-going'. For the working-man however religion was more likely to be concerned with the Christianity of the Sermon on the Mount and with a move away from dogma and theological or liturgical dispute to a concern for conduct and social and moral issues; it should be concerned as much with 'the poorest he' as with 'the richest he'. Such a concern was more likely to elicit a sympathetic response in nonconformity for most of the nineteenth century.

Spokesmen for the Established Church in Wales admitted that working-class support was very difficult to obtain and indeed stressed that the church must enlist the cooperation of working men by placing them in official positions in the church and on representative bodies.[34] A writer in the **Contemporary Review** in 1893 was of the opinion that the church had little to offer to that 'influential class of Welshmen .... the very elite of the middle and lower classes' from which the elders and deacons of nonconformist chapels were chosen.[35] The duties performed by chapel deacons were, in the church, confined to the ordained clergy. Despite this, it does seem that towards the end of the century the church became more and more conscious of having to play a more active social role among the working class. There may be some truth in the claim of propagandist churchmen that the church was **more** attentive to the claims of the working man than nonconformity at this time; that nonconformity was interested largely in those who could afford to give money for the building of chapels, so much so that nonconformity not only sought to build chapels in the midst of well-to-do populations, but when these latter began to migrate from over-crowded areas to suburban districts, nonconformists always began rapidly to make arrangements for closing and selling their chapels in order to build a new one in the 'rising' suburban district with the proceeds. In this way, it was claimed, the poor and over-crowded populations were largely left to the church to be taken care of: the church became the Poor Man's Church.[36]

In an article on the duty of Methodists to the masses in December 1884, **Y Goleuad** asked the question: What is the **raison d'etre** of non-

---

[34] For example, see the statement of the Revd. A. E. Campbell of Aberdare, **Report of the Llandaff Diocesan Conference, 1884** (Cardiff, 1884), p. 54.

[35] **Contemporary Review,** LXIII, June 1893, p. 819.

[36] **Aberdare Dawn of Day and Parish Magazine,** February 1886, p. 18.

conformity?[37] It answered that politically nonconformity was a protest
against constraint of conscience, and religiously, care for the poor and
fallen, which sought to raise them from degradation and ignorance, to set
before them higher ideals of life, and to obtain for them the means of grace,
the hope of glory, or in the words of the Bible, 'to exalt them of low degree,
and fill the hungry with good things'. This was described as the major ideal
which inspired the founders of sects. But religion proves the truth of the
aphorism that nothing fails like success; great dangers arose to the nonconformist from the 'accidental circumstances' of religious life. Religion encouraged patient labour, temperance and thrift, and so brought those who
practised it into comfortable worldly circumstances, so much so that they
were 'influenced by the ordinary ideal of raising their position in society'.
For such people religion became a mark of respectability, and the result of
the spread of worldly ease was loss of contact with those of 'low degree', the
people who had originally inspired the denomination.

The question was posed: is not Welsh nonconformity, like the church, in
danger of losing its hold on the working and poorer classes? The short
answer was yes. Calvinist theology, which dominated Welsh nonconformity
in the nineteenth century, did not help. 'This' life was only a preparation
for the one to come so what on earth (literally) was the point of tackling the
social grievances of the working population?[38] Calvinist theory resulted in
an attitude which took obedience to the Will of God as implying complete
satisfaction with, and acceptance of things as they were. Belief in a Providence of moral purpose could easily be maintained as an authority for
existing conditions, regardless of their moral justification. If abuses in the
system of industrialization and wretched social conditions were part of an
over-ruling purpose, decreed from eternity, what could mere human effort
avail to remove them? Religion became an apologist for social inequalities
instead of a critic with a new standard of values to impose upon the life of
men. This type of attitude towards life would make all human efforts at
improvement, material or spiritual, individual or collective, futile and unnecessary. If it was original sin that caused abuses to exist, what steps
could man, the sinner, take to remove them?[39]

The passion for personal salvation tended to produce the self-reliant

---

[37] See also **South Wales Daily News,** 6 January 1885.

[38] For a good exposition of other-worldliness see J. C. Campbell, **A Lecture on the Social
State of the Mineral Districts** (Cardiff, 1850), p. 15.

[39] On the general background to this paragraph see R. L. Hugh, 'The theological background
of Nonconformist social influence in Wales, 1800–1850' (University of London Ph.D thesis,
1951); G. Richards, 'A study of theological developments among the Nonconformists of Wales
in the nineteenth century' (University of Oxford B. Litt. thesis, 1956).

person who had little interest in social reform. But place responsibility on
the individual and seek to correct human and social ills by direct appeals
to personal conscience and one loses sight of the power of social condition-
ing. Many preachers in nineteenth-century Wales spoke vaguely of certain fundamental principles which must permeate society and which, if
followed, would automatically solve all problems. They found security behind such abstractions as 'love', 'justice', 'honesty' and 'soul' — vague
terms which possessed a mystical fascination, and which were not sufficient
in themselves to supply guidance to human conduct. Generally speaking,
nineteenth-century Welsh nonconformity was unable to define its 'principles'
in terms of attitudes towards wider social change because it believed that
'conditions do not make men, only a revolution in the individual spirit
towards God will transform the man and the world he lives in'.[40] As a
Welsh missionary working at Tredegar during the cholera outbreak of 1866
noted: 'Works are all important, but let them come in their proper order,
and received not as a **means** of salvation but as the result. Instead of
working for life we should work **from** life.'[41]

The Independents provide a good example of this attitude. During the
nineteenth century it was largely the miner, the labourer and the quarry-
man that filled the ranks of the denomination.[42] Independency's strongest
resources and its greatest leaders came from the working class. Williams of
Wern was the son of a cottager, Hiraethog was called from the plough, and
Thomas Aubrey came from the furnaces of Merthyr and north Monmouth-
shire. The Independents were fairly convinced of the value of the worker
and his importance in society. An article in an early number of **Y Gwerinwr** emphasised the dignity of every honest calling in life.[43] In 1859 **Y
Diwygiwr** severely criticized the custom of some middle-class people to
despise the workers.[44] But there were socially conservative elements in
Welsh Independency also. Although in 1852 Hiraethog admitted that the
Welsh nonconformists as a whole had been too long silent on matters of
general interest and had urged that the pulpit should teach the people their
social responsibilities as citizens of a free country, as well as their duties as
sinners and as Christians, it must be remembered that there were a number

---

[40] On this see E. T. Davies, op. cit., chapter 2, passim; C. R. Williams, 'The Welsh Religious
Revival of 1904–5'. **British Journal of Sociology**, 3, 1953, 243.

[41] Thomas, **Sunshine on the 'Hills'**, pp. 33–4.

[42] See R. T. Jenkins, **Hanes Cymru yn y Ddeunawfed Ganrif** (Cardiff, 1928), p. 52.

[43] **Y Gwerinwr,** May 1855, p. 42.

[44] **Y Diwygiwr,** 1859, p. 144.

of instances of complaint from Independents against any movement towards social and political reform.[45] As far back as 1831 the **Cymanfa** at Pantteg had urged the churches to pay more attention to the condition of the soul.[46] In 1837 the Revd. Evan Davies (Eta Delta) of Llanerchy-medd, complained in **Y Dysgedydd** that the best brains in the denomination were being dedicated to worldly affairs;[47] and in 1850 the letter from the Talybont **Cymanfa** of that year feared that zeal for cooperative action would prove disadvantageous to personal religion: 'We mean that excessive emphasis is being placed upon public remedies and social efforts. The public and social spirit of the age has operated to harmful excess in the church as well as in the world.'[48]

It is worthy of note that in the sphere of temperance reform the social conservatism in Welsh nonconformity expressed itself in an explicit attempt to distinguish between the social aspect of the temperance question and its religious aspect. The Calvinistic Methodist **Treasury** declared in 1870 that 'in the light of religion the stakes are far more important than they are in the light of mere social science because it is distinctly told us that the drunkard shall not inherit the kingdom of God'.[49] The drunkard would be cast away from the presence of God and this was 'a more lamentable feature of the evil effects of the drinking customs of our country than anything relating to this life'.[50] But in 'this' world drink 'despoils our Churches of members', and for these reasons earnest-minded Christians were exhorted to make great efforts to fight the evil. 'Upon social grounds alone the drinking habits of our country should be combatted with earnestly; but how much more so upon religious grounds! Especially by those who profess that they have at heart the eternal welfare of immortal souls and the success of Christ's kingdom in the world.'[51] This was a popular theme throughout the century: the man who has been addicted to drinking to excess will never bear the fruits of divine grace unless he abstains totally from drink. Although many Christian spokesmen stressed also that if the

[45] **Yr Amserau,** 11 August 1852.

[46] J. L. Jones, **Cymanfaoedd yn Annibynwr, Eu Hanes a'u Llythyrau** (Dolgellau, 1867), p. 449.

[47] **Y Dysgedydd,** 1837, p. 111.

[48] D. G. Williams, **Llythyrau a hanes cymanfaoedd dearllewin a deddwyrain yr Annibynwyr,** 1845–60 (Llanelli, 1927), pp. 69–70.

[49] **The Treasury,** 7, 1870, p. 119.

[50] Ibid.

[51] Ibid., p. 121.

salvation of man could not be attained because of drunkenness then 'it is a great thing, in our belief, to lessen the temporal ills of men and to improve their social happiness', the dominant view was that the evils done by drink to religion and to the spiritual welfare of men were more serious than the 'social ills which men suffer through their drinking habits because the latter are limited to this life alone'.[52] A Calvinistic Methodist, writing in 1890, recognised that the temptations to drink were inextricably intertwined with the habits and customs of society, but he still condemned drunkenness as a question, or a failing, of personal morality.[53]

One can only conclude that during the nineteenth century in Wales the attitude of the churches towards the drink problem was stern and moralistic, and that morality was conceived of in too negative and individualistic a fashion. Drunkenness was seen as a delinquency not as a disease. The Welsh denominational magazine was more likely to give its space over to barren theological polemics rather than to social questions. It is a statement, not a criticism, that the whole conception of religion seems to have been too narrowly individualistic, sabbatarian, bibliolatrical and otherworldly. A national temperance organisation complained in 1895 that the churches had been so much concerned with men's souls that in too many cases they had forgotten their bodies.[54]

To sum up thus far, it may be argued that many working men came to have no great liking for a religion whose chief blessings and rewards were only to be found in a future state of existence. Such an attitude became marked towards the end of the century. As a working man complained in 1891: 'A religion which is put into the pocket on Sunday night, to lodge there for six days at a time, is not likely to interest those who find their six-day work no sham, while the seventh is only dressed up for the occasion.'[55] The general feeling was that the Christianity preached from the pulpit was not the Christianity practised on the streets and in the place of work. The churches seemed not to take sufficient interest in the social and economic affairs of working-class members and sometimes made abusive comments on the drinking habits of union members. The **South Wales Labour Times** in March 1893 noted that working men increasingly could not reconcile the 'smug sentiments of brotherly love' which emanated regularly from the pulpit with the 'fawning' of the ministers on the prosper-

---

[52] Revd. Joseph Evans, **Arrows from a Temperance Quiver** (Carmarthen, 1864), pp. 12, 16.

[53] **Monthly Tidings: a repertory of Christian thought and a record of Christian work among the Calvinistic Methodists of Wales,** vol. 6, no. 1, January 1890, p. 4.

[54] **National Temperance League Annual,** 1843 (1843), p. 39.

[55] **South Wales Daily News,** 19 February 1891.

ous deacons and their 'lofty condescension' towards the poorer members. A working man said: 'They compare the silky tones and sanctimonious expression of the churchman on Sundays with his scowling face and brutal sneers among his workmen on Monday.'[56] During the 1890's working men were bound to see organized religion in such social and political terms.

Contemporaries believed that a major fault was the increasingly middle-class composition of the 'big seat': 'The modern deacon', it was said, 'is more intelligent but less spiritual'.[57] The working-class deacons had formed a bond of union and sympathy between the mass of people and the office-bearers, and it was claimed that churches where working men had been placed in positions of trust had a great hold on the working population in general.[58] But by the end of the century the composition of the 'big seat' was made up largely of the local trading community and the industrial management, if any, in the locality. It was a disappointed working-class candidate for the diaconate at Penuel Calvinistic Methodist chapel, Ebbw Vale, who said after the election: 'Do you not think that it is a pity that we did not elect just one deacon to represent not bricks and mortar and rent books at all, but Him who went about not collecting rents, but doing good, a homeless wanderer in his own world?'[59] During the 1880's and '90's the diaconate of the aforementioned Caersalem Baptist chapel at Dowlais included two coalmine agents, a stocktaker and a grocer interspersed among the working-class deacons.

A great bone of contention among working men in Wales in the 1890's was the failure or refusal of the churches to provide for the recreational needs of the working population. With the exception of prayer meetings, Bible classes and children's Bands of Hope, all of which had a strong recreational content, little recreation was offered by the churches and chapels. Ministers and deacons tended to frown on theatres and music halls. A working man pleaded in September 1892: 'I want somewhere to go in the evening, a place that's comfortable and warm and where I can find suitable company. I don't care for street corners, and, after all, you know, I am a total abstainer. Let it be a mutual improvement class, a debating class, or any class, and only a limited number of hymns.'[60] Another corres-

---

[56] **South Wales Labour Times,** no. 1, 4 March 1893, p. 3.

[57] **Welsh Weekly: an independent journal of religious and social life in Wales,** vol. 1, no. 2, 15 January 1892, p. 8.

[58] Ibid.

[59] Evan Price, **The History of Penuel Calvinistic Methodist Church, Ebbw Vale** (Wrexham, 1925), pp. 59–60.

[60] **South Wales Daily News,** 19 September 1892.

pondent from the Rhondda suggested that the 'palatial-looking chapels', which were practically closed for six days a week and the cost of which was paid by the mass of ordinary people, should be opened on week days for working men to spend their leisure time there. He advocated setting up chess and billiard rooms with newspapers as a counter-attraction to the public house.[61] His suggestion was regarded as being of particular importance if the eight-hour day was ever achieved in practice, a development which would give men more time to attend the pub.[62] But such appeals fell largely on deaf ears.

The rigid enforcement of a biblical Sabbath was a serious matter for some working men. As one commented: 'After serving an austere master on six days of the week, they are made to find in the Father of Love an austerer still.' Towards the end of the century, the good life was still thought of in such negative terms as teetotalism. Many workmen were openly blamed for desecration of the Sabbath, but the rich were equally guilty. In their clubs and homes the better-off had their own independent facilities for recreation, eating and drinking, but the poor had only the public facilities subject to legislative restriction. In this vein, a Merthyr workman attacked the blindness, arrogance and inhumanity of these respectable, religious people who had helped bring about the Sunday closing of pubs in Wales in 1881: 'How would these very good people like to live days, weeks, months underground without a sight of the sun, and then on a wet Sunday to keep within doors all the sunless hours, except while attending divine worship? Oh, these very generous people have their nice cosy clubs or homes which they enjoy every day. But the collier has to live in discomfort in a small home, and for near six months in every year never sees the sun except on the first day of the week.'[63] Many anti-sabbatarians who wished the Welsh Sunday to be improved for the working man but without its general character as a day of rest being endangered, argued that education or moral suasion and not legislative enactments, would be a more successful method of reducing Sunday drunkenness; that the opening of museums, theatres, coffee taverns and newspaper rooms on a Sunday at hours other than those of religious service would result in a more 'improved' working class amongst which drunkenness would not be so marked; indeed, that Sunday drunkenness was a direct result of the Sunday closing

[61] Ibid., 21 September 1892.

[62] See **Report of the Second Triennial Conference of the English Section of the Presbyterian Church of Wales, Liverpool, 1892** (Caernarvon, 1892), p. 25.

[63] **Merthyr Express,** 30 July 1881.

of places of public recreation.[64] But such proposals were largely ignored. Any effort made towards providing so-called rational (i.e. respectable) recreation for the working man on a Sunday was consistently blocked by sabbatarians and stigmatised as a conspiracy to deprive the working man of his day of rest.[65] The Sunday Closing Act exacerbated this tendency, for the clause in the Act which permitted **bona fide** travellers on a Sunday to obtain drink if they could prove they had travelled over three miles, led sabbatarians to oppose any form of entertainment on a Sunday so as to prevent any inducement to Sunday travelling.[66]

Indeed, it must be stressed that many working men in Wales were repelled by the churches' close identification with temperance. Some regarded teetotalism as an impudence to man's self-control; that to take the official teetotal pledge was an admission of man's weakness and a gross violation of his potentialities for self-control. Some of these men were not anti-religious. They believed that the temperance view that man's health could be brought under man's control conflicted with religious superstitions that disease was divinely ordained and could not be evaded by man's effort. The temperance view, which was shared by the secularist, was that man's health was governed by natural laws which every individual could perceive for himself. Secondly, total abstinence was linked to an optimistic view of human capacities scarcely compatible with orthodox doctrines of original sin. Thirdly, teetotalism elevated works over faith and turned away from the emphasis on doctrine towards an emphasis on moral reform.

Any exceptions to the prevailing attitude of the churches to working-class recreation seems to have come from the English nonconformist churches in Wales during the 1890's. In particular, the English churches of the Calvinistic Methodists became more attentive to the problems of working men. In his paper, **The Duty of the Christian Church in relation to the social life of the People**, read before the annual conference of the English Calvinistic Methodist churches of south Wales in 1890, the Revd. Ebenezer Davies maintained that Christ's religion involved duties towards all men, believers and non-believers, and that the church should pay attention to those duties. The church, he argued, should cater for the social recreation

[64] Cardiff Central Library, MS 2.560. Cardiff Society for the Impartial Discussion of Political and other Questions. Minute Book, vol. 1, 1886–88, **sub** 17 January 1887; J. P. Thompson, **Sunday Emancipation** (Cardiff, 1887), p. 11.

[65] See, for example, ibid., p. 4.

[66] See, for example, Report of the Commissioners appointed to inquire into the operation of the Sunday Closing (Wales) Act, 1881. **Parliamentary Papers,** 1890, XL, 1 (C. 1890), Q.11.304.

of the people rather than allow them to find it in directions and channels which were 'dangerous': drinking, sport and gambling.[67] The English churches of the Congregationalists in Wales witnessed that more was needed than the preaching of an orthodox theology in 'comfortable chapels'; the only way to reach the working class was to show practical sympathy with the problems of the day. 'Congregations', said the **North Wales Congregational Magazine** in 1891, 'will be regarded by working men as the conservators of effete superstitions if they do not step out from the formalism of their round of services into the midst of the struggling, starving, sorrowing, sinning world around them.'[68] To the predictable charge that such 'social Christianity' reversed the true order and placed society before the individual came the reply that the claims of the individual were the very life of social Christianity; that it was the 'absolute equality' of men that initiated the church's protest against the gulfs in society between man and man, class and class. As the Revd. Griffith Ellis claimed at the conference of the English churches of the Presbyterian Church of Wales at Cardiff in 1895: 'It is the high possibilities of manhood that Christianity discovers even in the drunkard that stimulate us to assist their developments by all means in our power. Throughout, we seek the salvation of society because we believe in the spiritual claims and possibilities of the individual.' For these Christians, but not for many more, social amelioration was regarded as being as important as spiritual culture for those degraded by poverty, crime and drunkenness.[69]

During the 1880's and '90's increasing numbers of urban workers in Wales were losing confidence in the churches as a means of social improvement and were becoming committed instead to trade unionism and political action. Welsh nonconformity did not give a lead to the aspirations of the workers; as has been hinted, the evidence I have found would tend to support Canon Davies' view expressed a decade ago that the English nonconformist churches of Wales took a greater interest in social amelioration, more especially during the last two decades of the century. Welsh nonconformity's antagonism to the early workers' unions, the benefit clubs and to certain manifestations of Chartism is well known. The concentration of Welsh nonconformity on disestablishment during and after the 1880's became less and less relevant to the problems of an industrial

---

[67] **Report of the Sixth Annual Conference of English Calvinistic Methodists of South Wales** (Carmarthen, 1890), p. 8.

[68] **North Wales Congregational Magazine,** vol. 2, no. 20, September 1891, p. 272.

[69] Revd. G. Ellis, 'The Church and Social Problems', **Report of the Conference of the English Churches of the Presbyterian Church of Wales at Cardiff, 1895** (Manchester, 1895), p. 34.

society. By the end of the century, workers concluded that they could best achieve their aspirations through their own industrial and political organizations, and they ceased to look to the chapels as their political allies. During the last two decades of the century miners' unions were comparatively weak. This was a period of cooperation between the owners and the workers during which most miners' leaders came from the ranks of nonconformity, Mabon was the key figure. The bitter strike of 1898 brought this phase to a close. Thereafter the struggle was for a minimum wage, and socialism and class welfare were the keynotes of the new industrial gospel. Thus the politics of Welsh nonconformity became irrelevant to many working men. Disestablishment had no place in workers' politics. Gradually they became less impressed by the nonconformist social pathology which traced the evils of man to drinking, gambling, whoring, a landed aristocracy and the lack of international arbitration.

One result of working-class disillusionment with organized religion was the formation of labour churches, a development brought about because, as a Cardiff labour church supporter put it, 'the old established churches are altogether too far committed to an endorsement of the worst aspects of latter-day industrialization'.[70] Supporters of the labour church believed that Christian morality and daily avocation had been separated. 'We join issue with the teaching that Christianity is a religion of comforting hope in the future. We say that unless it is of practical utility to us as we hew the coal and hammer the metal . . . . as we think and act, it is no religion for us. We say that Christ was essentially a practical teacher and therefore we treat with contempt the narrow theological hair-splitting which is making the churches of today the laughing stock of every thinking man.'[71] The labour church had no formal ministry, no dogma and no ritual beyond the structure of the barest preaching service. But, as Dr Kent points out: 'People who did not want institutionalized religion did not want an institutionalized form of that rejection.'[72] The failure of the labour church movement underlined the separation of the chapels from the demand for political and social change. In this view, and in sociological terms, the urbanization of south Wales, at least in the mid and late nineteenth century may have been a gradual process of liberation from ties paternalist and religious. The importance of the labour churches is that they provided a stepping-stone for some nonconformists on their way to socialism.

[70] A. G. Hobson, **Possibilities of the Labour Church. An Address to the Cardiff Labour Church** (Cardiff 1893), p. 4.

[71] Ibid., pp. 4–5.

[72] Kent, op. cit., p. 871.

   The Royal Commission which looked into the state of religion in Wales in the early twentieth century concluded that the evidence concerning agricultural districts, particularly Welsh-speaking agricultural areas, was quite conclusive that few habitually absented themselves from religious service, but for industrial areas the evidence varied.[73] But it certainly seems that by 1900 there had occurred a marked decline in the number of members and particularly of 'hearers' or 'adherents' of nonconformist places of worship, most of them working men.[74]

---

[73] Report of the Royal Commission appointed to inquire into the Church and other Religious Bodies in Wales, **Parliamentary Papers**, 1910, XIV, p. 55.

[74] See E. T. Davies, op. cit., pp. 151, 155.

WALTER RALLS

CHAPTER 6

THE PAPAL AGGRESSION OF 1850: A STUDY IN VICTORIAN ANTI-CATHOLICISM

F or those wishing to generalize about the Victorians the Great Exhibition of 1851 usually proves irresistible. But it does seem an obvious omission that so little is said about the disorders which kept the country upended during the preceding six months, that is, during the episode of the restoration of the Roman Catholic hierarchy, the 'Papal Aggression.' Christopher Dawson has urged that the one needs the other to symbolize properly the Victorian frame of mind. Here I wish to outline the underlying causes of this last great outburst of No-Popery feeling in an effort to trace the paradox of the aroused, angry, bigoted Guy Fawkes Day-men of November appearing the next summer as the staid, curious and progressive-minded citizens sunning themselves in the glory of all that glittering machinery so carefully displayed beneath the vaulted glass dome of their Crystal Palace.[1]

---

[1] Unfortunately, Christopher Dawson did not himself undertake such a study, but see his comments, 'The Victorian Background,' *The Tablet*, 23 September 1950, p. 245. For a satisfactory narrative account of the Papal Aggression, see ch. 4, 'Lord John Russell,' in Owen Chadwick, *The Victorian Church (London, 1966), 1*. The centennial volume, *The English Catholics, 1850-1950*, ed. G. A. Beck (London, 1950), has several pertinent articles, including Gordon Albion, 'The Restoration of the Hierarchy,' pp. 86–116. More monographic is E. R. Norman, *Anti-Catholicism in Victorian England* (London, 1968), pp. 52–79, and Thomas P. Joyce, 'The Restoration of the Catholic Hierarchy in England and Wales, 1850: A Study of Certain Public Reactions' (Ph. D. diss. Gregorian University, Rome, 1966). The recent literature on Victorian Catholicism is summarized by Josef L. Altholz, 'Writings on Victorian Catholicism, 1945–1970,' *The British Studies Monitor* 2, no. 3 (Spring 1972): 23–30. Altholz argues that while much is being published it remains excessively pietistic, favors biography (with studies of Newman, Acton and Manning still dominant) and, though much is scholarly, remains largely uncritical. For a broader coverage of recent Victorian religious history which includes some instructive comments on English Catholicism, see Richard A. Soloway, 'Church and Society: Recent Trends in Nineteenth Century Religious History,' *The Journal of British Studies* 11 (1972): 142–159. A comprehensive study of Victorian anti-Catholicism has yet to appear; Norman's brilliant essay only points the way, as does G. F. A. Best, 'Popular Protestantism in Victorian England,' in *Ideas and Institutions of Victorian Britain: Essays in Honour of George Kitson Clark*, ed. Robert Robson (London, 1967), pp. 115–142. Prior to these was Gilbert A. Cahill, *Irish Catholicism and English Toryism, 1832–1848: A Study in Ideology* (Ann Arbor, Mich.; University Microfilms, 1954). For the roles played by various leading individuals, see Brian Fothergill, *Nicholas Wiseman* (London, 1963); David Newsome, *The Parting of Friends, The Wilberforces and Henry Manning* (London, 1966): Meriol Trevor's massive *Newman: The Pillar of the Cloud* and *Newman: Light in Winter* (London, 1962). A more critical view of Newman during the crisis of the Papal Aggression is Ronald Chapman, *Father Faber* (London, 1961). Newsome's study is the model for what is required.

To begin, Lord John Russell, then prime minister, seems badly miscast as the leader of No-Popery sentiment, for he had attacked the Tories for decades for mixing anti-Catholicism with politics. Six years earlier during the bitter debate over the Maynooth grant (begun during the French Revolution for the support of an Irish Roman Catholic seminary) he had argued that it was no wonder Catholics refused to consider office under the Tories: 'I ask, what men of the smallest spirit would join a party which treats with such contumely, such insult and such flagrant injustice, the body of Roman Catholics, professing the ancient religion of Europe, and forming more than six millions of people of Ireland?' His career had been virtually punctuated by such statements as 'on the principle of general religious liberty.... I will give my support to any question that may come before the House.'[2]

But in his letter to the bishop of Durham, written on the eve of Guy Fawkes Day 1850, the stand of a lifetime was swept aside. The opening sentence was, 'My Dear Lord: I agree with you in considering the 'late aggression of the Pope upon our Protestantism' as 'insolent and insidious,' and I therefore feel as indignant as you do upon the subject.' The letter, made public to the nation, concluded, 'But I rely with confidence on the people of England and I will not bate a jot of heart or hope as the glorious principles and the immortal martyrs of the Reformation shall be held in reverence by the great mass of a nation which looks with contempt on the mummeries of superstition and with scorn at the laborious endeavours which are now making to confine the intellect and enslave the soul.'[3]

The occasion for this outburst was the reinstitution of a national hierarchy for Roman Catholics: England and Wales, after September 29, 1850, were to be divided among twelve dioceses headed by regular bishops under canon law with the highest authority being vested in the newly announced office of 'Cardinal-Archbishop of Westminster.' Since the seventeenth century, English Catholics had been under a type of church organization reserved for mission lands as in China, India and Oceania. It was a form of government headed by vicars apostolic instead of bishops, and directed immediately by the Congregation of Propaganda at Rome.

This change for English Roman Catholics would seem to have been

[2] *Debates* (Commons), 72 (13 February 1844). col. 699; 17 (23 March 1827) col. 14.

[3] *The Times*, 7 November 1850. This most famous of all Victorian assaults on English Catholicism is reprinted in *English Historical Documents*, ed. G. M. Young and W. D. Handcock (New York, 1956), 12 pt. 1:367-369. The bishop of Durham, Dr. Maltby, had publicly complained to Russell about the 'insolent and insidious' nature of the restoration of the hierarchy. Disraeli, assuming an amused attitude toward all parties, said, 'I am bound to state that ... I never knew a proceeding more free from the appearance of sublety and covin.' *Debates* (Commons), 114 (4 February 1851), col. 132.

unexceptional, especially since in the previous decade similar arrangements had been made for Quebec and Australia. In Ireland of course such a hierarchy had never ceased to function. However, when the papal brief announcing it was made known in England in late October 1850, there began a national outcry that swept along nearly every shade of the press and the pulpit with the established church and much of dissent joined in a most uncharacteristic show of unity.[4] The *Times* soon found the appropriate label and from then on it was everywhere known as the Papal Aggression. Thousands of petitions to the Crown urged some form of retaliatory action, as did some seven thousand meetings, chaired by indignant local leaders. From November and the publication of Russell's Durham Letter no event could rival its continued fascination for the public. The Parliament of 1851 wasted itself on efforts to create new No-Popery legislation, efforts which finally met some returning sense of proportions, for the Ecclesiastical Titles Bill when passed that August was only a sop to bigotry and remained quietly on the books until Gladstone, opposed to the furor from the first, secured its removal some twenty years later.

Here I wish to explore why the Protestant majority felt so threatened and made so much of the issue; why in fact England at mid-century proved a most inappropriate place for the Vatican to assert in any formal way a revival of Catholic authority. The question includes what led Englishmen at the height of their power to find in the ancient cry of 'No-Popery' so apt an outlet for their strongest fears and self-doubts.

There are four aspects to the nature of the Catholic threat. First there is the fact that the number of Catholic believers had increased some twenty-fold, from thirty thousand at the turn of the century to perhaps three-quarters of a million by 1850.[5] Nearly all of this was due to the Irish immigration and had come about within the last decade. The heart-breaking experience of the Irish arriving by the hundreds of thousands, penniless, half-starved, half-clad, living in squalid rooms unfortunately only worsened the prejudices already surrounding Roman Catholicism in England. During the severe social and economic discontent of the 1840s, the English poor found themselves in direct economic competition with this

[4] But see below for the ambivalence felt by many dissenters in thus supporting the claims of the national church.

[5] E. E. Y. Hales, *The Catholic Church in the Modern World* (New York, 1958), p. 108. *Census of Great Britian, 1851; Religious Worship: England and Wales* (London 1853), pp. cii, cxlvi, cxlviii, xlvi. G. Kitson Clark, *The Making of Victorian England* (Cambridge, Mass., 1962), pp. 165ff. A cautionary note on the use of the Religious Census of 1851 is in W. S. F. Pickering, 'The 1851 Religious Census — A Useless Experiment,' *British Journal of Sociology* 18 (1967): 382-407. This should be compared with David Thompson's earlier article, 'The 1851 Religious Census: Problems and Possibilities,' *Victorian Studies* 2 (1957): 87-97.

new labor force. Carlyle drew the stereotype when he wrote in his wild fashion: 'Crowds of miserable Irish darken all our towns ... He is the sorest evil this country has to strive with. In his rags and laughing savagery ... he lodges in any pig hutch or dog hutch, roosts in outhouses ... The Saxon man may be ignorant, but he has not sunk from decent manhood to squalid apehood.'[6] This merging of the Irish poor with the old stigma attaching to the ancient faith raised popular anti-Catholic feelings to a new intensity.

The second point is that during this period there is renewed insistence on the old charge that Catholicism was incompatible with English political institutions. Since the mid-thirties the Tories had made an attack on Catholicism, its priesthood and doctrines, a major part of their objection to the Whig-O'Connell connection. *The Times,* the *Quarterly Review,* the Protestant Association, Exeter Hall and a score of other sources reinforced the charge that Catholics were priest-dominated, owed their ultimate allegiance to a foreign power and were unable to fulfill their obligations as loyal citizens. Such charges and the replies they evoked from the Whigs, the Radicals and eventually the Peelites, made up a surprisingly large part of the political dialogue from 1835 to 1850.[7]

On the other hand liberal opinion though somewhat more careful of the niceties of civil and religious liberty was itself deeply opposed to Catholicism. A correct definition of liberalism according to Matthew Arnold in *Culture and Anarchy* must include as a cardinal tenet the 'Protestantism of the Protestant religion.'[8] According to this view the progressive nations of the world, economically and politically, were those with a predominately Protestant faith.

The *Dublin Review* which was founded in 1836 by Nicholas Wiseman and other leading Catholics largely to refute the more grotesque misunderstandings regarding their faith, and which hoped to meet the *Edinburgh* and *Quarterly* reviews on some level of parity in its critical and historical writing, returned repeatedly to this charge (despite its name, it was always published in London). In an article entitled 'Arbitrary Power, Popery, Protestantism', it was conceded that no article of the national creed had been inculcated more successfully than that both 'popery and arbitrary power'

---

[6] Thomas Carlyle, 'Chartism,' *Critical and Miscellaneous Essays* (London, 1907), 4:138. For a study of the Irish immigration in depth in one city (Cardiff) see John Hickey, *Urban Catholics: Urban Catholicism in England and Wales from 1829 to the Present Day* (London, 1967). A broader scope is attempted in Lewis P. Curtis, *Anglo-Saxons and Celts: A Study of Anti-Irish Prejudices in Victorian England* (Bridgeport, Conn., 1968). For a review of other recent studies in local social-religious history, see Soloway, pp. 151ff.

[7] Cahill has been most enterprising on this theme in his *Irish Catholicism and English Toryism, 1832–1848: A Study in Ideology.*

[8] Matthew Arnold, *Culture and Anarchy* (Ann Arbor, Mich., 1965), p. 106.

were 'inseparable.' This had been so long taught without contradiction, the article said, 'that we fear the majority of Protestants, in both kingdoms now regard it as a religious-political axiom.' And then the author sets himself the imposing task of proving that 'it has been from the earliest period the doctrine of Catholic writers, that the people were the only legitimate source of all civil authority.'[9] In a subsequent piece, 'Prejudices of our Popular Literature', it was observed that England was the 'slave of prejudice' despite her boasted liberty. It was the prejudice of both patriotism and religion, for in England these were one. 'It is the growth of centuries, deepening in its dye as each year rolled on, becoming every day more inveterate in its hold upon the public mind.'[10]

The third factor contributing to anti-Catholicism in 1850 was that during the previous decade Catholicism in England had become, rather suddenly, revitalized and impressive in its enthusiasm for challenging the position of the Protestant majority, and especially of the established church. To the old hereditary Catholics and the immigrant Irish there was added in the thirties and forties a remarkable group of young, well-born converts who brought intelligence, money, position and above all great enthusiasm for the task of winning England again for the faith.

A.W.Pugin, the famous proponent of neo-Gothic architecture and a recent convert, built the first monastery since the Reformation. It was followed by a variety of schools, chapels, churches and in 1848 the dedication of the first cathedral since the sixteenth century, St George's in Southwark. A score of prelates from the continent attended the brilliant ceremony and the publicity was nation-wide. Ambrose Phillipps and other rich converts helped bring various Italian monastic orders to engage in open-air

---

[9] Anon., *Dublin Review* 8 (February 1840): 6–10.

[10] *Ibid.*, p. 57. Protestant antagonism towards Catholicism extended as everyone knows far beyond the classical doctrinal differences. Best has been illuminating and amusing about the intense alarm Victorians experienced when confronted with the world of convents, monasteries and the confessional. Still, as he himself urges, these are important matters and as yet await extended treatment. No one, for instance, has explored the social meaning of that great body of early Victorian literature (popular and scholarly) on the prophetic interpretation of *Daniel* and the *Revelation* with their master symbols supposedly pointing to 'the mystery of iniquity' and the 'anti-Christ.' Even more neglected are the controversies over Saint Alphonsus Liguori (1696–1787) whose works were translated into English during this time. A major influence throughout nineteenth-century Catholic theology, Liguori is credited with shaping the definition of the dogmas of the Immaculate Conception and the infallibility of the pope. His *Theologia moralis* (9th ed., 1785) was fiercely attacked by Protestants for its handling of such sins as lying and theft. Even more disturbing to an age traumatized by any hint of sexual symbolism was his graphic devotional study (*Le glorie di Maria*, 1750) on the relation of the Virgin to Christ and the Father. The *Dublin Review* repeatedly comes to the defense of the great Redemptorist theologian. There was also considerable public interest (see almost any issue of the *Annual Register*) in the numerous law suits charging that property had been granted to the Catholic bishops (indirectly for the law forbade direct gifts) because of undue influence in the confessional. This, clearly, hardly begins the subject of Victorian anti-Catholicism.

missionary work. Here again there was much notice taken of the public processions in sandals and flowing robes, with statues of the Virgin in prominent display — sights not seen in England for hundreds of years, and accompanied now by frequent ugly mobs.[11] Among the monastic orders heretofore unknown to England were the Trappists, Redemptorists, Passionists and the Fathers of Charity, now all in their distinctive garb.[12]

The papacy, long out of touch with affairs in England, was led to believe, especially by the ebullient Wiseman, that a new day had indeed dawned, and after 1845 and the conversion of Newman and other Oxford Anglicans, there was a widely held opinion in Rome that all of England might return to the ancient faith. The journal of ultramontane French Catholicism, *L'Univers*, gave European prominence to these events, though the facts were somewhat less than these reports implied.[13]

At the center of this new activity was Nicholas Wiseman. Born at the turn of the century, he had a phenomenal career at Rome after attending a small parochial school in England. While still in his twenties he had become the head of the English College in Rome, agent for the vicars apostolic (among whom he got a bad reputation for politics), and still had time to win an international reputation as a scholar for his textual studies on ancient manuscripts in the Vatican library. At the same time his exuberant nature had carried him into the social world of Rome and he was early accounted a public figure and a great preacher. Everyone knew him. When the new English converts came to Rome in the thirties he proved a sympathetic advisor and friend, and he began to share their dream of the reconquest of England for the faith. The *Dublin Review* was to be the special instrument for this end, and it was important in convincing the later converts of the forties that Newman's doctrine of the *via media* was incompatible with a true history of the church. Newman, as is well known, credits one of Wiseman's articles as having started him on the road to Rome.[14] Wiseman

---

[11] Denis R. Gwynn, *The Second Spring: 1818–1852* (London, 1942); and by the same author. *Father Dominic Barberi* (London, 1947); Ambrose Phillipps (later de Lisle), 'Supplement: Letters of Father Dominic of the Mother of God', *The Life of the Blessed Paul of the Cross* (London, 1853), 3; Urban Young *Dominic Barberi in England* (London, 1935); E. S. Purcell, *Life and Letters of Ambrose Phillipps de Lisle* (London, 1900); Bernard Ward, *The Sequel to Catholic Emancipation* (London, 1915); Claude R. Leetham, *Luigi Gentili: A Sower for the Second Spring* (London, 1965).

[12] Protestants were not the only ones to take exception to this flowering of Italian Catholicism. The hereditary English Catholics (the 'Old Catholics') deeply resented these (to them) un-English and unnecessary innovations. See especially B. Ward and Leetham.

[13] James MacCaffrey, *History of the Catholic Church in the Nineteenth Century* (2nd ed., Dublin, 1910), 2: 49ff., is an extended review of Vatican-English Catholic relations in the generations before 1850.

[14] *Apológia Pro Vita Sua* (New York, 1956), p. 218.

had come to England permanently in 1840 and had thrown himself into the work of public lectures, organizing the new changes in ritual and worship along more Italian (and thus controversial) lines, raising money for Pugin's buildings, and trying to solve the problem of how best to assimilate the Irish into the English Catholic world. His style of writing and address ranged from carefully reasoned polemics to what even his contemporaries deemed lugubrious sentimentality. As his energies became ever more diversely directed the unfortunate tendencies in his style predominated. It is significant that after becoming cardinal-archbishop in 1850, his one major effort was the novel *Fabiola*, an immensely popular romance of the early Christians. As the choice in 1850 to head the new hierarchy, Wiseman's fondness for ornate display and his tendency towards orotund rhetoric made him an extremely visible target for Protestant antagonism. Brilliant, versatile, ambitious and dedicated as he was, still he could appear a pompous fool.[15]

My fourth observation has to do with the sharp contrast between a seemingly monolithic Catholic faith, revitalized and expanded, and the disarray in which Protestantism found itself at mid-century. This is a subject obviously unto itself, and here I wish to make only the broadest of connective statements. The established church was riven between the evangelical, the Arnoldian broad and the ritualistic high church factions. Central to the confusion was the Oxford Movement. Probe at virtually any point, and the bitterness and hostility will seem a hundred and twenty years later to be palpable and alive. From Dr. Arnold's first bitter attack in the *Edinburgh Review*, entitled 'The Oxford Malignants, and Dr Hampden', wherein he called the Tractarians 'the peculiar disgrace of the Church of England', through the publishing of Hurrell Froude's mildly scandalous *Remains*, and then the almost ludicrous effort to establish with the German Lutheran Church a joint bishopric of Jerusalem — bringing upon the British government in 1841 a protest from Turkey not dissimilar to that expressed by the English parliament ten years later against the 'Papal Aggression'[16] — through the issuing of *Tract 90* with the resultant outcry

---

[15] For depth of presentation Wilfred Ward, *The Life and Times of Cardinal Wiseman* (London, 1897), 2 vols., is richer than the recent work by Fothergill.

[16] Thus Faud Effendi put to Aberdeen, at the Foreign Office, a series of questions which closely parallel those put to Rome by the British ten years later: Did not the British government concede that the Jerusalem bishopric was unduly ambitious, including as claimed, all of Syria, Palestine, Chaldea, Egypt and Abyssinia? 'And since he exercised this 'jurisdiction' under the metropolitan control of a foreign pontiff', one question read, 'was not this violation of the sovereignty of the sultan in his dominions, a derogation, so to say, of the sultan's royal supremacy?' R. W. Greaves. 'The Jerusalem Bishopric, 1841,' *The English Historical Review* 64 (July 1949): 350.

from all sides, including those most kindly disposed toward the Tractarian movement (here the master of Trinity, Christopher Wordsworth, is typical when he cried, 'Oh, what a fall! Its perusal has lowered my opinion of the writer more than I could have thought possible'), there is an atmosphere of unrelieved tension which had not abated by 1850.[17]

The Puseyite ritualists, if no one else, were enough to keep raw nerves from healing. Every weapon was used against them: sarcasm, supercilious and frosty disdain, ecclesiastical censure and finally court action. But they held their own, an acerbating minority estimated as some five per cent of the clergy who were a constant reminder of the tendency toward Rome and the prior claims of the ancient church. It can be argued that there was more actual antagonism directed toward them during the uproar over the Papal Aggression than toward the Roman Catholics. Lord John Russell's loss of equilibrium can most directly be charged against his high irritation with the Puseyites, for in the Durham Letter he said, 'What, then, is the danger to be apprehended from a foreign prince of no great power, compared to the danger within the gates from the unworthy sons of the Church of England?'[18]

Still, the ritualists and the conversions to Rome were but part of the problems facing the Protestant majority by 1850. From the agnostic left came the new geology and earth sciences and by the forties a wide reading in German theology and the higher criticism to contest not only the Mosaic cosmology but classical Christian doctrine itself. Gladstone reported that for him reading Schleiermacher opened the 'sluices of the theological deep whether to deluge or to irrigate, I do not know.' This is not the place to explore how wrong G. M. Young was in writing that 'English divinity was not equipped to meet — for its comfort, it was hardly capable of understanding — the new critical methods of the Germans', but the evidence runs the other way.[19] And it is instructive that when Bishop Blomfield answered a petition signed by some seven thousand clergy regarding the Papal Aggression he chose to say, 'I cannot but think that we have more to

[17] Thomas Arnold, 'The Oxford Malignants and Dr. Hampden,' *The Edinburgh Review* 63 (April 1836): 235. For the Wordsworth quotation, A. B. Webster, *Joshua Watson: the Story of a Layman, 1771–1885* (London, 1954), p. 108.

[18] Young and Handcock, 12, 1:368.

[19] John Morley, *The Life of William Ewart Gladstone* (New York, 1903), 1:166. G. M. Young, *Victorian England* (New York, 1954), p. 114. See Duncan Forbes, *The Liberal Anglican Idea of History* (Cambridge, Mass., 1952). On the early recognition of German textual criticism, see Merton A. Christensen, 'Taylor of Norwich and the Higher Criticism,' *The Journal of the History of Ideas* 20 (April 1959): 183. See also A. O. J. Cockshut, *The Unbelievers: English Agnostic Thought, 1850–1890* (London, 1964); Anthony Symondson, *The Victorian Crisis of Faith* (London, 1970).

apprehend from the theology of Germany than from that of Rome; from that which deifies human reason, than that which seeks to blind or stifle it.'[20]

Further anxiety was occasioned by the widespread concern over the proper definition of church-state relations. The profound impact of Coleridge and his view of the common identity of church and state had met a sharp setback in the post-1832 (the Great Reform Bill) world of ecclesiastical commissions and the newly insistent voice of dissent that the Anglican church shoud be disestablished. Church and dissent had since the seventeenth century never been further apart; one of the great authorities on the period (Kitson Clark) refers to 'the hatred entertained for the Church of England by many of those who dissented from it.'[21] Examined individually, the various denominations and sects were either experiencing a sharp contest for authority within their ranks as in Methodism, or an unsettling decline in growth relative to the population. All dissent of course still suffered grave social and educational disadvantages. It would not be until later in the next decade that a new wave of enthusiasm and growth would begin for the nonconforming bodies. At the time of Papal Aggression dissent shared with the established church a crisis of confidence which made the Catholics appear all the more formidable.[22]

Significantly, dissent, though early swept along by the mighty surge of No-Popery, soon had second thoughts. For them to join the national church in a protest against the Catholic challenge to its jurisdiction in England would only serve to strengthen the former. Caught between two, not one, ancient enemies, the leading dissenting parliamentary spokesman, John Bright, vigorously opposed Russell's Ecclesiastical Titles Bill, which the government introduced early in the life of the parliament of 1851. He had of course other grounds for opposition: Russell's speech on the seventh of February he found 'very good if delivered some 300 years ago' and along with many thinking members of the house (Gladstone, Graham, most of the Peelites and of course the other Radicals, Roebuck and so on) condemned the illiberality and inanity of forbidding under penal threats any ecclesiastical organization other than the established church from assuming territo-

---

[20] *The Morning Chronicle*, 4 November 1850.

[21] Clark, p. 158.

[22] Ibid., especially ch. 6, 'The Religion of the People.' See also Elie Halévy, *A History of the English People in the Nineteenth Century*, Vol. 4: *Victorian Years, 1841–1895* (London, 1961): 337–414. Maldwyn Edwards, *After Wesley* (London, 1943). E. R. Taylor, *Methodism and Politics, 1791–1851* (Cambridge, 1935). John T. Wilkinson, *1662 and After: Three Centuries of English Nonconformity* (London, 1962); John Kent, *The Age of Disunity* (London, 1966) is excellent on Methodism.

rial titles. But Bright also spoke for dissenters when he argued: 'The measure is nothing better than a sham. I believe the only effect of it can be an attempt to bolster up the ascendency so long maintained by the Church Establishment.'[23]

No-Popery in 1850 then may be explained in part by the four factors of 1) the Irish immigration; 2) the old charge of Catholic alienation from true English values intensified by the politics of the thirties and forties; 3) the publicity given Wiseman and the converts; and 4) the unsettled condition of Protestantism. The evidence would appear to support Halévy's judgment: 'By birth or choice, Catholics were aliens at home. The history of the growth of English Roman Catholics is no part of the English history.'[24]

The simplicity of this statement is, however, misleading. As an observation that in the nineteenth century (the period Halévy focused on) Catholicism in England led a life of its own and Catholics were only partially assimilated into the dominant culture of the Protestant majority, the statement stands. But surely one is not left to infer that Catholicism may be eliminated from a study of the Victorian world. For one thing the Victorians were saturated with a sense of history, far more than we who have the alternative rhetoric of the social sciences to rely upon. History for them was virtually the only instrument of investigation and analysis and in the hands of Macaulay, Lecky, Froude and others, it produced the Whig interpretation that England's present pre-eminence was closely associated with the values and ideas of Protestantism. And in their pages invidious anti-Catholic comparisons abound.

Yet for all their belief in 'progress' the Victorians clearly were uneasy. Their novelists and prophets were only too aware that the authority of Protestantism was under severe attack. What would replace it, or possibly renew it, had not yet appeared. Then for the ancient authority at Rome to be experiencing a 'second spring' was doubly disturbing. And when the Vatican sent the first Cardinal the English had seen since the Reformation to rule a church now announced as coterminous with the established church, all the old associations of No-Popery were sharply intensified.

Several events in 1850 made that year most unpromising for such a venture. Vatican policy and Catholic affairs generally in Europe were harshly regarded in England. While at home the Gorham Judgment proved the most unsettling event since Newman's defection to Rome. In Ireland there was the seemingly interference in secular matters by the Catholic hierarchy, a considerable cause of alarm to the government, for since the death of O'Connell (1847) and the sudden demise of Smith O'Brien and the

---

[23] George Macaulay Trevelyan, *The Life of John Bright* (New York, 1913), p. 193.

[24] Halévy, p. 376.

Militant Young Irelanders (1848) there was a vacuum of leadership, which if filled by the Catholic clergy would mean trying days ahead.

As regards the pope, Pius IX had begun his reign in 1846 with an almost popular press in England. The *Times* playfully referred to him as 'Pio Nono' and applauded his first mildly liberal measures in the papal estates. But the revolutions of 1848 killed this mood when he had had to make his hasty and ignominious flight to Naples, a place widely regarded in England as having the most corrupt, reactionary government in Europe. Gladstone in 1850 had just returned from there, 'boiling with indignation' over the plight of liberal Neapolitan politicians wasting in dark solitary confinement.[25] As always Gladstonian indignation was good press. And bad for the pope for having sought asylum there. Nor did his recent return to Rome in the spring of 1850 under the protection of French troops help, for it revealed how unpopular his leadership had become to his own people. His angry struggle that summer with the liberal Sardinian government of d'Azeglio completed English disillusionment. It was this pope, then, who issued the papal rescript, derisively called the 'Papal Bull',[26] in October establishing Wiseman and his hierarchy in England.

At home Palmerston was in his most John Bullish mood and his refusal either to receive General Haynau, the leader of Austrian conservative forces in 1848, or to apologize to him or his government after the workers at Barclay's Brewery gave him a mild but nasty roughing, was generally regarded by Englishmen with fond approval. As for his great four-hour 'Don Pacifico' speech in the House of Commons earlier that year, no expression of the pride in being English was to be so remembered throughout the century. The peroration it will be recalled ended with the stirring assertion that an Englishman anywhere in the world should be able to use his citizenship to invoke respect, just as in ancient times a Roman could rout opponents with the cry, 'civis Romanus sum.'[27] 1850 clearly was an

---

[25] Ibid., p. 317.

[26] In Vatican usage the document was referred to as a *rescript* or *brief*, but never a *bull*, which of course has a higher order of authority. These niceties were lost in the heat of the moment: 'Papal Bull' certainly sounded more threatening, and the homonymic possibilities of such a word proved widely irresistable. *Punch* for weeks carried endless puns and cartoons about strayed, lost, charging and wounded bulls. The most famous cartoon, perhaps is a scene at a cattle show of an enormous bull with the face of Pius IX and the English public contemptuously walking away. The caption read, 'Great Cattle Show: The Roman Bull that Didn't Get the Prize.' Equally abounding were the puns on 'Wise-man' and 'New-man.' *Punch* threw itself with such vehemence into the uproar that their most distinguished artist, Dicky Dole, felt called upon to resign. Denis R. Gwynn, *A Hundred Years of Catholic Emancipation: 1829–1929* (London, 1929), p. 107.

[27] Halévy, p. 305.

awkward time for any foreign potentate to insult, no matter how unknowingly, English patriotism.

No-Popery feelings were even more directly aroused when the prolonged investigation of the theology of the Rev. G. C. Gorham came to a controversial end in 1850. An especially acerbating aspect was the fact that the final decision was handed down by a lay court, the Judicial Committee of the Privy Council. The Gorham case touched on all sides of the religious issue, but the most prominent feature was the ranging of the Puseyite wing solidly against Gorham. When the government validated his orthodoxy a storm broke over the head of the prime minister. Russell, who had systematically appointed only anti-Puseyite men to high ecclesiastical position now made no bones about his opposition and fear of the high church party. They were not only traitors to the church, he said, but also guilty of a 'shocking profanation' by 'turning a service of remembrance into an offensive spectacle.'[28]

The Gorham Judgment was the occasion for a stream of new defections to Rome, Manning and Robert Wilberforce being only the more prominent members of this new party of converts who found their high church hopes crushed by this final intolerable event. A measure of the intense excitement the issue raised is the British Museum's collection of over two hundred books and pamphlets written in 1850 and the following year on the Gorham Judgment.[29]

On the personal side, the ritual controversy had come to Russell in 1850 in a rather intense way. St Paul's, Knightsbridge, where he and his wife worshipped, had become since its consecration in 1843 one of the most fashionable parishes in London. The curate-in-charge was W. J. E. Bennett, an able man, much dedicated to the social side of his ministry. As a consequence he asked his wealthy congregation to back the building of a church for the poor. This was completed and had just been consecrated on 11 June 1850 as St. Barnabas, Pimlico, or rather, according to the new style as S. Barnabas. Russell approved this work and gave it support.

At St. Barnabas, Bennett indulged his tendency toward high church ritual by installing a small college for choristers and four priests. His services included all the niceties of address and usage employed by the more daring Puseyites. After Russell wrote his Durham letter the press

[28] Spencer Walpole, *The Life of Lord John Russell* (London, 1889), 2: 116.

[29] Though some ritualists joined in the general No-Popery cry (for reasons that may be imagined), many felt that they were the true point of attack and there began a general retreat from the time-honored policy of appealing to the secular power for support in sustaining the church. Gladstone who was frequently ranked with them said he voted against the Ecclesiastical Titles Bill on its second reading 'for the purpose of entering my protest against all attempts to meet the spiritual dangers of the Church by temporal legislation of a penal character.' This is certainly an important by-product of the Papal Aggression. *Debates* (Commons), 115 (23 May 1851), col. 566.

picked up charges recently made by Bennett's superior, the redoubtable Bishop Blomfield, against Romanizers in the church and focused on Bennett as a prime example. There was an ugly riot at St. Barnabas on the third Sunday in November. A mob broke in and the police were called. Bennett received threatening letters and a package filled with dung. Early in December he wrote a public *Letter to Lord John Russell* which pointed out that these were the true consequences of the prime minister's appeal to No-Popery, and, more telling, he related that for the past few years high church services which Russell now termed 'mummeries of superstition' had been weekly practiced in St. Paul's, with no noticeable protest from his most distinguished parishioner. The *Letter* went through seven editions, and it could only have added to the difficulty Russell was having in keeping a sense of perspective on the issue of anti-Catholicism.[30]

Finally, perhaps the most alarming previous event of 1850 for Russell and his government regarding Catholic power took place in August at the Synod of Thurles. No such Irish national synod had been held since the early seventeenth century, and that now assembled was seen from Westminster as a peculiar instance of revived papal authority. When the primate of all Ireland, the archbishop of Armagh, died late in 1849, Pius IX passed over the three names recommended by the Irish clergy and had instead appointed Dr Cullen, a still youthful churchman then serving as head of the Irish College in Rome. Dr Cullen was seen not only as a new broom — there had been some debilitating divisions in the Irish hierarchy — but as sharing that ultramontane spirit which so moved Wiseman and the English converts. The Russell government was made to feel his presence in an especially uncomfortable way: 'One alarming spectacle of the present times', the new primate told the assembled prelates, 'is the propagation of error through a godless system of education.'[31]

This attack was aimed at the efforts of Peel and now supported and continued by Russell and the Whigs to make up for the inadequacies of Dublin University. This ancient institution, established in the closing years of Elizabeth I, had but one college, Trinity, and though more or less open by the nineteenth century to attendance by others than members of the established church, in fact very few Presbyterians and fewer Catholics went there. Peel in 1845 had successfully introduced legislation to establish three new Queen's Colleges at Belfast, Galway and Cork. It called for an initial endowment of £100,000 for the buildings and £6,000 annually for upkeep. It was to be non-sectarian.

---

[30] Frederick Bennett, *The Story of W. J. E. Bennett* (London, 1909). For a succinct account, see Chadwick, 1: 301ff.

[31] Peadar Mac Suibhne, *Paul Cullen and His Contemporaries, with their letters from 1820–1920* (Kildare, 1962), 2: 56.

This principle of undenominational education ran counter to virtually all English schools at the time, from primary to the two older universities. Predictably a protest was made by nearly all camps on the right when Peel introduced his bill. That ardent champion of low church feeling, Sir Robert Inglis, called it 'a gigantic scheme of godless education', and the phrase 'godless colleges' stuck.[32] Now Dr. Cullen was using those very phrases. While at Rome he had been privy to the conflicting response the Irish hierarchy experienced when faced with this generous proposal. For Rome, however, there was only one correct position and the Sacred Congregation of Propaganda issued late in 1847 a papal rescript condemning the colleges. A year later in October a second rescript reiterated the prohibition. Lord Clarendon, then Irish Viceroy, rather desperately tried to reach an accommodation, for his government was going ahead with the buildings and the question was who was going to use them. Now at the Synod of Thurles six separate decrees were issued; the first prohibited anyone in orders from participating in the Queen's Colleges in any way, and in the sixth, the laity were warned 'to repudiate and shun them on the ground they involved grave and intrinsic dangers to faith and morals.'[33] It was not an absolute prohibition, but it was enough to render the scheme a failure (by 1858 the government reckoned over some £380,000 had been spent with less than 262 students taking degrees — the 'godless colleges' were dissolved in 1882).[34]

When early in the life of the parliament of 1851 Russell defended both his unwonted No-Popery and the need for penal legislation, he cited the recent Synod of Thurles as the kind of ecclesiastical interference which must be prevented. He referred to the 'unusual manner' in which Rome had selected their own man as primate:

> a clergyman who had long been resident at Rome ... conversant with the habits and opinions of Rome. I must ask whether this House and the Government of this country can be entirely indifferent, when they see that an archbishop has been thus named ... and that the first proceeding he carries into effect is to hold forth to odium an Act of Parliament passed by this country for the purpose of educating the people of Ireland ... This I think, is an instance at all events, that we have not to deal with purely spiritual concerns; that that interference ... has been attempted as a beginning, no doubt, to be matured into

[32] *Debates* (Commons), 80 (9 May 1845), col. 378.

[33] Fergal McGrath, *Newman's University: Idea and Reality* (London, 1951), p. 74.

[34] Ibid., pp. 80, 81.

other measures, and to be exerted on some future occasion with more potent results.[35]

Everyone could understand this argument, whether agreeing or not. To the Catholic mind it was manifestly unfair, for the decisions taken at the Synod of Thurles were entirely appropriate to the pastoral functions of their bishops. But for most Protestants it meant that a major piece of social legislation, developed for the sole end of improving Ireland, had been repudiated and rendered ineffective by an authority unknown to the constitution and one accountable to no power in the Queen's realm. Some weeks earlier the *Times* addressed itself to the question of the Synod of Thurles: 'Is it not the very essence of this jurisdiction to insinuate itself into that of the State ... Did not these spiritual and ghostly 'governors' of Ireland denounce and nullify the best-conceived measures of Her Majesty's Ministry for improving that miserable country?' And then making the jump to the Vatican's quarrel with the liberal government of d'Azeglio, the editorial continued, 'Are not the same 'authorities' at this moment defying the Government and laws of Sardinia and waging open war there with the Crown?'[36]

These are some of the circumstances, then, surrounding Russell's and many others' loss of perspective and equilibrium when the papal rescript, *Universalia Ecclesiae*, announcing the new hierarchy, was published in full in the *Times*. Unfortunately for everyone it was Wiseman who had composed this solemn document, and to the question, 'What was the Papal Aggression?', one must look as much to the matter of style as to the events themselves. For the infuriating element was not so much how the Roman Catholics organized their community in England, but rather the inflated and arrogant language used in announcing these changes. This 'Papal Bull' dismissed the established church in such phrases as 'the Anglican schism of the sixteenth century' and then declared 'after having weighted the whole matter most scrupulously ... we have resolved and do hereby decree the reestablishment in the kingdom of England, and according to the common laws of the church, of a hierarchy of bishops deriving their titles from their own sees, which we constitute by the present letter in the various apostolic districts.' It concluded with a direct challenge: 'We decree that this apostolic letter shall ... always be valid and firm, and hold good to all intents and purposes, notwithstanding the rights of former sees in England ... We likewise decree that all which may be done to the contrary by anyone

---

[35] *Debates* (Commons), 114 (7 February 1851), col. 187–190.

[36] *Times*, 27 November 1850. A careful account of the 'godless colleges' is in McGrath, pp. 1–83. See also J. H. Whyte, *The Independent Irish Party, 1850–9* (London, 1958).

whoever he may be, knowing or ignorant, in the name of any authority whatever, shall be without force.'[37]

The *Morning Chronicle* said it appeared that all other ecclesiastical authority had been 'stigmatized ... as schismatic and intrusive.'[38] And the extreme element in the Catholic press only made matters worse. The French ultramontane journal *L'Univers* declared that 'since the promulgation of the Papal brief, the sees of Canterbury, of York, of London, and any other sees established before the reformation have ceased to exist. The persons who in the future may assume the titles of Archbishop of Canterbury, or Bishop of London will be nothing less than intruders, schismatic priests, without spiritual authority.'[39] The radical Catholic newspaper *The Tablet*, published then in Dublin but written primarily for the English, said that 'Rome has more than spoken ... all baptized persons, without exception ... are openly commanded to submit themselves in all ecclesiastical matters, under pain of damnation, and the Anglican sees, those ghosts of realities long passed, are utterly ignored.'[40] These and other comments were extensively quoted in the English press.

But worse was to come: a week after the publication of the papal rescript, the *Times* on October 29 carried a copy of Wiseman's first pastoral letter to English Catholics. He wrote it while still traveling in Europe and before he knew of the outcry against *Universalis Ecclesiae* breaking in England. Read today this first pastoral does seem an unbelievably grandiloquent document. He announced himself to be, 'Nicholas, by the Divine mercy of the Holy Roman Church [known] by the title of St. Pudentiana Cardinal Priest, Archbishop of Westminster, and Administrator of the Diocese of Southwark.' (Newman on reading it asked, 'Who in the world is St. Pudentiana?'[41]) The pastoral went on to claim that, 'at present and till such time as the Holy See shall think fit otherwise to provide, we govern, and shall continue to govern, the counties of Middlesex, Hertford, and Essex, etc.' Wiseman continued, 'England has been restored to its orbit in the ecclesiastical firmament, from which its light has long vanished, and begins now anew its course of regularly adjusted action round the centre of unity, the source of jurisdiction, of light and vigour.' And then, in a burst of

---

[37] *The Times*, 21 October 1850.

[38] 25 October 1850.

[39] Quoted in the *Morning Chronicle*, 23 October 1850.

[40] *The Tablet*, 26 October 1850.

[41] Wilfred Ward, *Life of Newman* (London, 1912), 1: 168. Apparently no one has ever successfully answered Newman's question; the good saint was found questionable in the early 1960s. and removed from the roster.

prose: 'How much the Saints of our country, whether Roman or British, Saxon or Norman, look down from their seats of bliss, with beaming glance.' Their former sadness at 'the departure of England's religious glory' was over 'as they see the lamp of the temple again enkindled and rebrightening, as they behold the silver links of that chain which has connected their country with the see of Peter in its vicarial government changed into burnished gold . . .'[42]

The *Times* assumed a contemptuous tone: 'that mongrel document, which reads like a cross between an Imperial rescript and a sermon addressed to the victims of an *auto-da-fe.*' The *Morning Chronicle* declared that 'nothing under heaven — no science and no art — can be pursued by Catholic and Protestant in common. Everywhere the old spiritual war cry is heard.'[43] Many Catholics were embarrassed and disheartened. Wiseman, who was still out of the country, had sent the pastoral to his assistant in London, Dr Whitty, who was close to panic over the outcry already created by the publication of the papal brief. To Bishop Ullathorne he explained, 'I could not withhold it. Still less could I dare suppress or tamper with any of its expressions at my own discretion. On the other hand, not a few were beginning to apprehend a repetition of the Gordon riots. . . . After a short prayer for light, I decided on publishing the Pastoral just as it was.' Ullathorne commented to Newman that he wished Whitty had asked 'for a little human light as well.'[44]

But predictably the language used in reply and in the appeals to the government to take retaliatory action was just as intemperate. Mass meetings, over one million signatures on petitions to the crown, declarations of civic and religious organizations, burnings of effigies and some ugly mob

---

[42] *The Times*, 29 October 1850, printed Wiseman's Pastoral 'Out of the Flaminian Gate,' issued October 7, 1850; it appears in Young and Handcock, 12, 1: 364–367.

[43] *The Times*, 29 October 1850. See also 4 November 1850; *The Morning Chronicle*, October 29; see also November 3, 4, 1850.

[44] William Bernard Ullathorne, *An Autobiography* (London, 1891), 2: 296. The old Catholics were especially dismayed. Their most prominent lay figures, the Duke of Norfolk and his son, gave up the faith, and the Duchess of Norfolk wrote a letter of embarrassed indignation to the Queen. See Arthur C. Benson, *Letters to Queen Victoria, 1837–1861* (New York 1907), 2: 325. The papal secretary, Mgr. Talbot, writing to Nassau William Senior said, 'If we had had the slightest suspicion of the storm which we were about to excite, it would have been easy to avoid.' See E. E. Y. Hales, *Pio Nono: A Study in European Politics and Religion in the Nineteenth Century* (London, 1954), p. 142. As for the Old Catholic dream, and partly Wiseman's too, of finding acceptance without bigotry within the structure of English culture, that too was lost as the alienation so dramatically intensified by the Papal Aggression continued. Christopher Hollis has observed that 1850 'killed Roman Catholicism politically. It was all but impossible for a Catholic to get an English constituency to elect him.' See his 'Catholics in English Politics: 1850–1950,' *The Tablet*, 23 September 1950, pp. 252–253.

scenes[45] and finally the excesses of the parliamentary debates over the Ecclesiastical Titles Bill in the session of 1851 all indicate that it was not simply Wiseman and Lord John Russell who had lost their balance.

We thus return to our opening remarks concerning the difficulty of understanding the Victorian balance: its enormous swing between things spiritual and things material. Within six months of the height of the Papal Aggression tumult the pendulum swung to another extreme, and the nation was absorbed in an entirely different national experience, that of the Crystal Palace and the Great Exhibition. Here, on display to the world, were sufficient grounds for their confident belief in progress, sufficient proof to support the many prophets who had held that social and political and above all material advancement was the true business of man. Some fifteen years before Macaulay had written, 'To make men perfect was no part of Bacon's plan. His humble aim was to make imperfect men comfortable.'[46]

But the Victorians could not rest on this side of the equation either. Far more representative than Macaulay was the experience of Charles Kingsley. The Crystal Palace, he said, moved him to tears. To him 'it was like going into a sacred place.' And four days later in an exuberant sermon he announced, 'If these forefathers of ours could rise from their graves this day they would be inclined to see in our hospitals, in our railroads, in the achievements of our physical science, confirmation of that old superstition of theirs, proofs of the kingdom of God, realization of the gifts which Christ received for men, vaster than any of which they had dreamed.'[47] On the other hand, earlier that year he published his novel *Yeast* in which the hero Lancelot Smith is moved to write to a cousin recently converted to Rome:

> When your party compare sneeringly Romish Sanctity, and English Civilization, I say, 'Take you the Sanctity, and give me the Civilization! ... Give me the political economist, the sanity of the reformed, the engineer; and take your saints and virgins, relics and miracles. The spinning-jenny and the railroad, Cunard's liners and the electric

[45] This is hardly the place to detail these ragged events; Guy Fawkes Day came at a most awkward moment, for the newspapers and various ecclesiastical meetings and charges had already begun to fill the air by then with the old No-Popery passions — Russell's Durham letter, however, though dated November 4, did not reach the press until after the Guy Fawkes riots had occurred, though it was blamed then, and in many subsequent accounts, for having set fire, as it were, to that waiting tinder box: the annual celebration of the ancient victory over the Gun-Powder Plot.

[46] Thomas Babington Macaulay, 'Francis Bacon,' *Critical and Historical Essays* (London, 1961), 2: 371.

[47] *Letters and Memories*, 1: 239, 240; quoted in Walter Houghton, *The Victorian Frame of Mind* (New Haven, 1957), p. 44.

telegraph, are to me, if not to you, the signs that we are, on some points at least, in harmony with the universe; that there is a mighty spirit working among us, who cannot be your anarchic and destroying Devil, and therefore may be the Ordering and Creating God.[48]

The Crystal Palace made many Victorians besides Kingsley uneasy[49] for it raised the question whether the universe could be explained and its value measured by glass and iron. While some would shrug with Macaulay, many more would rather smother the question, as Kingsley did, in the language of sentimental religion, and with him conclude that while one would opt for civilization over a false and superstitious sanctity, in a higher sense, civilization was sanctity. This of course is what Victorians tended to do with every important issue: smother it in the rhetoric of religiosity. It was their chief hedge against the new world of science, technology and bureaucracy.

As already indicated, central to an understanding of the Papal Aggression is the role played by this kind of rhetoric. The papal brief, Wiseman's pastoral, Russell's Durham Letter, the press and pulpit all elevated the issue to a level of principalities and powers unmatched by anything here below. Wiseman strove through words to realize the great dream of conquering England again for the faith and by exalted language to cover the miserable quarrels and petty factional disputes which actually constituted the English Catholic scene.

But such words touched all the deepest feelings of the Protestant majority, and for a brief season they were able to luxuriate in the ancient battle with popery. By the spring of 1851 the language of alarm and outrage had become threadbare, and nothing is clearer than the embarrassment of Russell and his government when stuck in the parliament of 1851 with an issue from which all sensible minds had turned away.

Finally it should be noted that in their quite different ways, both the Papal Aggression and the Crystal Palace presented the perennial problem

---

[48] *Yeast* (New York: 1851), ch. 4 pp. 79, 80.

[49] Pugin's virtually unique effort at the exhibition to preserve a Gothic unity and chasteness of style — his 'Medieval Court' was set apart from the other displays, so full of Victorian bulges and curves and gutta-percha affronts to taste — has occasioned a modern authority to muse: 'Gothic gloom or Crystal Palace, 1851 had two faces Candles and gaslight and dreams of electricity; medieval armor and Birmingham hardware; pyramids of soap and cries of 'No-Popery' — all these were part of 1851.' Asa Briggs, *Victorian People: A Reassessment of Persons and Themes, 1851–67* (Chicago, 1955), p. 37. At one point John Bright came upon Sir James Graham looking bemused. He explained that as he walked through the displays dedicated to the twin themes of 'peace and civilization' his mind kept reverting to the previous autumn and the storm of the Papal Aggression. It must have been a reflection common to many thoughtful Victorians.

of authority. One pointed forward, to all those *-isms* of the future: nationalism, industrialism, imperialism, and the *-ism* having for the later Victorians the most authoritative vocabulary of all, scientism. No-Popery, however, pointed backward, to the authority of an impeccable Protestant Bible, to a history rich in Spanish armadas, Gun Powder plots and Gordon Riots, to their own nightly sermons on the Whore of Babylon in the huge auditorium of Exeter Hall and more profoundly to the world of Coleridge and the early Gladstone wherein there was found a divinely joined identity of church and state.

Either direction could and often did lead to bigotry, intellectual dishonesty and on occasion a desperate unease. As Sir Llewellyn Woodward some years ago wrote regarding the various levels of meaning the Great Exhibition represented, 'The visibility of progress was undoubted.... Nevertheless something is wrong, or I should say, something is missing from the vision of progress. For one thing, there is too little sense of mystery. The warning that the range of the known is and must remain far smaller than the range of unknown recurs as something which could not be said too often in the writings of the greatest Victorians. The Victorians were living dangerously, far more dangerously than they knew. The world was much stranger than their machinery, and the nature of man more fragile and at the same time more unfathomable.'[50]

[50] Ernest Llewellyn Woodward, '1851 and the Visibility of Progress,' in B. B. C. Third Program, *Ideas and Beliefs of the Victorians, An Historical Revaluation of the Victorian Age* (London, 1949), p. 62.

JENNIFER F. SUPPLE

CHAPTER 7

ULTRAMONTANISM IN YORKSHIRE, 1850–1900

'ULTRAMONTANISM', a term which can be used simply to describe a particular attitude towards the Papacy, is frequently used to describe certain kinds of devotional practice, and is sometimes used in connection with other aspects of Catholicism, such as attitudes towards poverty, charity and Protestants, and the growth of authoritarianism in the Church. The second half of the nineteenth century is portrayed as the period during which the Ultramontane clergy took control of the Catholic Church from the hands of the old English clergy and laity, symbolised in the appointment of the Ultramontane Manning to Westminster in 1865 rather than the old English Bishop Clifford: 'the victory of Ultramontanism and Romanisation'.[1] If this was true of England as a whole, then it must surely be true of Yorkshire, where in 1861 the 'thoroughly Roman'[2] Robert Cornthwaite became Bishop of Beverley? Ultramontanism, in all its guises, certainly had an important influence on the Catholic Church in Yorkshire during this period, but there is also evidence of a continued attachment to old English attitudes and practices, even as late as the 1890s. What took place in Yorkshire was not the triumph of Ultramontanism but a gradual acceptance and assimilation of two different kinds of Catholicism, as the gentry who had formerly dominated the Yorkshire Church, and the old English clergy who served them, came to terms with the most Ultramontane of the English bishops and the younger priests who followed his example.

Loyalty and devotion to the papacy was the first mark of an Ultramontane, and there is clear evidence of this in Yorkshire among bishops, priests and people. The first Bishop of Beverley, John Briggs, was suspected by Wiseman of Gallicanism, largely because he would not follow the Archbishop's lead in everything, but there is evidence that he was certainly not deficient in loyalty to the Pope. In 1850 he encouraged all Yorkshire Catholics to take advantage of the Jubilee Indulgence in thanksgiving for the return of the Pope to Rome, though the manner in which he ordered

---

[1] E. I. Watkin, *Roman Catholicism in England from the Reformation to 1950*, (1957), p. 194.

[2] F. J. Cwiekowski, *The English Bishops and the First Vatican Council*, (Louvain 1971), p. 52.

prayers for 'our Chief Bishop Pius'[3] shows something less than the adulation accorded to the Pope by the extreme Ultramontanes. However, nine years later Briggs was urging his flock to pray for the Pope in his time of trial, and encouraging the organisation of meetings, resolutions and addresses of sympathy for 'the good, gentle and saintly Pope Pius the Ninth'.[4] Nevertheless, Briggs was not averse to ignoring the Pope's wishes when these clashed with his own inclinations, as shown by his determined refusal, over several years, to appoint a coadjutor, even when informed that the Pope himself desired this.

Of the loyalty and devotion of Briggs' successor, Robert Cornthwaite, there can be no doubt. Described by John Morris, Wiseman's secretary, as 'the best Bishop in England',[5] Cornthwaite, accepting his appointment to Beverley, stated that 'the main point to be put forth, defended and enforced is the See of Peter and its prerogatives',[6] and in his first address to the people of Yorkshire he urged them to pray for the defeat of those seeking 'the destruction of the Holy See and of the august Personage whose apostolic virtues are now adding to it a new lustre'.[7] Cornthwaite, for several years Rector of the English College, Rome, had frequently met Pius IX and, like many others, had been captivated by what Newman called 'the magic of his presence'.[8] Throughout his episcopate Cornthwaite, in letters to clergy and people, was to demonstrate his great devotion to the papacy and his determination that his flock should show a similar loyalty and devotion to Rome. This was especially evident at the time of the Vatican Council, when his pastoral letter explaining and defending the doctrine of papal infallibility, 'a doctrine about which we candidly acknowledge, we have neither difficulty nor doubt',[9] was praised and published by the strongly Ultramontane *Tablet*. Cornthwaite's devotion did not end with the death of 'the ever magnificent and magnanimous Pontiff'[10] Pius IX, but continued under his successor, Leo XIII.

[3] Leeds Diocesan Archives (L. D. A.), *Pastorals*, Bishop John Briggs, 28 November 1850.

[4] L. D. A., Dr. Briggs' correspondence 2007B, Letter of Briggs to the Archbishop and Bishops of Ireland on the Plight of the Pope, 1859.

[5] E. Norman, *The English Catholic Church in the Nineteenth Century*, (Oxford 1984), p. 260.

[6] L. D. A., copies from Talbot MSS, 146, Cornthwaite to Talbot, 6 September 1861.

[7] Acta Diocesiana Beverlacensia (A. D. B.), Vol. 1, pastoral letter, 10 November 1861.

[8] C. Butler, *The Life and Times of Bishop Ullathorne, 1806–1889*, Vol. 2, (1926), p. 299.

[9] A. D. B., Vol. 2, pastoral letter, 25 October 1869.

[10] A. D. B., Vol. 6, pastoral letter, 28 February 1878.

With the division of Yorkshire into the Leeds and Middlesbrough dioceses in 1878, the Catholics of the North and East Ridings gained a new bishop, Richard Lacy. Formerly a priest under Cornthwaite, it is hardly surprising that Lacy should share his attitude towards the papacy. In 1882 the Bishop of Middlesbrough wrote a pastoral letter on 'The Loyalty due to the Holy Father', published in the *Tablet*, defending the temporal power of the Pope. Five years later, on Pope Leo's golden sacerdotal jubilee, Lacy wrote of the 'great and glorious Pontiff' who 'by his great learning, profound wisdom, deep piety, knowledge of his age and varied gifts, sheds an exceptional lustre on the Apostolic See and thereby upon the Universal Church'.[11]

William Gordon, who succeeded Cornthwaite in the Leeds diocese in 1890, made far fewer references to the papacy in his letters than his predecessor, but this does not necessarily mean that he was less devoted to the pope: rather that loyalty to Rome was now taken for granted. Like his predecessors, Bishop Gordon ensured that Papal Encyclicals were passed on to the clergy to be read to the people, urged all to be generous to the annual collections for Peter's Pence, and as late as 1900 was still defending the temporal power of the papacy.

The bishops expected their own loyalty to the Pope to be shared by priests and people, and there were certainly priests in Yorkshire who had a great devotion to the papacy. Those who had passed through the seminaries from the 1840s onwards imbibed Ultramontane ideas there, while priests educated in earlier years were not deficient in loyalty. The devotion of the clergy to the papacy was particularly evident during the early sixties, when the Pope was resisting the unification of Italy and the loss of the Papal States. It was usually the mission priest who organised meetings at which clergy and laity agreed to send addresses of sympathy, and financial aid, to Rome. Canon Fisher, speaking in defence of the temporal power on one such occasion, expressed his love and sympathy for the Pope, who 'had no equal upon earth'.[12] In 1875 Father John Curry of Bradford received the Pope's special blessing 'on account of his able essay'[13] in reply to Gladstone's pamphlet attacking papal infallibility, while thirteen years later, at a Papal Jubilee Tea, Father Andrew Burns of Selby spoke of Leo XIII as 'the friend of all, both high and low', who draws 'the hearts of the whole world, both Catholic and Protestant, to himself in a most wonderful manner'.[14]

[11] *Tablet*, 26 November 1887.

[12] *Tablet*, 16 January 1864.

[13] *Tablet*, 10 April 1875.

[14] *Tablet*, 10 March 1888.

Throughout the period, prayers for the Pope were said at Mass and Wiseman's hymn 'God Bless our Pope' was sung in Yorkshire churches. Yet is there an indication that not all priests shared their bishops' devotion to the papacy in the reluctance shown by some to carry out the annual collection for Peter's Pence in their churches? A study of the amounts received annually reveals that each year a number of missions failed to send any contribution. Poverty may, in some cases, have been the reason for this, for Father George Keasley, at the poor mission of Yarm, remarked that, although they sent the Pope £4 each year, 'if his Holiness knew to what extent their money was needed at home, he would say — By all means keep it'.[15] Yet in 1884 only seventeen out of a total of eighty-four missions in the Diocese of Leeds contributed to Peter's Pence, while in 1898 Bishop Gordon remarked 'that in some congregations no collections of Peter-Pence are ever made'.[16] However, although Yorkshire had its share of troublesome priests, there is no evidence of any priest openly challenging the prevailing attitude towards the papacy, nor of any clash between Ultramontane and Gallican clergy.

One might expect the laity to follow the lead of bishops and priests in devotion to the papacy, and to a large extent they did, although there were exceptions. In 1850 Lord Beaumont of Carlton Towers and his brother John Stapleton agreed with Protestants that the restoration of the hierarchy represented unwarranted papal interference in English affairs, and both subsequently left the Church. Although this was an extreme case, there was a tendency among the Yorkshire gentry to believe that they, not the Pope nor the Bishop, knew best how to run the Yorkshire Church. This tendency was evident in 1878, when several prominent laymen objected to the division of Yorkshire into the dioceses of Leeds and Middlesbrough. They wrote to the Bishop, suggesting that their own schemes for the division be considered and that devised by Propaganda set aside, although most quickly backed down in the face of episcopal disapproval. Another example of the independent attitude of the Yorkshire gentry can be seen in the determination of some to send their sons to university, despite Rome's prohibition, which was made clear by the bishops. Nevertheless, during the 1860s many of the sons of the Yorkshire gentry went to Rome to fight in the Papal Zouaves, while their families at home were prominent in protests on behalf of the papacy against the invasion of Rome and the loss of the Papal States. In 1874 a number of the Yorkshire gentry defended the Pope against Gladstone's attack on infallibility, while one of them, Lord Herries, on his death two years later, was said to have had 'an exquisite sense of loyalty to

[15] L. D. A., Visitation Returns, St Mary's, Yarm, 1871.

[16] Acta Ecclesiae Loidensis (A. E. L.), Vol. 10, ad clerum, 6 June 1898.

the Vicar of Jesus Christ'.[17] However, as with the clergy, the collections for Peter's Pence indicate that the laity were by no means as devoted to the papacy as the Ultramontanes would have them be. With the exception of jubilee years and other special occasions, there was a general decline in the amounts collected, and the bishops were constantly complaining that the laity were failing to contribute in accordance with their means and with the needs of the Pope.

Was then, the Yorkshire Church Ultramontane in its attitude towards the papacy? If Ultramontanism implies *excessive* devotion towards the papacy, then not every Yorkshire Catholic was an Ultramontane, but Bishop Cornthwaite certainly was, Bishop Lacy most probably was, and a number of priests and people followed their example. Nevertheless, old English Catholicism, with its far less adulatory attitude towards the papacy, its habit of taking the papacy for granted 'without particular interest, reverence or romanticism',[18] and its tendency to question papal directives, can also be found in Yorkshire, in Bishop Briggs and in several of the Yorkshire gentry, at least up to 1878. However, by the end of the century the general attitude towards the Pope in Yorkshire was one of unquestioning loyalty and obedience, without the excessive adulation of the Ultramontanes of earlier years, while the reluctance to send money to Rome was probably no more than a typical Yorkshire reluctance to part with hard-earned 'brass'. In Yorkshire, therefore, a middle way, acceptable to most, had been found.

Ultramontane devotions found a ready acceptance in Yorkshire, even under the allegedly Gallican Bishop Briggs. It was during the 1840s that Briggs introduced the continental practices of the Quarant'Ore devotion and processions of the Blessed Sacrament into Yorkshire churches, while during the fifties he encouraged devotion to the Sacred Heart. Despite Milburn's assertion that conservative north countrymen 'rejected the too exuberant and flamboyant'[19] devotions, these were soon to be in evidence in Yorkshire, with the flamboyant Faber himself preaching on the Virgin Mary in Sheffield in 1850. In his sermon at St Marie's his concluding words 'which impressed the crowded congregation, were: "*Sanctus, Sanctus, Sanctus*"'.[20] There was certainly plenty of flamboyance at the Corpus Christi procession held in Leeds in 1876. The papal flag flew from St Mary's Church, while the route of the procession was marked by garlands on poles. The Guild of the Immaculate Conception marched in blue cloaks,

[17] *Tablet*, 18 November 1876.

[18] J. C. H. Aveling, *The Handle and the Axe*, (1976), p. 355.

[19] D. Milburn, *A History of Ushaw College*, (Durham 1964), p. 152.

[20] C. Hadfield, *A History of St Marie's, Sheffield*, (Sheffield 1889), p. 112.

veils and medals, and the Children of Mary in black uniforms, white veils
and blue ribbons. Boys and girls in white scattered flowers along the route,
while the Blessed Sacrament was surrounded by a guard of honour of
twelve men with drawn swords. At a May Festival in Holbeck in 1895,
during which a statue of the Blessed Virgin was crowned, a Protestant
commentator remarked 'one felt for the time being as if a sudden trans-
portation into a Roman Catholic country had taken place'.[21]

While such public processions were extraordinary affairs, other devotions coming from the Continent, or directly from Rome, became very
popular in Yorkshire, including devotion to the Sacred Heart, to Mary
under various titles, to St Joseph, and later to the Holy Family. Devotion to
the Sacred Heart was shared by bishops, priests and people. In 1873, in
an ad clerum letter published in the *Tablet*, Cornthwaite gave instructions
for the celebration of the feast of the Sacred Heart, to which the diocese
had recently been dedicated, and recommended all the clergy to obtain a
picture or statue of the Sacred Heart. Many priests had already done so,
moved perhaps by earlier pastorals of Briggs, who encouraged daily devotion to the Sacred Heart, and of Cornthwaite, who asked 'who does not feel
especially drawn to the Sacred Heart, centre as it is of all his love for us?'[22]
In 1868 Father Andrew Burns of Middlesbrough spent the large sum of £60
on a picture of the Sacred Heart, while many Yorkshire missions not only
had pictures, statues, shrines or chapels of the Sacred Heart, but also
recited the Litany of the Sacred Heart at evening prayers and had established confraternities of the Sacred Heart. A pilgrimage to Paray-le-Monial
in 1873, as an act of reparation to the Sacred Heart, was attended by
Bishop Cornthwaite, several Yorkshire priests and a number of the Yorkshire laity. During the 1890s Mrs Elizabeth Reynard, offering to build a
church at Scarborough, asked that it be dedicated to the Sacred Heart in
thanksgiving for favours received. Although this plan fell through, by the
end of the century nine Yorkshire churches and chapels were so dedicated,
and few, if any, churches did not contain some representation of the Sacred
Heart.

While devotion to the Sacred Heart made steady progress in Yorkshire
during this period, that to St Joseph enjoyed a sudden and enormous burst
of popularity. Cornthwaite himself remarked that devotion to this saint had
grown 'in a way and in a measure that has no parallel in our past
history'.[23] In fact, the rapid spread of this devotion owed much to Pius IX,

[21] *Leeds Mercury*, 11 May 1895.

[22] A. D. B., Vol. 1, pastoral letter, 5 February 1864.

[23] A. E. L., Vol 2, pastoral letter, 20 April 1882.

who was greatly attached to the saint. In 1868 Cornthwaite asked his clergy to promote devotion to St Joseph among the laity, and they were apparently successful in this, for in 1870 a petition from Yorkshire joined others sent to Rome asking the Pope to proclaim St Joseph patron of the universal Church, with which request he was only too delighted to comply. By the 1880s there were twenty churches in Yorkshire dedicated to St Joseph, as well as the diocesan seminary, while many churches had a statue of the saint, and priests included prayers to St Joseph in their evening services. Still, in 1884, Cornthwaite was urging even greater devotion to the saint, reminding his flock that St Joseph had 'a place apart' among the saints, for 'he displayed such a beauty of holiness as the world has never seen, excepting only our Blessed Lady'.[24] The devotion apparently became popular with the laity, for priests appealing for financial support in the *Tablet* applied to friends or clients of St Joseph, John Earnshaw of Bradford referring to him as the 'friend of the Sacred Heart',[25] while many Yorkshire Catholics, priests and people, contributed towards the memorial church of St Joseph at Mill Hill. Mrs Apollonia Bland, providing the financial backing for a church at Stokesley, asked that it might be dedicated to St Joseph, her 'special patron'.[26]

Devotion to the Virgin Mary was by no means new in the Catholic Church in England, but the Ultramontanes invested it with greater fervour and enthusiasm, using a variety of titles, including the Immaculate Conception, Our Lady of Perpetual Succour, Our Lady of Lourdes and Our Lady of Mount Carmel. The definition of the Immaculate Conception was welcomed in Yorkshire, even by those not generally regarded as Ultramontanes. Describing Mary as 'the beautiful lily among the briars',[27] Briggs wrote of the great joy which the feast of the Immaculate Conception ought to give to all Christians. Two Yorkshire churches were dedicated to the Immaculate Conception, while the Oblates of Mary Immaculate were welcomed to Yorkshire by Briggs. It was in the Middlesbrough Diocese that devotion to Our Lady of Perpetual Succour became particularly strong, encouraged by Bishop Lacy who believed that he had been cured of an illness through Mary's intercession. Throughout Yorkshire as a whole, Marian enthusiasm increased during these years. There was scarcely a church which did not have a statue of the Blessed Virgin, or a picture of

[24] A. E. L., Vol. 3, pastoral letter, 19 April 1884.

[25] *Tablet*, 30 June 1883.

[26] L. D. A., Bishop Cornthwaite's correspondence 1870–79, Apollonia Bland to Cornthwaite, 13 February 1871.

[27] L. D. A., *Pastorals*, Bishop John Briggs, 10 May 1855.

Our Lady of Perpetual Succour, while some had quite elaborate shrines. St Marie's, Sheffield, already had one Marian shrine when in 1878 a new oratory dedicated to Our Lady of Mercy was opened. This contained a statue of the Virgin, flanked by angels, and a stained glass window showing the coronation of Our Lady. During May, Mary's month, most priests provided additional evening services in her honour, while some organised May processions during which young girls crowned statues of the virgin. Later in the century, October Devotions, consisting of the rosary and benediction, took place in most churches during the month dedicated to the Holy Rosary. Several priests also said the rosary and recited the Litany of the Blessed Virgin each Saturday evening, the day which became dedicated to Mary. The laity joined the Children of Mary and the Confraternity of Our Lady of Perpetual Succour, and those who could afford it took part in the English pilgrimage to Lourdes in 1883.

Towards the end of the century another devotion came to Yorkshire, with the special recommendation of Rome; this was the devotion to the Holy Family. In 1892 Leo XIII established the Pious Association of the Holy Family, 'an association of families who consecrated themselves to the Holy Family of Nazareth' and who nightly prayed before 'a representation of the Holy Family'.[28] There were numerous indulgences for all enrolled in the Association, and Gordon appointed a priest to ensure that the Association was established in every mission in the Diocese of Leeds.

Many of these new devotions were encouraged by members of the religious orders who visited Yorkshire to give missions during this period. The Redemptorists promoted devotion to the Virgin Mary, particularly to Our Lady of Perpetual Succour, enrolling members into the Confraternity, while at a mission in Sheffield in 1883 they organised 'a grand devotional service in honour of the Blessed Virgin'.[29] The Redemptorists also received members into the Confraternity of the Holy Family during missions in Hull, Batley and York. At a Praemonstratensian mission in Howden in 1885 many members of the congregation were enrolled in the Association of Perpetual Adoration of the Blessed Sacrament, while almost all the Catholics of the area were invested with the scapular of Our Lady of Mount Carmel.

Ultramontanism, then, added a new vigour and gave a new variety to the spiritual life of Yorkshire Catholics. There were new ways of worshipping Christ and honouring his mother, different saints to invoke, new confraternities, a plethora of statues and shrines, processions and pilgrimages. Not everyone appreciated this, however, and a few made clear their

[28] A. E. L., Vol. 7, Letter from the Bishop of Newport and Menevia, August 1892.

[29] Tablet, 29 September 1883.

dislike of the new ways. At St Mary's, Middlesbrough, in 1871, about one hundred and fifty people left the church before the beginning of devotions to the Sacred Heart. One of them, James McNamee, explained in the local press his objections to the veneration of the picture of the Sacred Heart 'which to many Catholics seems, to say the least, a ridiculous form of devotion, and the pennies required to be thrown at the foot of the picture a dubious means of raising money'.[30] Others, while accepting the new, still clung to the old. Bishop Briggs recommended the daily reading of a chapter of Challoner's *Think Well On't*, while many priests continued to include in their evening services prayers from the medieval Jesus Psalter, popular during the penal period. However, it was Canon Samuel Walshaw of St Marie's, Sheffield, who made his church into the showpiece of English Catholic worship.

In 1891 Canon Walshaw wrote to the *Tablet* pressing for a revival of the custom 'familiar in old Catholic days' of intercessory prayer for the dead and those in deadly sin, known as 'The Bidding of the Beads'. He remarked that 'we have *now* many and varied forms of modern devotions, some perhaps trifling and weak, some perhaps affected or insipid, even mawkish; not so the olden prayers'.[31] Walshaw had already done a great deal to revive old Catholic practices in Sheffield. At St Marie's all the singing was entrusted to a surpliced chancel choir which specialized in Gregorian chant, 'the devotional badge of the "English" Catholics'.[32] Walshaw introduced Gothic vestments, and revived the ancient practice of Relic Sunday, while Holy Week services were carried out according to 'the most ancient and devotional liturgy of the Catholic Church'.[33] Instead of the more modern evening services, at St Marie's, one could attend Gregorian Vespers. One of the severest critics of 'Italianism' in the English church, St George Mivart, wrote that St Marie's 'for the beauty and appropriateness of its appointments and services might set an example to all of England'.[34] Yet unlike Mivart, Walshaw was not motivated by Gallicanism or Modernism, but simply by a love of the past, shown in his interest in medieval religious literature, and the holidays he spent brass-rubbing. He simply challenged the view that 'as certain fashions prevail in modern Rome, it becomes our duty, in reverence to the Holy Father, to float downwards with the current

---

[30] *Middlesbrough Gazette*, 2 October 1871.

[31] *Tablet*, 21 February 1891.

[32] E. Norman, *The English Catholic Church in the Nineteenth Century*, (Oxford 1984), p. 237.

[33] *Tablet*, 4 April 1891.

[34] *Dublin Review*, Vol. 12, 1884, p. 80.

144

of the present tide'.[35] Walshaw did not reject all that was new, for St Marie's was noted for the great number of devotional aids in the Church, pictures, statues and shrines, including an elaborate oratory of Our Lady of Mercy, and a shrine of the Sacred Heart. Procession also took place in St Marie's, while Walshaw defended the pilgrimage to Paray-le-Monial in honour of the Sacred Heart against the sneers of the Protestant press, denying their assertion that pilgrimages were un-English.

Walshaw's attitude seems to have been shared by most Yorkshire Catholics. Rather than involving themselves in controversies over different types of worship, they clung to what they liked from the past, and adopted the Ultramontane devotions which suited them. Bishop Briggs did this in the fifties, welcoming the new Marian devotions, yet adhering to Challoner's *Think Well On't*. Priests did this throughout the period when they combined the Litany of the Sacred Heart and the singing of 'God Bless our Pope' with prayers from the Jesus Psalter and extracts from Challoner's *Meditations*. Bishop Gordon did this at the end of the century when he looked back nostalgically to old-fashioned 'Garden of the Soul Piety' which he believed had kept the Faith alive during the penal period, while happily accepting the newer devotions to the Immaculate Conception, the Sacred Heart and the Holy Family. Clearly, there was not an Ultramontane takeover of the devotional life of the Yorkshire Church; instead, old and new co-existed peacefully.

The same was true of architecture, often regarded as a symbol of devotional differences, for in Yorkshire there seems to have been no clash between Gothic and Classical styles. Although Norman states that English Catholics insisted on Gothic, while Ultramontanes wanted Roman buildings for the new Italianate style of worship, in Yorkshire the Gothic style predominated regardless of the Ultramontane views of bishops and clergy. The Church of the Immaculate Conception, erected for the Oblates of Mary Immaculate at Sicklinghall in 1854 was a Gothic design, while the Oblates also chose Gothic architects, Hansom and E. W. Pugin, for the church they built in Leeds with the financial support of the St Saviour's converts. However, some years earlier a member of the old English gentry, Lord Herries, chose the Italian style for his private chapel at Everingham Hall. Architecture seemed to be a matter of personal taste in Yorkshire, with most priests choosing Gothic because it was fashionable, cheap and quickly constructed.

The Ultramontanes had a new attitude towards poverty, which was certainly out of step with that prevalent in Victorian England. Reviving the ancient idea that poverty was holy, the Ultramontanes proclaimed poverty

[35] *Tablet*, 3 February 1894.

as 'the will of God'[36] and maintained that to be poor could be regarded as a blessing. Whether the poor themselves were able to share this view is doubtful, but two of the Yorkshire bishops clearly did to a certain extent. Cornthwaite, in a pastoral letter of 1877, remarked that 'It is, indeed, a dispensation of Providence that there shall always be poor ...', but added that the rich are 'commanded by God to help them'.[37] Bishop Gordon went even further, declaring that because Christ 'chose to be poor, poverty, therefore, must be good', adding that it 'delivers a man from many temptations'.[38] While some priests shared their bishops' views, others who had to deal directly with the poor had a less idealised view of holy poverty. Sister Mary Ignace, of the Convent of the Assumption, Richmond, writing of the poor who attended mass at the Convent chapel, commented 'We get only a halfpenny from each; it does not even pay for cleaning up the dirt they make'.[39] Some priests remarked that, far from being holy, the poor were the most lax in religious observance. Nevertheless, the saints of poverty found a place in Yorkshire, in particular St Francis and St Vincent de Paul. From the 1880s the Third Order of St Francis flourished there, in accordance with the wishes of the Pope, and with the encouragement of Bishops Cornthwaite, Lacy and Gordon. Lacy recommended both clergy and laity to study the life of St Francis as 'an antidote against the soul-destroying spirit of worldliness',[40] while Gordon was publicly received into the Third Order during a Capuchin mission at Pontefract. Two churches in the Leeds diocese were dedicated to the saint, both on the outskirts of Leeds where so many of the poor lived.

St Vincent de Paul became known in Yorkshire chiefly through the Society bearing his name. The St Vincent de Paul Society was the work of the French Ultramontane revival, and perfectly in accord with the Ultramontane view of charity which advocated personal contact between rich and poor. The Society was active in York in the early fifties, not only helping the poor, but allegedly 'connecting classes of society, too prone to mutual jealousies, in bonds of friendship and charity'.[41] In Sheffield the

---

[36] S. Gilley, 'Heretic London, Holy Poverty and the Irish Poor 1830–70', *Downside Review* 89, no. 294, January 1971, p. 66.

[37] A. D. B., Vol. 5, pastoral letter, 30 November 1877.

[38] A. E. L., Vol. 8, pastoral letter, — November 1894.

[39] Middlesbrough Diocesan Archives (M. D. A.), Richmond, Sister Mary Ignace to Cornthwaite, 24 June 1866.

[40] M. D. A., pastoral letter, Advent 1882.

[41] *Tablet*, 10 February 1855.

Society did excellent work for the poor throughout the period, maintaining personal contact by regular visits to the homes of the poor, giving Christian instruction to poor boys, and helping unemployed men find work. In the late 1880s the Catholic Ladies' Association of Charity was founded in Sheffield, under the presidency of Lady Mary Howard, 'for the purpose of visiting the sick poor in their own homes'.[42] However, the type of charity condemned by the Ultramontanes, balls, bazaars and subscription-lists, appealing to 'snobbery and self-advertisement',[43] also flourished in Yorkshire. In Hull a Catholic Charity Ball was held each year, attended by the prominent laity of the area and fully described in the local press. Bazaars, with stalls manned by the prominent ladies of the diocese, were a frequent method of raising money for the poor and other worthy causes throughout Yorkshire, while the bishops published lists of sums contributed by individuals to diocesan charities. Once again, in Yorkshire, one can see a mingling of old and new.

It has been claimed that Ultramontanism brought with it a 'new Catholic sectarian consciousness', an exclusiveness which brought to an end the English Catholic liberal tradition of co-operation with Protestants. Ultramontane Catholics insisted upon having their own schools, institutions and charitable organisations, refusing to co-operate with Protestants. That Catholics everywhere did set up their own institutions cannot be disputed, but that this was a sign of 'exclusive Ultramontane triumphalism'[44] is by no means certain. In Yorkshire there is much evidence that Catholics were determined to have their own institutions, but this was for more practical reasons. Only in Catholic schools and reformatories could children receive a Catholic education; only Catholic charitable organisations ensured that help was given to the Catholic poor, for the Protestant philanthropic societies were simply unable to cope with the mass influx of the Irish poor in the middle of the century, while in some cases Protestant prejudice denied help to the Catholic poor. Bishop Cornthwaite made the provision of education for all Catholic children in the diocese one of his major concerns, and during the crisis period following the Education Act of 1870, when Catholics had either to provide school accommodation or see their children swept into the new Board Schools, Beverley came second only to the large diocese of Liverpool in the number of extra school places provided. By 1874

---

[42] *Tablet*, 27 April 1889.

[43] S. Gilley, 'English Catholic Charity and the Irish Poor in London', *Recusant History* 11 (1971–72), p. 256.

[44] S. Gilley, 'Protestant London, No Popery and the Irish Poor 1850–70', *Recusant History*, 11 (1971–72), p. 37.

the bishop was able to report that there was now 'ample room for all'.[45] Yorkshire Catholics also had their own reformatories, one for boys at Market Weighton, opened in 1856, and another for girls in Sheffield, opened in 1861. Ten years later an orphanage for girls was opened in Leeds, and in 1880 a home for destitute boys was also established there. It was in Yorkshire that the only Catholic school for the deaf and dumb was founded in 1870. Nevertheless, despite the establishment of separate schools and institutions, there is still much evidence of co-operation between Catholics and Protestants in Yorkshire. They worked together in times of distress to help the poor of all denominations, as in Middlesbrough during the nineties, when local priests were active members of inter-denominational committees formed to alleviate the sufferings of the unemployed and their families. Despite differences of opinion, Catholics and Protestants managed to co-operate on School Boards in order to increase educational opportunities for all children. The contribution made by Catholic members was acknowledged by their Anglican and Nonconformist colleagues, as in the case of Canon Gordon of Halifax, regarded as 'a source of strength to the Board' because of his wide experience in education, as well as 'his genial presence'.[46] Denominational boundaries were readily crossed by those attempting to convince the poor of the benefits of temperance. In Hull, in 1857, Father John Motler gave a lecture on temperance to a mixed audience at the Oddfellows' Hall, which 'eloquently and practically brought the matter home to everyone'.[47] Far from showing an Ultramontane exclusivity, the majority of the Catholics of Yorkshire, with the support of their bishops, were eager to work with Protestants for the common good, providing that this involved no risk to the Catholic faith.

Finally, Ultramontanism has been seen as the cause of increased authoritarianism in the Church during this period, Gilley claiming that this was the reason for 'a degree of sacerdotal authority unknown to recusant Catholicism'.[48] There certainly was a strengthening of authority within the Yorkshire Church during this period. Bishop Cornthwaite imposed his authority on the priests of the diocese to a far greater extent than Briggs, and consequently met with a certain degree of resentment. One priest, undergoing an investigation regarding the finances of his mission, remarked that he had never experienced such treatment from Cornthwaite's

---

[45] *Tablet*, 28 March 1874.

[46] *Tablet*, 18 July 1896.

[47] *Hull Advertiser*, 14 February 1857.

[48] S. Gilley, 'English Catholic Charity and the Irish Poor in London', *Recusant History*, 11, p. 261.

'venerable predecessor'.[49] Other priests, however, soon realised that they could rely on Cornthwaite to uphold their own 'pastoral authority' and 'the dignity of the priesthood',[50] as the authority which they themselves claimed increased. Yorkshire priests now resisted the commands of the gentry if they believed that these prevented them from carrying out their spiritual duties, and this, too, was often resented. Thomas Constable, writing to Cornthwaite concerning the chaplain at Burton Constable Hall, regretted that the obliging disposition and deferential attitude of earlier priests no longer prevailed. Mission priests also abolished lay committees, taking full control for mission finances themselves. By the end of the century, if not before, the mission priest had become the acknowledged and respected leader of the people, with few instances of the laity resisting sacerdotal authority in matters of faith or morals. To some extent Ultramontanism may have been responsible for the clergy's own perception of the dignity of their position, for the spiritual vigour of religious Ultramontanism which had taken root in the seminaries during the forties and fifties seemed to breathe a new life and activity into the clergy. However, there are reasons totally unconnected with Ultramontanism for the increase in sacredotal authority, which, as Norman claims, 'was already coming into existence long before the Ultramontanes put their stamp upon the process'.[51] It seems probable that lay ascendancy in the Church declined as a result of the change in the composition of the Catholic community. While the gentry remained independent in outlook, they were, from the early years of the nineteenth century, becoming a minority within the Church; and by this period they were overwhelmed by the Irish poor who, of necessity, looked to the clergy for temporal as well as spiritual guidance, and so accepted the leadership of the mission priest. Furthermore, both bishops and priests recognised the need for a firm hand to keep the Irish masses in order, and for increased diocesan organisation to keep control of a rapidly expanding Church. The increase in authority was, therefore, accepted as a practical necessity, rather than a matter of dogma.

Practical necessity and sensible compromise do much to explain the changes which took place in the Catholic Church in Yorkshire during this period. Yorkshire Catholics were certainly not 'forced . . . into a position of Ultramontane "romanizing" conformity'.[52] Papal authority was accepted because, as a Scarborough priest, Arthur Riddell, commented in a letter to

[49] M. D. A., Beverley, T. A. Smith to Cornthwaite, 5 November 1873.

[50] M. D. A., Brough Hall, L. Burke to Cornthwaite, 3 March 1864.

[51] E. Norman, *The English Catholic Church in the Nineteenth Century*, (Oxford 1984), p. 5.

[52] F. Heyer, *The Catholic Church from 1648 to 1870* (1969), p. 202.

the *Tablet*, the matter had been settled by the Vatican decree on Infallibility, and to reject this would make one either a Protestant or a heretic. Practical necessity also led to the acceptance of increased authoritarianism within the Church in Yorkshire. In other matters, such as attitudes towards poverty, charity and Protestants, a sensible compromise between old and new was achieved, while in spiritual affairs Yorkshire Catholics apparently accepted the idea 'that a Catholic Church could, should and did, include many varieties of devotion and artistic expression'.[53] In Yorkshire, then the Ultramontane revival certainly had an effect, but there was no 'victory of Ultramontanism'. If this is what happened in Yorkshire, might it not be true of England as a whole?

[53] E. I. Watkin, *Roman Catholicism in England from the Reformation to 1950* (1957), p. 183.

[54] E. I. Watkin, *ibid*, p. 194.

JOSEF L. ALTHOLZ

CHAPTER 8

THE WARFARE OF CONSCIENCE WITH THEOLOGY

T HE most important thing to remember about religion in Victorian England is that there was an awful lot of it. The nineteenth century was marked by a revival of religious activity unmatched since the days of the Puritans. This religious revival shaped that code of moral behavior, or rather that infusion of all behavior with moralism, which we still call, rightly or wrongly, 'Victorianism.' Above all, religion occupied a place in the public consciousness, a centrality in the intellectual life of the age, which it had not had a century before and did not retain in the twentieth century.

That is the second important thing to remember about the Victorian religious revival: that it did not last. It was not merely that the churches lost, or rather had never had, the growing working classes of their increasingly urbanized society; they could hardly be blamed for being defeated by demographics. But the striking thing about the decline of the Victorian religious revival is that it took place, in the latter decades of the century, within that very middle class whose virtues it sanctified. Most importantly, those special segments of the middle class which served as culture-bearers to their age and shapers of the next, the intellectual and professional classes, had their faith eroded in a distinctive and decisive manner.

The crisis of intellectual faith, which may be dated about 1860, had a deceptive appearance of suddenness. The 1850s had been a period of relative religious calm, in which unquestioning churchgoers had little to trouble them except the growth of Popery and ritualism, the dissidence of Dissent, and the strange absence of the poor from the churches. Then in 1859 appeared Darwin's *Origin of Species*, the most famous but not the most important of the challenges to faith, which questioned both the literal accuracy of the first chapters of Genesis and the argument from design for the existence of God. In 1860 appeared a book entitled *Essays and Reviews*, six of whose seven authors were clergymen of the Church of England, which brought to Britain the techniques and startling hypotheses of German biblical criticism. In 1862 the Mosaic authorship of the Pentateuch was denied by no less than a bishop, John William Colenso. In 1864 and 1865 the courts decided that nothing could be done about these subversives within the Church, and in 1869 one of the Essayists and Reviewers became a bishop. Naturalistic, non-miraculous lives of Jesus appeared: Renan's *Vie de Jésus* in 1863, J. R. Seeley's *Ecce Homo* in 1865. Meanwhile the scientists pressed their challenge: in 1863 Huxley's *Man's Place in Nature* and Lyell's *Antiquity of Man*, and finally in 1871 Darwin's *Descent of Man*, stripped away the uniqueness of mankind. To retain a traditional Bible-centered faith in the 1870s, an educated man had either to deny the findings of biblical criticism and natural science, supported by an increasing mass of evidence, or else to re-create that faith on a new basis which few were able to construct.

Because this crisis was brought on and highlighted by challenges external to orthodox faith — because the normal posture of the churches during the crisis was one of denial and resistance in the face of the triumphant advance of science and criticism — it is natural to see these events in terms of the inevitable progress of the human mind and the advancement of science. Certainly, if we understand by 'science' what the Germans call *Wissenschaft*, not merely the natural sciences but social and humane studies scientifically treated, what transpired was a victory for science. This is the traditional approach to the subject, immortalized in the phrase of Andrew Dickson White, 'the warfare of science with theology.' This approach presupposes a clear and direct confrontation between geological, biological, and historical science on the one hand and religion on the other, with science ultimately prevailing because of its intrinsic merits.

I wish to propose an alternative approach, which treats the conflict not as a struggle of faith against its external enemies, but as a crisis within religion itself. The real point of the conflict was not the challenge of science but the response of religion. The scientific challenges laid bare certain weaknesses of the Victorian religious revival, and the victory of science was largely due to elements within the religious position. The most important such factor was the latent conflicts between the sensitivity of conscience stimulated by the religious revival and the crude and harsh statement of the dogmas to which such sensitive consciences were expected to give their allegiance.[1] The spokesmen of orthodox faith narrowed the ground on which Christianity was to be defended and allowed their scientific opponents to appear more honest than themselves. In these conflicts, the position of orthodox doctrine was, as presented by its upholders, not only less valid but less moral than that of irreligious science. As events unfolded,

[1] The first scholar to explicate this point was Howard R. Murphy, 'The Ethical Revolt against Christian Orthodoxy in Early Victorian England,' *American Historical Review*, 40 (July 1955), 800–817: 'the Victorian religious crisis was produced by a fundamental conflict between certain cherished religious dogmas ... and the meliorist ethical bias of the age' (pp. 800–801). See also James C. Livingston, *The Ethics of Belief* (AAR Studies in Religion no. 9; Missoula, 1975).

not merely the intellect but the moral sense, particularly the sense of truthfulness, revolted against orthodoxy. This may be called 'the warfare of conscience with theology.'[2]

It is possible to analyze this conflict as a 'class struggle' of sorts, if this be understood not as a struggle between classes but as a struggle within the middle class, between the clergy on the one hand and the secular professions on the other, for the minds of the rising generation.[3] The nineteenth century saw the rise and definition of the professions, including the clerical profession itself. The eighteenth-century clergyman could not be said to have had a vocation. He was a country gentleman, or hoped to be one; his few religious duties left him ample time to mingle in society, to be a magistrate, a naturalist, an essayist, or a sportsman. If he did not much improve his world, he was very much a part of it. But the evangelical revival changed all that. The evangelicals (the 'serious' Christians, as they called themselves) insisted that clergymen be serious, attend to their religious duties, and expand the definition of those duties until they were capable of absorbing their entire time and energy: two sermons on Sunday, weekday services, frequent visiting of the poor. To this the tractarians added the sense of a distinct vocation and separation of the priesthood from the laity. By the 1840s, even among those who were neither evangelical nor tractarian, the professional ideal of the clergy had won out.

All Victorians were earnest; it was important to be earnest; but clergymen were distinctively and preeminently earnest. They hunted not, nor did they attend the theater; they wore black unrelieved by the slightest hint of gray; and from the 1860s they adopted that ultimate badge of clericalism, the dog collar. Such a hard-working clergy accomplished much and deserved to have accomplished more. But this professionalism came at a price. Fully occupied by work which was absorbing but specialized, concentrating their minds on the 'one thing only' that mattered, most of the clergy withdrew from that wider intellectual life of England of which they had once been a central part. At the very time that Coleridge formulated his ideal of the 'clerisy' to embrace all the educated classes, the clergy was separating from the 'clerisy' and withdrawing behind the impregnable

[2] This phrase and certain other passages have been borrowed, with the permission of the Bobbs-Merrill Co., from the chapter 'Science and Conscience' in Altholz, *The Churches in the Nineteenth Century* (Indianapolis, 1967).

[3] See Frank M. Turner, 'Rainfall, Plagues, and the Prince of Wales: A Chapter in the Conflict of Religion and Science,' *Journal of British Studies*, 13 (May 1974), 46–65. For the pivotal role of the professions, see Harold Perkin, *The Origins of Modern English Society 1780–1880* (London, 1969).

fortress of Holy Scripture and Paley's *Natural Theology*. A closed mind had become, as much as the black coat, part of the professional equipment of a clergyman.

At the same time the secular professions had also developed their distinctive specialized training and functions and esprit de corps, and the physical and natural sciences, though still largely in the hands of amateurs, were beginning to develop similarly professional standards. Now what distinguishes these sciences, and their aspiring brethren in the social sciences, is a preeminent concern with fact — fact that is verifiable and applicable. To the gentlemen of the factual professions, it was galling to see the precedence and prestige accorded to a clergy which had come to define itself by the blinkers it wore. In their struggle to impress scientific ideas, and, more important, the idea of science itself on the minds of the rising generation of intellectual young men, it was inevitable that they would come into conflict with the obstacle of clerical narrowness. And in this conflict they found themselves armed with a weapon which even clergymen were taught to fear, the weapon of truth.

It is difficult to avoid the conclusion that these rival professionalisms — the growth of an Anglican clericalism coinciding with the awakening of a self-conscious intellectual laity — provide necessary predisposing conditions for the conflict that was to develop. However, there are certain difficulties which limit the usefulness of this class analysis in terms of conflicting elements in the intellectual middle classes. The first arises from the professionalism of science itself: scientific facts require scientific minds to appreciate them, and they could have only a peripheral effect as long as education remained classical rather than scientific. Second, as we shall see, the heaviest blows to clerical orthodoxy were dealt, not by scientific outsiders, but by dissident clergymen, those who felt entrapped by the narrowness of their profession and sought to break out to a broader culture. After all, Lyell's geology and Darwin's biology, even if absolutely true, affected only a few chapters of Genesis, leaving the rest of the Bible untouched; but biblical criticism, even in the hands of devout clergymen, affected the whole text and inspiration and authority of the Bible and perhaps of the Christian faith. Most important, however, is the fact that what ultimately alienated the rising intellectual generation was, not the external challenge of science or criticism, but the response of the spokesmen of orthodox religion. It was the failure of orthodoxy, not the strengths of heresy or infidelity, which lost the intellectual classes to religion.

The orthodoxy of Protestant England, common to Anglicans and most Dissenters, was the product of the evangelical revival. It is impossible to overstate the pervasiveness and intensity of the moralism which the evangelicals had infused into every aspect of Victorian life. Indeed, what separates us from the Victorians is, not so much the difference in our moral judgments, as their readiness to make moral judgments and our readiness to suspend them. Our objectivity is their immorality. The sensitivity of conscience thus produced, the self-consciousness and introspection thus fostered, were awesome things; and the moral crises which are so frequent in both the literature and the life of the educated classes did not always pass through the approved channels of evangelical conversion and a strenuous but safely moral life.

One of the moral virtues most frequently inculcated (and regarded as distinctively English) was the virtue of truth. Now truth is a two-edged sword. For one thing, there was a fundamental confusion in the Victorian concept of 'truth.' In one sense the word refers to objective truth, the factual reality; in another sense it means truthfulness, that is, the honesty of a person. It is characteristic of the Victorians that they were more interested in truthfulness than in truth; they were more concerned with the moral character of the speaker than with the factual correctness of his statement. A result of this attitude is that the debates over biblical criticism have a curious ad hominem character. Thus, criticism is opposed because it seems to impugn the truthfulness of God as the author of the Bible;[4] or the Essayists and Reviewers are condemned as dishonest because the conclusions they reached contradicted the promises they made at their ordinations. The trouble with this mode of reasoning is that it draws attention to personalities and away from the actual issues of debate; it is the practice of evasion in the name of honesty.

This practice was not uncommon among the clergy. It contributed, in the middle decades, to a growing (though rarely articulated) distrust of their preaching, a loss of influence which paralleled their increasing professionalism. This is best stated by a Broad Church clergyman, Arthur Stanley, later Dean of Westminster:

> I believe that the besetting sin of the clerical profession — that to which its peculiar temptations may lead — is indifference to strict truth.... There is also a habit of using words without meaning, or with only a half-belief, or for the sake of a convenient argument and of filling up an awkward gap, or with a love of things established ... which leads in part, I am convinced, to that deep-rooted indifference to sermons, and that vast separation between faith and outward

[4] Thus Canon Liddon as late as 1889: 'The trustworthiness of the Old Testament is, in fact, inseparable from the trustworthiness of our Lord Jesus Christ.' Quoted in W. Neil, 'The Criticism and Theological Use of the Bible, 1700–1950,' in *The Cambridge History of the Bible: The West from the Reformation to the Present Day*, ed. S. L. Greenslade (Cambridge, 1963), p. 267.

belief, and that distrust of all that the clergy say, and that intolerable arrogance which so many of them feel towards lay people.[5]

Stanley's friend Benjamin Jowett put it more concisely: 'I never hear a sermon scarcely which does not seem equally divided between truth and falsehood.'[6] Preaching, to be sure, has problems as well as temptations; there are a limited number of conclusions which may safely be arrived at in an unlimited number of sermons, and facility in achieving this may correlate negatively with religious depth. By 1860 it was noticed that the really ablest men were no longer proceeding to holy orders; and Frederick Temple, like Jowett an Essayist and Reviewer, was struck by the 'extraordinary reticence'[7] on religious matters of the young men at the universities.

Part of this reticence, this reluctance to express and examine doubts and perplexities in religion, was the frequently inculcated belief that religious doubt was in itself sinful. The duty of avoiding doubt, whatever intellectual operations might be needed to accomplish this, was put with characteristically eloquent crudity by Samuel Wilberforce, later Bishop of Oxford:

> Whilst irreverence and doubt are the object of your greatest fear; whilst you would glady retain a childlike and unquestioning reverence by abasing, if need were, your understanding, rather than gain any knowledge at the hazard of your reverence; you are doubtless in God's hands, and therefore safe.... Fly, therefore, rather than contend; fly to known truths.[8]

As his biographer remarked, 'In an age that pressed desperately for the answers to all sorts of questions, Wilberforce believed they were better left unasked.'[9]

---

[5] Stanley to Hugh Pearson, Sept. 21, 1841, in Rowland E. Prothero and G. G. Bradley, *The Life and Correspondence of Arthur Penrhyn Stanley, Late Dean of Westminster*, 2 vols. (New York, 1894), 1, 302.

[6] Jowett to Stanley, Aug. 17, 1846, in Evelyn Abbott and Lewis Campbell, *The Life and Letters of Benjamin Jowett*, 2 vols. (New York, 1897), I, 150.

[7] Quoted in Ernest G. Sandford, ed., *Memoirs of Archbishop Temple, by Seven Friends*, 2 vols. (London, 1906), I, 303.

[8] A sermon in the 1830s, quoted in Standish Meacham, *Lord Bishop: The Life of Samuel Wilberforce* (Cambridge, Mass., 1970), p. 229. Also p. 225: 'God intended revelation to train the heart, not to gratify the intellect.' Significantly, Wilberforce published in 1861 a volume of sermons entitled *The Revelation of God the Probation of Man*. Goldwin Smith, a layman, responded with *The Suppression of Doubt Is Not Faith*.

[9] Meacham, *Lord Bishop*, p. 228.

One reason for the non-asking of questions was the belief that doubt was not only sinful but that it rendered the doubter miserable in this life as well, the absence of faith producing emptiness and unhappiness. Men of much faith projected what they would feel if deprived of their faith; and no factual evidence of serene agnostics and happy atheists could shake their conviction that doubt was a state of misery. Even the usually sensible Newman could exclaim, 'Consider the miseries of wives and mothers losing their faith in Scripture.'[10] It became a duty to prevent this, to suppress one's own doubts and discourage the doubts of others. But could the rising generation, self-consciously devoted to truth but increasingly aware of disturbing facts, be expected indefinitely to contain their doubts and profess an assurance which was decreasingly real? This was the point of tension, the poison in the theological atmosphere which had to come out.

The issue on which the intensity of Victorian religion first began to turn inward on itself was, not an external challenge of science or criticism, but a felt conflict between the morality which the evangelicals had cultivated and the theological doctrines which they taught. Victorian morality was not merely stern, it was also humanitarian; though the evangelicals doubted whether the mass of mankind could be saved, they preached the duty of active benevolence; they freed the slaves and improved the conditions of factory labor. There was already a discrepancy here between the essentially otherworldly character of their faith and the contemporary aspirations, in which they often shared, towards the progress and improvement of human society. More important, the humanitarian values thus engendered were incompatible with the commonplace theology of the day. Here we must note that the word *theology* is and was used loosely; nineteenth-century England was not a home of systematic theology as Germany was; the best of its religious thinkers were self-taught amateurs. The theology espoused by most evangelicals, and generally accepted by most others, was a sort of unsystematic and semiconscious quasi-Calvinism, positing the Atonement rather than the Incarnation as the central fact of Christianity, and stressing the sterner and harsher Christian doctrines: original sin, reprobation, vicarious atonement, eternal punishment. The unbalanced emphasis of these essentially unattractive themes was bound to come into conflict with the sentimental and humanitarian spirit of the age, itself largely a product of the religious revival.

[10] Newman to Malcolm McColl, Mar. 24, 1861, in Charles S. Dessain, ed., *The Letters and Diaries of John Henry Newman*, XIX (London, 1969), 488. Newman, with the detachment of a Roman Catholic, could observe that 'The religion of England depends, humanly speaking, on belief in "the Bible and the whole Bible," etc., and on the observance of the Calvinistic Sabbath. Let the population begin to doubt in its inspiration and infallibility, where are they?'

The conflict between humane ethics and rigorous dogma was responsible for some of the more spectacular losses of faith in the 1840s. How could a benevolent and sensitive conscience accept the morality of a Jehovah who behaved, as the young Darwin put it, like a 'revengeful tyrant'[11] and who condemned the majority of his human creatures to an eternity of torment disproportionate to their wickedness or based on no personal fault at all? These were the issues which provoked theological crises in the 1850s. F. D. Maurice, perhaps the most prophetic mind of the century, was deprived of his professorship in 1853 for questioning the eternity of punishment. Jowett's 1855 commentary on St Paul, denouncing the conventional presentation of the Atonement, brought a storm of criticism foreshadowing the later denunciation of *Essays and Reviews*. Let me quote Jowett to show the depth of the indignation which Victorian quasi-Calvinism could produce in a usually calm mind: 'God is represented as angry with us for what we never did; He is ready to inflict a disproportionate punishment on us for what we are; He is satisfied by the sufferings of His Son in our stead.... The imperfection of human law is transferred to the Divine.' After this Jowett 'cannot but fear whether it be still possible so to teach Christ as not to cast a shadow on the holiness and truth of God.'[12]

The erosion of faith caused by this ethical revulsion against cruel dogmas crudely stated is perhaps the clearest example of what I have called 'the warfare of conscience with theology.'[13] The classic statement of this revulsion is that of John Stuart Mill: 'I will call no being good, who is not what I mean when I apply that epithet to my fellow creatures, and if such a being can sentence me to hell for not so calling him, to hell I will go.'[14] This sentiment was not confined to such eminent cases as Darwin, Francis Newman, James Anthony Froude, or George Eliot; it can be found in many

---

[11] Quoted in William Irvine, *Apes, Angels, and Victorians* (New York, 1955), p. 109.

[12] These passages from 'On Atonement and Satisfaction' are quoted in Geoffrey Faber, *Jowett, a Portrait with Background* (London, 1957), p. 219, and Abbott and Campbell, *Life of Jowett*, I, 234.

[13] This point is made by Murphy, 'The Ethical Revolt,' p. 811. Another illustration of the state of mind which produced this revulsion is the case of Tennyson, who vividly remembered an aunt saying, 'Alfred, Alfred, whenever I look at you I think of the words, "Depart from me, ye cursed, into everlasting fire."' A Catholic critic remarked, 'It is the Calvinistic idea of God and hell which is at the bottom of it.' Maisie Ward, *The Wilfrid Wards and the Transition* (London, 1934), I, 167–68.

[14] Mill, *An Examination of Sir William Hamilton's Philosophy* (4th ed., London, 1872), p. 129. The reference was specifically to Mansel's philosophy, discussed later in this essay. Mill's phrase seems to echo James Anthony Froude in 1849: 'oh, I would sooner perish for ever than stoop down before a Being who may have power to crush me, but whom my heart forbids me to reverence.' Froude, *The Nemesis of Faith* (New York, 1879), p. 17.

elements of society.[15] The apparent immorality of the Bible and the Creed provided stock arguments for atheists; more important, it provided grounds for that perplexity of faith about which professed believers were so unwholesomely reticent. It is possible that the science and criticism of the 1860s had such effect because they provided stimuli and rationales for minds already unsettled and alienated on these moral grounds. At any rate, the ethical challenge preceded and transcended the scientific challenge. Perhaps the Victorian religious revival had made men too moral to be orthodox, too humanitarian to be Christian.

The ground was thus prepared for the first onslaughts of science and criticism. Biblical criticism, to be sure, was slow to reach England; it was a German product. But science, especially biology and geology, had a respectable English pedigree. Country clergymen observed plants and animals; country gentlemen looked at rocks; and so we have biology and geology. But the close observation of nature produced some problems. How could these geological strata and fossils of extinct species be squared with a six-day Creation dating, according to Archbishop Ussher's chronology printed in the margins of the authorized Bible, from only 4004 B.C.? The question was focused by Sir Charles Lyell in his *Principles of Geology*, which advanced the convincing hypothesis that geological formations were the results, not of sudden catastrophes such as Creation and the Flood, but of the slow operation of uniform processes of change. The uniformitarian hypothesis required a much longer time-span than seemed to be allowed by the biblical account of Creation. The response of churchmen was not, in the 1830s, directly hostile; rather they sought to show that the biblical texts could be harmonized with the new science. Unfortunately, the various 'harmonies,' such as those which treated the 'days' of Genesis as geological eras, proved to be nearly as incompatible with the developments of geology as the literal biblical text itself. And those fossils, which suggested transformations in biology as vast as those in geology, were awkward to get over: a religious scientist was reported to have concluded that fossils had been deliberately placed by God to test man's faith.

More serious problems would arise when the concept of development was extended from geology to biology. The idea of evolution, though not yet acceptable to most biologists, was in the air. In 1844 Robert Chambers, an amateur, published anonymously a book called *Vestiges of the Natural History*

---

[15] A student of hymnology has pointed out that references to hell in revival hymns had almost disappeared by the 1870s; and the Congregationalist divine R. W. Dale said in 1874 that eternal punishment had been relegated to 'the house of beliefs which we have not rejected, but which we are willing to forget.' G. Kitson Clark, *An Expanding Society: Britain 1830–1900* (Cambridge, 1967), p. 104; H. G. Wood, *Belief and Unbelief since 1850* (Cambridge, 1955), p. 32.

of Creation, which maintained that each species had not been specially created by God but had evolved according to general laws. This rather unscientific work, a sort of Darwin without discipline, was written in a reverent spirit. It was received, however, with a storm of theological criticism which anticipated the more famous debate later excited by Darwin. The book was criticized by scientists no less strongly than by clergymen, but many sensitive laymen were curiously attracted by the idea of evolution. The storm over *Vestiges of Creation* was a sign of the uneasiness of the times, the unsettlement of minds produced by the scientific picture of impersonal nature functioning without direct divine interposition, a picture difficult to accept, yet increasingly difficult to resist. The poet Tennyson was one of the fascinated readers of *Vestiges of Creation*, and *In Memoriam* shows both its influence and the problems it posed:

> Are God and Nature then at strife,
> > That Nature lends such evil dreams?
> > So careful of the type she seems,
> So careless of the single life;
>
> That I, considering everywhere
> > Her secret meaning in her deeds,
> > And finding that of fifty seeds
> She often brings but one to bear,
>
> I falter where I firmly trod,
> > And falling with my weight of cares
> > Upon the world's great altar-stairs
> That slope through darkness up to God,
>
> I stretch lame hands of faith, and grope,
> > And gather dust and chaff, and call
> > To what I feel is Lord of all,
> And faintly trust the larger hope.
>
> (LV)

In Memoriam, published in 1850, stands as a monument of the Victorian mind at equipoise, unable to deny the results of science, yet hopefully (if 'faintly') placing its faith in 'the truths that never can be proved.'

But these first glimmerings of doubts and difficulties did not produce a direct conflict between science and religion. Indeed, it was almost an article of faith that such a conflict could not occur, that the conclusions of reason would ultimately harmonize with the dicta of revelation, that the facts of nature discovered by science could not contradict the Word of God who was the creator of nature. A clear position on this matter had been worked out in the conflicts with the rationalists of the eighteenth century, when it was the glory of the Church of England that its thinkers had met the deists and freethinkers on their own rational grounds and more than held their own. A line of Anglican apologists, from Berkeley through Butler to Paley, had used the language of the Enlightenment to justify the ways of God to man. The culmination of this process came, at the end of the eighteenth century, in the work of Archdeacon William Paley. His *Natural Theology* (1802) demonstrated the existence of God by the argument from design. As the existence of a watch proves that there must have been a watchmaker, so the complexity and perfect interrelationships of nature prove that it must have been designed by an intelligent creator. The smoothness and closeness of Paley's arguments had a certain fatuous charm, and the abundance of his detailed illustrations from nature impressed the young Darwin and may have influenced his style. Another of Paley's works, *The Evidences of Christianity* (1794), rested the case for the specific Christian revelation primarily on the argument from miracles. These works became standard textbooks at the universities and provided the staple apologetic theology for generations of clergymen.

The argument from design and the evidence of miracles and prophecies seemed to have met not only the challenge of eighteenth-century rationalism but all future argumentative needs, enabling the clergy to disregard most external challenges to religion. Paradoxically, the success of the Paleyan apologetic was to prove disastrous in the 1860s: it was precisely the argument from design and miracles and prophecies (the 'external evidences') that were devastated by the new science and criticism. But evangelicalism and tractarianism had turned the clerical mind from more original researches in apologetics to matters internal to the Church. The one exception, the Bridgewater treatises of the 1830s, proved to be restatements by religious scientists of the argument from design.

Meanwhile philosophy had moved beyond the positions of the Enlightenment to new rationalisms, whether the utilitarianism of Bentham and Mill or the German metaphysics of Kant and Hegel. The external evidences for Christian faith on which Paley had relied were being pushed aside by a new emphasis on inward religious experience, more profound but less verifiable, whose spokesman in England was Coleridge. In his distaste for the formal evidences and dogmas of Christianity, Coleridge spoke for many sensitive religious intellectuals, and he provided the philosophical underpinning for much of later Broad Church biblical criticism. Orthodox clergymen were vaguely aware of these challenges to their position, but they were unable to respond with more than denunciations.

Then, in 1858, emerged a new champion of orthodoxy who seemed to have finally refuted all unbelievers and heretics with the most up-to-date philosophical weapons. H. L. Mansel, in his Bampton lectures on *The Limits of Religious Thought*, employed the then-current philosophy of Sir William Hamilton to place the Christian faith permanently beyond the reach of rational challenge. Mansel argued that the Absolute, the Unconditioned, the Infinite (in other words, God), was utterly beyond the power of human reason to understand, either to defend or to deny. He thus dismissed summarily both Paley's demonstration of the existence of God and the rationalists' attempts to disprove it. From this supreme skepticism, Mansel immediately passed to the most complete orthodoxy. What man's reason could not do, God could do and did in his revelation. Regardless of intellectual or ethical difficulties, man must accept revelation as God gives it; he can examine not its contents but only its evidences. And the evidences Mansel offers are none other than the external evidences of Paley: miracles and prophecies. We must accept revelation on these evidences and we must accept it in its entirety, with no exceptions or qualifications.[16]

This now-forgotten book of 1858 is important because it shows the state of mind of the most intelligent upholders of orthodoxy on the eve of their most formidable challenges. Mansel's book was hailed as having definitively put down rationalism, with the result that the 'religious world' was in a state of false security just before the crises of 1859 and 1860. His admirers could perhaps be excused for not having anticipated that Hamilton's philosophy of the Unconditioned, on which Mansel's logical structure depended, was shortly to be demolished by John Stuart Mill. They were more culpable for disregarding the ease with which Mansel's philosophical skepticism could be accepted by those who, like Herbert Spencer, saw no need to proceed beyond it to Christianity. But the great danger in Mansel's argument was that it identified the Christian faith with the text of the Bible and rested the authenticity of the Bible solely on external evidences such as miracles and prophecies. While removing faith safely beyond the reach of philosophy, Mansel had exposed it directly to the attack of science and biblical criticism. The prevailing acceptance of the Paleyan evidences made Mansel and others blind to the vulnerability of a faith which rested solely on such external supports.

Mansel's successor as Bampton lecturer was to assert that the Bible was, as history, 'absolutely and in every respect true.' Another held that every

---

[16] 'If the teaching of Christ is not in any one thing the teaching of God, it is in all things the teaching of men.' H. L. Mansel, *The Limits of Religious Thought* (Oxford, 1858), p. 155. A good discussion of the Mansel controversy is R. V. Sampson, 'The Limits of Religious Thought: The Theological Controversy,' in *1859: Entering an Age of Crisis* (Bloomington, Ind., 1959), pp. 63–80.

word in the Bible was 'the direct utterance of the Most High.'[17] The clear implication of such statements was that, if any text of the Bible could be shown to be scientifically or historically erroneous, not only that text but the entirety of revelation must be given up. Never had traditional Christianity been so self-confident or so vulnerable.

We may now turn to the first of the great challenges to orthodox Christianity, the publication of Darwin's *Origin of Species* in 1859. This work became the most successful exposition of the doctrine of evolution because, first, it offered a coherent and detailed presentation of the evidence and, second, it provided for the first time a satisfactory explanation of the mechanism of evolution, the theory of natural selection. Although Darwin hesitated to apply his theory to the case of man, its applicability was immediately recognized and became the focus of the public debate. 'Is man an ape or an angel?' asked Disraeli; being a politician, he was 'on the side of the angels.'[18] While some scientists found objections to evolution, the attack on Darwin turned on his denial of the special creation of each species by direct divine action and his refusal to assign to man a unique place distinct from the rest of animal creation. Philosophically Darwin was even more subversive: his concept of random variations challenged not only the literal text of Genesis but also the argument from design of Paley and the deists.

The controversy over the *Origin of Species* took the unfortunate form of a direct confrontation between religion and science. The great majority of religious spokesmen condemned the doctrine of evolution, often without regard to its scientific merits, on the ground of its repugnance to the text of the Bible and its tendency to degrade man to the level of the beasts. A majority of scientists, on the other hand, accepted evolution as at least a probable hypothesis, and some, notably Huxley and Tyndall, were goaded by their clerical opponents to take an increasingly anti-religious position. Both sides seemed to identify the substance of Christianity with the text of Genesis.

The most famous confrontation occurred at Oxford in 1860. Samuel Wilberforce, a fine bishop but an over-ardent controversialist, went beyond the scientific arguments in which he had been briefed to refute evolution by sarcasm, asking Huxley 'was it through his grandfather or his grandmother

---

[17] George Rawlinson and J. W. Burgon, respectively, cited in Neil, 'The Criticism and Theological Use of the Bible,' pp. 260, 283.

[18] At a meeting of the Society for Increasing Endowments of Small Livings in the Diocese of Oxford, Nov. 25, 1864; W. F. Monypenny and G. E. Buckle, *The Life of Benjamin Disraeli, Earl of Beaconsfield*, 6 vols. (London, 1910–20), IV, 374.

that he claimed his descent from a monkey?' Huxley's reply was simple but devastating: 'He was not ashamed to have a monkey for his ancestor; but he would be ashamed to be connected with a man who used great gifts to obscure the truth.'[19] The audience (largely clerical) applauded. By relying on the supreme virtue of truthfulness, Huxley turned Victorian morality against Victorian orthodoxy. When it came to the test, the defenders of orthodoxy were not interested in truth, and the defenders of truth were not interested in orthodoxy.

The direct effects of this debate have been exaggerated, but it holds a great symbolic significance. The clergy in the audience may have merely applauded a good debate, or they may have enjoyed the put-down of a bishop whose outspokenness had made him many enemies; but the young laymen saw the contrast between the shallowness of a reverend bishop and the reverence for truth of an irreligious scientist. It was this contrast, more than the actual issues of the debate over evolution, which gave rise to the feeling that science was the wave of the future and religion a thing of the past. The effect of the victory of science in the evolution debate was not a headlong abandonment of faith by those who had previously been religious, but rather a confirmation of doubts that already existed and a general turning of attention to the more meaningful issues of the secular world.

The challenge of evolutionary biology, serious though it might be, was superficial compared with the challenge of biblical criticism, which ranged over the entire text and interpretation of the Bible and touched more deeply the sources of the Christian faith. This was an internal problem, not an external one. While textual criticism was relatively uncontroversial, the same could not be said of the so-called higher criticism, the analysis of the authorship, sources, motivation, and accuracy of the biblical writings. The results of such analysis might well disconcert those who believed in the direct and literal divine inspiration of the biblical writings; and the cool and detached manner of historical research seemed hardly compatible with a lively faith.

What was worse, biblical criticism was un-English, lacking in native roots and challenging the prevailing insularity. It was a German product. Hardly anybody read German; most did not think it worth reading; and what they heard of German thought was not encouraging. Virtually the first work of German criticism which reached England was D. F. Strauss's *Life of Jesus*, which treated the Gospels as mythological rather than

---

[19] Accounts of this debate vary; the standard account, made famous in Leonard Huxley's life of his father, is taken from [Isabel Sidgwick], 'A Grandmother's Tales,' *Macmillan's Magazine*, 78 (Oct. 1898), 433. A minimizing account is given by Owen Chadwick, *The Victorian Church*, 2 vols. (London, 1966–70), II, 10–11.

historical and scandalized even Germans; translated by George Eliot in 1846, it affected a few sensitive, already doubting souls, but served for most who heard of it as a warning that criticism led to infidelity. England was unprepared for biblical criticism; 'the Bible, and the Bible alone' was the watchword of English Protestantism. The extreme sensitiveness to any questioning of the authority of the Bible was exacerbated in the 1860s by the coincidence of the arrival of biblical criticism with the challenge of evolutionary science.

Seven men, six of them clergymen of the Church of England, sought to break through the reticence of the educated on matters of faith by 'a free handling, in a becoming spirit, of subjects peculiarly liable to suffer by the repetition of conventional language, and from traditional methods of treatment.'[20] The resulting composite volume, modestly entitled *Essays and Reviews*, was published in 1860. The five essays and two reviews, independently written, varied in character and quality: one was a rewritten sermon, another a learned, cold, but unexceptionable historical monograph. The one layman wrote a devastating critique of the attempted 'harmonies' between Genesis and geology. Rowland Williams, a feisty Welshman, wrote a provocative essay on Baron von Bunsen in which 'justification by faith' was turned into 'peace of mind.' Baden Powell, a mathematician, flatly denied the possibility of miracles. H. B. Wilson gave the widest possible latitude to subscription to the articles of faith and questioned the eternity of damnation. The entire work was capped by Jowett's tremendous though wayward essay 'On the Interpretation of Scripture,' in which he urged that the Bible be read 'like any other book' and made an impassioned plea for freedom of scholarship: 'The Christian religion is in a false position when all the tendencies of knowledge are opposed to it.'[21]

Much of what the Essayists and Reviewers wrote is now commonplace theology, and the work would not have attracted much attention even in 1860 but for the fact that its authors were clergymen. Once again the ad hominem element prevailed. How could a clergyman hold such views consistently with the Thirty-Nine Articles and his ordination vows? Once again Samuel Wilberforce led the attack, supported by evangelicals and High Churchmen in a rare display of unanimity. From all quarters the volume was denounced: some 150 replies fill three pages of the British Museum catalogue. Wilberforce pressed for a synodical condemnation by the bishops, which he obtained tentatively in 1861 and formally in 1864. Williams and Wilson, the two Essayists who were subject to deprivation, were prosecuted in the church courts and partially condemned in 1862. But here

---

[20] 'To the Reader,' introductory note to *Essays and Reviews* (London, 1860).

[21] Jowett, 'On the Interpretation of Scripture,' *Essays and Reviews*, p. 374.

the peculiarities of the English legal system intervened, demanding a strict construction of church formularies while giving the most liberal interpretation to the accused writings, and the conviction was reversed by the Privy Council in 1864. The Privy Council, someone quipped, 'dismissed Hell with costs, and took away from orthodox members of the Church of England their last hope of eternal damnation.'[22] Ironically, the liberty of thought within the Church of England was saved by the subjection of the Church to the state.

Hard on the heels of the clergymen of *Essays and Reviews* came a bishop, albeit a colonial bishop, with a more direct though less competent attack on the literal interpretation of the Bible. John William Colenso had been brought up to believe that every detail of the Bible is literally true; he had a simple, numerical mind which led him to write textbooks of arithmetic; sent out as bishop to Natal in 1853, he was an effective missionary among the Zulus. Natives, however, lack the knowledge given to civilized men that certain questions ought not to be asked; and so, when they were translating the story of the Flood, one African innocently enquired: 'Is all that true? Do you really believe that all this happened thus?' Colenso was an honest man; and he knew, having read Lyell, that geologists had disproved the universal Flood. He began to reexamine the first books of the Bible, with the aid of a few German works and a lot of arithmetic, and he found that the statistics given in the Bible, with their magnificent oriental rotundity, were simply impossible. His method was absurd, but his conclusion was irresistible: the Pentateuch was unhistorical, and most of it was written by someone other than Moses. He had to speak out, though many would be shaken by such statements from a bishop: 'Our duty, surely, is to follow the Truth, wherever it leads us, and to leave the consequences in the hands of God.' So he published *The Pentateuch Critically Examined* in 1862, telling a shocked England that 'the Bible itself is not 'God's word'; but assuredly 'God's word' will be heard in the Bible, by all who will humbly and devoutly listen for it.'[23] Having said this, he claimed the right to remain a bishop of the Church of England.

Pious ears were offended; orthodoxy was outraged. The prevailing sentiment was expressed by Bishop Lee of Manchester: 'the very foundations of our faith, the very basis of our hopes, the very nearest and dearest of our consolations are taken from us when one line in that Sacred Volume on

[22] The mock epitaph on Lord Westbury containing this phrase is attributed to Sir Philip Rose, but the phrase itself is said to have been coined by Charles Bowen, one of Jowett's favorite pupils. J. B. Atlay, *The Victorian Chancellors*, 2 vols. (London, 1906–8), II, 264.

[23] The quotations are from the preface to part I and the 'Concluding Remarks' of part II of Colenso, *The Pentateuch and Book of Joshua Critically Examined*, 2 vols. (New York, 1863), I, 8; II, 301–2.

which we base everything is declared to be unfaithful or untrustworthy.'[24]
Bishops demanded the removal of their heretical colleague. The Bishop of
Cape Town, who claimed jurisdiction over Natal, held a synod which
deposed Colenso, Colenso appealed to the Privy Council, where the matter
was promptly diverted from a religious question to the technical issue of the
legal status of colonies. In the end, without ever resolving the doctrinal
issue, the Privy Council held that Colenso could not be deposed. The
Bishop of Cape Town, acting on his own, consecrated another bishop for
Natal; most of his clergy repudiated Colenso; but he held on, and the result
was a local schism which lasted for decades.

The legal judgments on *Essays and Reviews* and Colenso made it not
illegal for a clergyman to deny the literal inspiration and infallibility of the
Scriptures, but that did not mean that it was tolerable for him to do so in
the eyes of most of the clergy and many even of the laity. There was a
double standard of belief, or rather of honesty, for clergymen and laymen.
Indeed it is possible that the outspokenness of the Essayists and Reviewers
actually retarded, by provoking so powerful a reaction, the advent of that
freedom of thought in matters of faith for which they strove.

The turning point came when Temple, the least offensive of the Essayists
and Reviewers, was nominated to be Bishop of Exeter in 1869 and consecrated despite strong efforts to prevent it. Eventually the theological
climate would change: evolution became generally acceptable in the 1880s
and, with the publication of *Lux Mundi* by a group of High Churchmen in
1889, it became evident that even conservative clergymen would have to
deal with the problem of biblical criticism. But by then it was too late.
What clergymen had belatedly discovered, intellectual laymen had known
all along.

There had been something exaggerated and even slightly comical in the
reaction against biblical criticism. Here, as with the response to Darwin, it
seemed as if the defenders of orthodox faith were afraid of the impartial
search for truth. As Tennyson said: 'There lives more faith in honest
doubt,/ Believe me, than in half the creeds.'

The Essayists and Reviewers, Colenso, and a few others such as F. D.
Maurice and Archbishop Tait — not doubters themselves, but critics —
were concerned to bridge the gap separating professed faith from the frank
inquiry of educated laymen. One of these laymen, the philosopher Henry
Sidgwick, spoke for many when he wrote: 'What we all want is, briefly, not
a condemnation, but a refutation. . . . A large portion of the laity now . . .

[24] *The Guardian* (1863), p. 302, cited in Bernard Reardon, *From Coleridge to Gore* (London,
1971), p. 343, n. 1.

will not be satisfied by an *ex cathedra* shelving of the question, nor terrified by a deduction of awful consequences from the new speculations. For philosophy and history alike have taught them to seek not what is 'safe', but what is true.'[25]

The failure of the spokesmen of orthodoxy to respond to such appeals, to enter into a creative dialogue with the new ideas, was more important than the new ideas themselves in alienating the rising intellectual generation. As Jowett said: 'Doubt comes in at the window when inquiry is denied at the door.'[26] From the 1860s, the intellectual leadership of England turned, first tentatively and in single cases, then in a growing flood, away from that deep concern with matters religious which had characterized mid-Victorian England. I am not speaking of that minority which, as in previous generations, was naturally attracted by philosophical radicalisms. I speak of those who yet retained much of the evangelical heritage, particularly in morality, but who, becoming increasingly suspicious of an orthodoxy so ineptly defended, drifted away from formal Christianity. A novel of 1888, *Robert Elsmere* by Mrs. Humphry Ward, tells the story of a clergyman who, because he can no longer believe in the creed of his church, resigns his office and devotes his life to social service. Robert Elsmere was the type of many young men of the late nineteenth century, some maintaining an outward conformity while thinking freely, others leaving organized religion altogether. Christianity had now become an 'open question.'[27]

As the natural sciences, soon joined by the social sciences, continued their progress, a limited number became outright atheists, needing no religion to explain a universe which could now be understood in purely natural terms. More common, though not always articulated, was the position for which Huxley invented the term 'agnostic.' As Huxley described it, there was a good deal of residual Christianity in agnosticism: 'a deep sense of religion was compatible with the entire absence of theology.... Science seems to me to teach in the highest and strongest manner the great truth which is embodied in the Christian conception of entire surrender to the will of God. Sit down before the fact as a little child, be prepared to give up every preconceived notion, follow humbly wherever and to whatever abysses nature leads, or you shall learn nothing.'[28]

[25] *The Times* (London), Feb. 20, 1861.

[26] 'On the Interpretation of Scripture,' p. 373.

[27] Goldwin Smith: 'a certain number of men may be growing up, not exactly in infidelity, but in the belief that Christianity is an open question.' Earl of Selborne, *Memorials*, ed. Lady Sophia Palmer, 2 vols. (London, 1896), II, 64–65.

[28] Huxley to Charles Kingsley, cited in Irvine, *Apes, Angels, and Victorians*, pp. 131, 129.

Truthfulness had replaced belief as the ultimate standard; but the abandonment of faith did not necessarily represent an abandonment of morality. Indeed it was an outraged moral sense that had led in many instances to the rejection of the Christian faith; and Victorian morality could, at least among the elite, survive the collapse of the Victorian creed. In the writings of George Eliot, as in the practice of numerous positivists, agnostics, and atheists, a humanized evangelical morality — the creed of duty, service, and love — stood alone and triumphant, unsupported by belief in God or the hope of personal immortality:

> O may I join the choir invisible
> Of those immortal dead who live again
> In minds made better by their presence; live
> In pulses stirred to generosity,
> In deeds of daring rectitude, in scorn
> For miserable aims that end with self,
> In thoughts sublime that pierce the night
>   like stars,
> And with their mild persistence urge man's
>   search
> To vaster issues.
>   So to live is heaven:
> To make undying music in the world,
> Breathing as beauteous order that controls
> With growing sway the growing life of man.
> . . . .
>   May I reach
> That purest heaven, be to other souls
> The cup of strength in some great agony,
> Enkindle generous ardour, feed pure love,
> Beget the smiles that have no cruelty —
> Be the sweet presence of a good diffused,
> And in diffusion ever more intense.
> So shall I join the choir invisible
> Whose music is the gladness of the world.

In such pure expression, the morality of the unbelievers could rival that of Christianity. The search for truth in science and in life is an activity as religious in spirit, if not in form or object, as the search for truth in religion. Thus one may speak of the 'religion of unbelief' — the faith of those who found the prevailing orthodoxy incompatible with the truths of which they were convinced, and who followed the truth they saw wherever it led them. The heritage of the Victorian religious revival had passed to those who had kept the morality when they could not keep the faith.

But they were living on the ethical capital of the Christianity which they had abandoned. In the long run, as the defenders of orthodoxy had pointed out, it was impossible for any but a small elite to sustain a morality without the foundation of faith. By the twentieth century, Victorian morality had gone the way of Victorian orthodoxy. But it did not go with joy: after the first flush of release, there was a sense of loss, a feeling of failure. We can 'hear the ghost of late Victorian England whimpering on the grave thereof'[29] in the words of Oscar Wilde: 'I would like to found an order for those who cannot believe; the Confraternity of all the Fatherless I might call it, where on an altar, on which no taper burned, a priest, in whose heart peace had no dwelling, might celebrate with unblessed bread and a chalice empty of wine.'[30]

---

[29] G. M. Young, *Victorian England: Portrait of an Age* (Garden City, N. Y., 1954), p. 277.

[30] Wilde to Lord Alfred Douglas, *The Letters of Oscar Wilde*, ed. Rupert Hart-Davis (London, 1962), p. 468.

FRANK M. TURNER

CHAPTER 9

THE VICTORIAN CONFLICT BETWEEN SCIENCE AND RELIGION: A PROFESSIONAL DIMENSION

W AS there a conflict between science and religion in late Victorian England? T. H. Huxley, Bishop Wilberforce, John Tyndall, Francis Galton, W. K. Clifford, and William Gladstone certainly thought so. Other contemporaries, such as Lord Tennyson, E. B. Pusey, Frederick Temple, Frederic Harrison, and Herbert Spencer, feared so but hoped not. Sermons criticizing the arrogance of scientists and articles decrying the ignorance of clergy, as well as books such as John Draper's *History of the Conflict between Religion and Science* (1874) and that of his fellow American Andrew White, *The Warfare of Science* (1876), with a preface by British physicist John Tyndall, suggested a bitter controversy between spokesmen for religion and science. Early-twentieth-century writers including J. M. Robertson, J. B. Bury, Bertrand Russell, and Arthur Balfour assumed that a conflict had raged over the subject a generation or so earlier.[1]

Later commentators have been less certain about the existence of the struggle, its dimensions, and even its issues. Robert Ensor regarded it parenthetically as '(real enough at the time).'[2] Charles Raven contended the debate over science and religion amounted to little more than 'a storm in a Victorian tea-cup.'[3] R. K. Webb explained that the number of people

---

[1] T. H. Huxley, *Collected Essays* (London: Macmillan, 1894), Vols. IV and V; E. B. Pusey, *Un-science, Not Science, Adverse to Faith* (London: J. Parker, 1878); Frederick Temple, *The Relations between Religion and Science* (New York: Macmillan, 1884): Herbert Spencer, *First Principles* (4th ed.: New York: D. Appleton, 1896, pp. 3–136: J. W. Draper, *History of the Conflict between Religion and Science* (New York: D. Appleton, 1874); Andrew Dickson White, *The Warfare of Science* (London: Henry King, 1876) (White's book kept growing until it eventually became two volumes entitled *A History of the Warfare of Science with Theology in Christendom*); Standish Meacham, *My Lord Bishop: The Life of Samuel Wilberforce, 1805–1873* (Cambridge, Mass.: Harvard University Press, 1970), pp. 207–234: J. M. Robertson, *History of Freethought in the Nineteenth Century* (London: Watts, 1929), Vol. I, pp. 313–342: J. B. Bury, *History of Freedom of Thought* (London: Oxford University Press, 1957; originally published 1913), pp. 141–185; Bertrand Russell, *Religion and Science* (New York: Holt, 1935); Lord Balfour, Introduction, in Joseph Needham, ed., *Science, Religion, and Reality* (New York: Macmillan, 1928), pp. 1–18.

[2] Robert K. Ensor, *England, 1870–1914* (Oxford: The Clarendon Press, 1936), p. 162.

[3] Charles E. Raven, *Science, Religion, and the Future* (Cambridge: Cambridge University Press, 1943, reprinted 1968), p. 33.

whose religious faith was shaken by scientific discoveries was 'probably fairly small' but consisted of 'people whose opinions counted for much.'[4] Owen Chadwick drew the important distinction 'between science when it was against religion and the scientists when they were against religion.'[5] The discoveries and theories of science might cast doubt on the accuracy of the Bible, but a scientist could also use a scientific theory to attack the Bible or to discredit the clergy for reasons that had little or no intrinsic relationship to theory. Considerable validity attaches to each of these assessments, particularly that of Chadwick. Yet to reduce the proportions of the dispute, while useful for achieving better perspective, still fails to account for its character, causes, or significance. Those problems — the brew in Canon Raven's teacup — remain.

The most common approach to the substantial issues of the debate has assumed the existence of an enduring and probably necessary conflict between scientific and religious modes of perceiving the world. Antagonism may arise because the naturalistic explanations of science dispense with the metaphysical presuppositions of theology, or because particular scientific theories contradict the literal reading of passages in the Bible, or because religious dogma and authority interfere with scientific research.[6] George Gaylord Simpson succinctly outlined the major features of this interpretation:

> The conflict between science and religion has a single and simple cause. It is the designation as religiously canonical of any conception of the material world open to scientific investigation.... The religious canon ... demands absolute acceptance not subject to test or revision. Science necessarily rejects certainty and predicates acceptance on objective testing and the possibility of continual revision. As a matter of fact, most of the dogmatic religions have exhibited a perverse talent for taking the wrong side on the most important concepts of the material universe, from the structure of the solar system to the origin of man. The result has been constant turmoil for many

---

[4] R. K. Webb, *Modern England from the 18th Century to the Present* (New York: Dodd, Mead, 1970), p. 413.

[5] Owen Chadwick, *The Victorian Church* (New York: Oxford University Press, 1970), Vol. II, p. 3.

[6] *Ibid.*, Vol. II, pp. 1–9; William H. Brock and Roy M. MacLeod, "The 'Scientists' Declaration': Reflections on Science and Belief in the Wake of Essays and Reviews, 1864–5," *British Journal for the History of Science*, 1976, 9: 60.

centuries, and the turmoil will continue as long as religious canons prejudice scientific questions.[7]

There can be no doubt that such disputes arising from epistemological differences over the role of theology as an intellectual authority were major issues at the center of the Victorian conflict of science and religion. By the second quarter of the nineteenth century substantial developments in geology, physics, biology, physiological psychology, and philosophy of science challenged or cast into doubt theological assumptions and portions of the Bible. During those years both Charles Lyell and Charles Darwin complained about the hindrance to scientific advance raised by metaphysics and theology. After midcentury Huxley, Tyndall, Joseph Dalton Hooker, Henry Maudsley, and others continued to press against the influence on scientific work of metaphysical and religious categories of thought and to urge the authority of critical reason and empirical verification against the authority of the Bible and natural religion.[8]

However, without questioning the presence, validity, or significance of the epistemological disagreements, it is possible to question the adequacy of the enduring conflict approach as a wholly satisfactory historical interpretation of the Victorian conflict between science and religion. This interpretation, if not further supplemented, takes too much at face value the statements of polemical interchange. The epistemological dichotomy, proclaimed at the time in such phrases as G. H. Lewes 'Religion and Science, — the two mightiest antagonists,' was an integral part of the debate and has come by default to provide an explanation for it.[9] While defending Darwin's *Origin of Species*, Huxley might declare, 'Extinguished theologians lie about the cradle of every science as the strangled snakes beside that of

[7] George Gaylord Simpson, *This View of Life: The World of an Evolutionist* (New York: Harcourt, Brace and World, 1964), p. 214.

[8] Charles Lyell, *Principles of Geology* (London: John Murray, 1830), Vol. I, pp. 1–91; *Life, Letters and Journals of Sir Charles Lyell, Bart.*, edited by his Sister-in-Law, Mrs. Lyell (London: John Murray, 1881), Vol. I, pp. 263, 316–317, 445–446; Charles Darwin, *The Origin of Species and the Descent of Man* (New York: The Modern Library, n.d.), pp. 122, 135, 319–324, 367–374; Huxley, *Collected Essays*, Vol. I, pp. 18–41; Joseph Dalton Hooker, 'Presidential Address,' *Report of the Thirty-eighth Meeting of the British Association for the Advancement of Science* (London, 1869), pp. lxxiii–lxxv; Henry Maudsley, *Body and Mind* (New York: D. Appleton, 1875), p. 275; Charles Coulston Gillispie, *Genesis and Geology: A Study in the Relations of Scientific Thought, Natural Theology and Social Opinion in Great Britain, 1790–1850* (New York: Harper Torchbook, 1959), pp. 217–228; Frank Miller Turner, *Between Science and Religion: The Reaction to Scientific Naturalism in Late Victorian England* (New Haven: Yale University Press, 1974), pp. 8–37.

[9] G. H. Lewes, *Problems of Life and Mind, First Series* (Boston: Osgood, 1874), Vol. I, p. 2.

Hercules.'[10] But the history of science has been more complex and problematical.

Statements such as Huxley's emerge from an ideology of science as well as from an attempt to account for disagreements between religious and scientific spokesmen. To pursue this track is to posit historically concrete forms for the theological and positive stages of Comte or for the mythopoetic and critical-rational epistemological dichotomy so brilliantly delineated by Ernst Cassirer. So far as the internal development of modern science is concerned, this juxtaposition of good progressive science against evil retrogressive metaphysics and theology fails to account for false starts on the part of scientists, their adherence to incorrect theory, the overlooking of evidence that might have led to further discovery, and the enduring influence of metaphysics and religion on scientific work that continued well into the nineteenth century. Moreover, the progressionist ideology also ignores the frequent hostility of scientific authorities and the scientific community, as well as that of theologians and clergymen, to new theories that challenge existing paradigms and reputations.[11]

To penetrate other levels of the Victorian conflict of religion and science, it is necessary to recognize that the epistemological redefinition of science to mean critical research based on empirical verification constituted only one element in a broader redefinition of the entire scientific enterprise in Great Britain. The debates over particular theories and methods were part of an extensive ongoing discussion about the character of the Victorian scientific community, its function in society, and the values by which it judged the work of its members. These latter issues largely determined why spokesmen for religion and science clashed when they did and as they did.

In 1873 physicist James Clerk Maxwell inquired rhetorically about the condition of British science and replied,

It is simply this, that while the numbers of our professors and their emoluments are increasing, while the number of students is increasing, while practical instruction is being introduced and text-books

---

[10] Huxley, *Collected Essays*, Vol. II, p. 52.

[11] Ernst Cassirer, *Language and Myth* (New York: Dover, 1946) and *The Philosophy of Symbolic Forms*, 3 vols, (New Haven: Yale University Press, 1953–1957): T. S. Kuhn, *The Copernican Revolution* (Cambridge, Mass.: Harvard University Press, 1957) and *The Structure of Scientific Revolutions (Chicago: University of Chicago Press, 1962);* Stephen Toulmin, *Human Understanding* (Princeton: Princeton University Press, 1972); Jerome R. Ravetz, *Scientific Knowledge and Its Social Problems* (Oxford Clarendon Press, 1971), pp. 11–74; Bernard Barber, 'Resistance by Scientists to Scientific Discovery' *Science*, 1961, *134*; 596–602; James Friday, 'A Microscopic Incident in a Monumental Struggle: Huxley and Antibiosis in 1875.' *Brit. J. Hist. Sci.*, 1974, 7: 61–71.

multiplied, while the number and calibre of popular lecturers and popular writers in Science is increasing, original research, the fountain-head of a nation's wealth, is decreasing. . . .[12]

Maxwell's concern about the paucity of research was widely shared at the time. But for the purposes of this essay the activity he did observe was more significant. The expansion in the numbers of professional scientists and the widespread dispersion of scientific ideas on the popular level and within institutions of education meant science was forging ahead in British society if not necessarily in British laboratories. The result of this process, according to A. W. Benn, who witnessed it, was 'a transfer of authority from religious to naturalistic belief.' In turn, as naturalistic belief grew, 'a great part of the reverence once given to priests and to their stories of an unseen universe has been transferred to the astronomer, the geologist, the physician, and the engineer.'[13] It was this shift of authority and prestige, noted by numerous other contemporaries, from one part of the intellectual nation to another that caused the Victorian conflict between religious and scientific spokesmen. Recognition of this development may explain why the Cambridge philosopher Henry Sidgwick termed the debate 'a great and prominent *social* fact of the present age.'[14]

The primary motivating force behind this shift in social and intellectual authority, which deeply involved the epistemological controversy, was activity within the scientific community that displayed most of the major features associated with nascent professionalism. As characterized by Bernard Barber, these include

> . . . a high degree of generalized and systematic knowledge; primary orientation to the community interest rather than to individual self-interest; a high degree of self-control of behavior through codes of ethics internalized in the process of work socialization and through voluntary associations organized and operated by the work specialists themselves; and a system of rewards (monetary and honorary) that is

[12] W. D. Niven, ed., *The Scientific Papers of James Clerk Maxwell* (New York: Dover, 1965), Vol. II, p. 356.

[13] A. W. Benn, *A History of English Rationalism in the Nineteenth Century* (London: Longmans, Green, 1906), Vol. I, p. 198.

[14] Henry Sidgwick, 'Presidential Address to the Society for Psychical Research, July 16, 1888,' in *Presidential Addresses to the Society for Psychical Research* (Glasgow: Society for Psychical Research, 1912), p. 35 (italics added).

primarily a set of symbols of work achievement and thus ends in themselves, not means to some end of individual self-interest.[15]

During the early stages of professionalism an elite from the emerging professional group attempts to project a new public image by formulating codes of ethics, strengthening professional organizations, establishing professional schools, penetrating existing educational institutions, and dispersing information to the general public. These leaders may simply be seeking to improve their social or economic position rather than self-consciously attempting to organize a profession. But to the extent that they are successful in improving their condition through these kinds of activities, their occupational group will assume to a greater or lesser degree the features of a profession.

Normally, pursuit of these ends requires the professionalizing elite to engage in conflict with persons inside and outside the existing occupational or amateur group. Within the group they must raise standards of competence, foster a common bond of purpose, and subject practitioners to the judgment of peers rather than external social or intellectual authorities. Outside they must establish the independence of the would-be professional group, its right of self-definition, and its self-generating role in the social order. Consequently, there are usually disputes between professionals and amateurs and between professionals and outsiders who wish to impose their own definition on the group or who presently carry out the social functions that the professionalizing group wishes to share or to claim as its own exclusive domain. The mid-Victorian scientific community experienced such pangs of professionalization, and the conflict of science and religion was one of the byproducts.

During the first half of the nineteenth century the major characteristics of British science were amateurism, aristocratic patronage, minuscule government support, limited employment opportunities, and peripheral inclusion within the clerically dominated universities and secondary schools. The Royal Society was little more than a fashionable club as befitted a normally amateur occupation of gentlemen. In 1851 Charles Babbage complained, 'Science in England is not a profession: its cultivators are scarcely recognized even as a class. Our language itself contains no *single* term by which their occupation can be expressed.'[16] Reverend

---

[15] Bernard Barber, 'Some Problems in the Sociology of the Professions,' *Daedalus*, 1963, 92: 672, See also J. A. Jackson, ed., *Professions and Professionalization (Cambridge: Cambridge University Press, 1970);* E. Mendelsohn, *'The Emergence of Science as a Profession in Nineteenth Century Europe,'* in K. Hill, ed., *The Management of Scientists* (Boston: Beacon Press, 1964), pp. 3–48.

[16] Charles Babbage, *The Exposition of 1851, or Views of the Industry, the Science, and the Government of England* (London: John Murray, 1851), p. 189.

William Whewell, the Cambridge mathematician and philosopher of science, had invented the word *scientist* in 1834 and reasserted its usefulness in 1840, but the term enjoyed little currency until very late in the century. Even the Devonshire Commission in the seventies found it necessary to define *science* to mean physical rather than moral science. Except for Babbage, other spokesmen in the 'Declinist' controversy, and Sir Robert Peel, all too few people within or without the scientific world related the advancement of physical science to national health, physical well-being, military security, or economic strength.[17]

Although before midcentury the utility of science for manufacturing, agriculture, and improvement of the working class received attention in the Mechanics Institutes, the Society for the Diffusion of Useful Knowledge, and University College London, still scientific knowledge as a buttress of natural theology figured most prominently among the justifications for its pursuit. Many scientists considered the moral and metaphysical imperatives of natural theology as a proper and integral part of their vocation and not as an intrusion of extraneous categories imposed by outside institutions.[18] Early presidents of the British Association repeatedly urged the interdependent relationship of science and theology. For example, in 1849 Reverend Thomas Romney Robinson, an astronomer, reminded the Association that

> ... science is not necessarily wisdom. To know, is not the sole nor even the highest office of the intellect; and it loses all its glory unless it act in furtherance of the great end of man's life. That end is, as both reason and revelation unite in telling us, to acquire the feelings and habits that will lead us to love and seek what is good in all its forms, and guide us by following its traces to the first Great Cause of all, where only we find it pure and unclouded. If science be cultivated in congruity with this, it is the most precious possession we can have —

[17] Sydney Ross, "'Scientist': The Story of a Word," *Annals of Science*, 1962, *18*: 65–86; *Third Report of the Royal Commission on Scientific Instruction and the Advancement of Science* (1873) in *British Parliamentary Papers, Education: Science and Technology* (Shannon: Irish University Press, 1970), Vol. IV, p. 15; G. A. Foote, 'The Place of Science in British Reform, 1830–1850,' *Isis*, 1951, *42*: 192–208.

[18] Gillispie, *Genesis and Geology*, pp. 3–49, 184–228; David L. Hull, *Darwin and His Critics: The Reception of Darwin's Theory of Evolution by the Scientific Community* (Cambridge, Mass.: Harvard University Press, 1973), pp. 37–67; Arnold Thackray, 'The Industrial Revolution and the Image of Science,' in Arnold Thackray and Everett Mendelsohn, *Science and Values: Patterns of Tradition and Change* (New York: Humanities Press, 1974), pp. 3–20; Arnold Thackray, 'Natural Knowledge in Cultural Context: the Manchester Model,' *American Historical Review*, 1974, 79: 672–709; David Layton, *Science for the People: The Origins of the School Science Curriculum in England* (New York: Science History Publications, 1973); George Foote, 'Science and Its Functions in Early Nineteenth Century England,' *Osiris*, 1954, *11*: 438–454; see also the annual reports of the British Association.

the most divine endowment. But if it be perverted to minister to any wicked or ignoble purpose — if it even be permitted to take too absolute a hold of the mind, or overshadow that which should be paramount over all, the perception of right, the sense of Duty — if it does not increase in us the consciousness of an Almighty and All-beneficent presence, — it lowers instead of raising us in the great scale of existence.[19]

Such convictions were not mere rhetorical window dressing. They influenced the behavior of men of science in their capacity as practicing scientists, defined the scope and intellectual context of scientific work, and frequently determined the kinds of questions and conclusions deemed appropriate or inappropriate for research.

Natural theology, whether derivative of the mechanical reasoning of William Paley and the *Bridgewater Treatises* or the idealist metaphysics of Richard Owen, could pose a major intellectual barrier to the further advance of critical empirical theory in science. A thoroughly naturalistic approach to the investigation of the universe was thwarted by considerations that had no intrinsic relationship to the undertaking. By midcentury many scientists had come to question or to reject the epistemological limitations established by regard for natural theology; yet those influences remained present throughout much of the scientific community. This division of opinion about the method and scope of science displayed itself in the debates over geology, natural selection, and the place of humankind in nature. However, as Robinson's statement indicates, the impact of religion extended beyond the strictly intellectual issue of epistemology. Scientific research stood subordinate to moral values, a concept of God, and a view of human nature that had been formulated by clergy and religious writers. Certain questions, areas of inquiry, methods of research, and conclusions were discouraged or proscribed because they carried the implication of impiety, immorality, or blasphemy. These limitations reflected the social context of early-nineteenth-century science in which clergy and laymen with strong religious convictions controlled access to much scientific patronage and employment. On more than one occasion practitioners of science, such as Charles Lyell and William Lawrence, had curbed or modified expression of their opinions for fear of offending both clerical and scientific colleagues.[20] The pervasive influence of natural theology and the derivative

---

[19] *Report of the Nineteenth Meeting of the British Association for the Advancement of Science* (London, 1850), pp. xliii–xliv.

[20] Leonard G. Wilson, *Charles Lyell, the Years to 1841: The Revolution in Geology* (New Haven: Yale University Press, 1972), pp. 310–315; Peter G. Mudford, 'William Lawrence and the Natural History of Man,' *Journal of the History of Ideas*, 1968, *29*: 430–436.

influence of the clergy meant the early Victorian scientific community was not yet self-defining in regard to its own function.

From the 1840s onward the size, character, structure, ideology, and leadership of the Victorian scientific world underwent considerable transformation and eventually emerged possessing most of the characteristics associated with a modern scientific community.[21] Between 1850 and 1880 the memberships of all the major scientific societies markedly increased, with many of them doubling their numbers. Total memberships during that period grew from 4,597 to 12,314. Even allowing for multiple memberships, there can be little doubt that the numbers of scientists rose considerably during the third quarter of the century. This increase in the size of the scientific community finds further confirmation in the expansion of the physics and chemistry faculties. In 1850 there were seventeen physics professors and two other faculty members teaching physics in the United Kingdom. By 1880 the figures had risen to twenty-eight and twenty-two respectively. The number of chemistry professors in 1850 was eleven, with four other chemistry faculty members. By 1880 the university chemistry faculties had expanded to twenty-five professors and thirty-four other instructors. Figures for the other sciences when calculated will probably reveal similar magnitudes of expansion.[22]

Directly tied to the growth of the scientific community was a new direction and character in its leadership. In 1847 the rules for membership in the Royal Society were reformed to favor the future inclusion of men whose achievements were scientific rather than social. That reform also included provisions for reducing the size of the society by limiting new memberships to fifteen annually. The long-term result would be a smaller society composed of practicing men of science. The year of the Royal Society reforms also saw the formation of the Philosophical Club, whose membership was limited to forty-seven persons each of whom had to be a researching and publishing scientist.[23] From the 1850s onward a group of newly arrived scientists whom Leonard Huxley later called 'the young guard of science'

[21] "... the 'scientist' is himself a social construct of the last hundred years or so. And, as usually understood, so are 'science,' 'the scientific community,' and 'the scientific career.'" Steven Shapin and Arnold Thackray, 'Prosopography as a Research Tool in the History of Science: The British Scientific Community, 1700–1900,' *History of Science*, 1974, *12*: 3.

[22] Dr. Roy M. McLeod has very generously furnished these figures to the author. The membership figures include the Chemical, the Geological, the Royal Anthropological, the Royal Astronomical, the Royal Entomological, the Royal Microscopical, the Royal Statistical, and the Zoological societies.

[23] Henry Lyon, *The Royal Society, 1660–1940* (Cambridge: Cambridge University Press, 1944), pp. 260–263, 282–283; T. G. Bonney, *Annals of the Philosophical Club* (London: Macmillan, 1919), pp. 1–3.

took up the public championship of professionalized science from the hands of persons such as Charles Babbage and the jurist William Grove.[24] The 'young guard' included as its chief spokesmen T. H. Huxley, John Tyndall, Joseph Dalton Hooker, George Busk, Edward Frankland, Thomas Archer Hirst, John Lubbock, William Spottiswoode, and Herbert Spencer, all of whom composed the X-Club, and Henry Cole, Norman Lockyer, Francis Galton, and Lyon Playfair.[25]

By the 1870s, in terms of editorships, professorships, and offices in the major societies, these men had established themselves as a major segment of the elite of the Victorian scientific world. Lockyer was the chief editor of *Nature* from its founding in 1869 until 1919. Hooker, Spottiswoode, and Huxley occupied the presidency of the Royal Society from 1873 until 1885. At one time or another between 1850 and 1900 one or more of this coterie served as president of the British Association for the Advancement of Science, the Anthropological Society, the Chemical Society, the Royal College of Surgeons, the Institute of Chemistry, the Ethnological Society, the Geological Society, and the Mathematical Society. They also held key positions in the Royal School of Mines, the Royal Institution, University College London, the Royal Botanical Gardens at Kew, the Royal Naval College, and the Solar Physics Observatory. They were also frequently consulted by the government on issues of scientific research, industry, and education.[26]

Such achievements had not been easy. These scientists had generally grown up on the peripheries of the English intellectual establishment. With a few exceptions they had not been educated in the English universities

[24] Leonard Huxley, *Life and Letters of Sir Joseph Dalton Hooker* (London: John Murray, 1918), Vol. I, p. 541.

[25] Other names, such as John S. Burdon-Sanderson, might obviously be added to this group. Three of the persons included may seem problematical. Galton held no professional offices, but worked consistently for the practical application of science and for its professional organization. Henry Cole was not a scientist, but as Secretary of the Department of Science and Art was one of the persons most vocal in calling for links between science and industry. Herbert Spencer was also no scientist, but he was treated by his contemporaries as a scientific figure and constituted a strong voice in the advancement of science.

[26] Consult the relevant articles in the *Dictionary of National Biography* and the *Dictionary of Scientific Biography*. See also D. S. L. Cardwell, *The Organization of Science in England* (rev. ed.; London: Heinemann, 1972), pp. 84–98, and the following series of important articles by Roy M. MacLeod: 'The Alkali Acts Administration, 1863–1884: The Emergence of the Civil Scientist,' *Victorian Studies*, 1965, *9*: 85–112; 'Science and Government in Victorian England: Lighthouse Illumination and the Board of Trade, 1866–1886,' *Isis*, 1969, *60*: 4–38; 'The X-Club: A Social Network of Science in Late-Victorian England,' *Notes and Records of the Royal Society of London*, 1970, *24*: 305–322; 'Of Medals and Men: A Reward System in Victorian Science,' *Notes and Recs. Roy. Soc.*, 1971, *26*: 81–105; 'The Support of Victorian Science: The Endowment of Research Movement in Great Britain, 1868–1900,' *Minerva*, 1971, *9*: 197–230.

but in their Scottish counterparts or in London medical schools, the civil service, the military, or in provincial dissenting communities. Although gifted and often brilliant, they had possessed no ready access to the higher echelons of Victorian society. There were all too few jobs that depended on merit rather than patronage. Neither public opinion nor government policy at midcentury generally recognized their social utility as scientists. The key to their own future social and financial security was the establishment of a greater public appreciation for science and its contribution to the welfare of the nation.

As expressed in 1868 in the prospectus of a short-lived journal called *Scientific Opinion*, such ambitious young scientists needed to advocate 'the cause of Science and the interests of scientific men in England, to enforce ... the claims of science upon the general public, to secure her followers their proper need of recompense and social distinction and to help them in their daily pursuits.'[27] To those professionalizing ends 'the young protagonists in science'[28] both individually and on occasion collectively participated in the Royal Society, the Philosophical Club, the British Association, and more specialized societies, delivered popular lectures to a variety of audiences, wrote textbooks, were active in the establishment of the unsuccessful *Reader* and the spectacularly successful *Nature*, served on and testified before government commissions for furthering scientific education, campaigned for the national endowment of research, and attempted to protect future physiological and medical research by doing battle with the antivivisectionists.[29] They repeatedly sought to relate the advance of science and of its practitioners to the physical, economic, and military security of the nation, to the alleviation of social injustice, to the Carlylean injunction for a new aristocracy of merit, and to the cult of the expert inherited from their utilitarian forerunners.[30]

Championship of the 'vigilant verification' of the empirical method and of a thoroughly naturalistic approach to science was integrally related to

[27] Quoted in *Nature*, 1969, *224*: 435.

[28] L. Huxley, *Life and Letters of Hooker*, Vol. II, p. 54.

[29] John Francis Byrne, *The Reader: A Review of Literature, Science, and the Arts, 1863–1867* (Ann Arbor: University Microfilms, 1965); Arthur Jack Meadows, *Science and Controversy: A Biography of Sir Norman Lockyer* (Cambridge, Mass.: M.I.T. Press, 1972), pp. 1–38; Richard D. French, *Antivivisection and Medical Science in Victorian Society* (Princeton: Princeton University Press, 1975), pp. 60–111.

[30] MacLeod, 'The Support of Victorian Science'; Roy M. MacLeod, 'The Ayrton Incident: A Commentary on the Relations of Science and Government in England, 1870–73,' in Thackray and Mendelsohn, *Science and Values*, pp. 45–80; Frank M. Turner, 'Victorian Scientific Naturalism and Thomas Carlyle,' *Vic. Stud.*, 1975, *18*: 325–343.

these professionalizing efforts.[31] The positivist epistemology constituted both a cause and a weapon. The 'young guard' agreed among themselves that science should be pursued without regard for religious dogma, natural theology, or the opinions of religious authorities. But neither such critical science nor its practitioners could flourish where the religious beliefs of clergy and other scientists could and did directly influence evaluation of work, patronage of research, and appointments in scientific institutions, the universities, and the public schools. By claiming their own epistemology as the exclusive foundation for legitimate science and as the correct model for knowledge generally, the professionalizing scientists sought to undermine the intellectual legitimacy of alternative modes of scientific thought and practice. Positivist epistemology provided an intellectual solvent to cleanse contemporary science of metaphysical and theological survivals. By excluding the kinds of questions as well as the answers that might arise from theological concerns, it also served to discredit the wider cultural influence of organized religion. Intellectual and social advance went hand in hand. For as the advocates of professional and critical science came to enjoy greater social prestige, their view of the purpose and character of science became more widely accepted, though not necessarily for philosophical or scientific reasons.

The drive to organize a more professionally oriented scientific community and to define science in a more critical fashion brought the crusading scientists into conflict with two groups of people. The first were supporters of organized religion who wished to maintain a large measure of control over education and to retain religion as the source of moral and social values. The second group was the religiously minded sector of the preprofessional scientific community, which included both clergymen and laymen. The debate within the scientific world deserves prior consideration because much of the harshest rhetoric stemmed from the determination of the aggressive, professionally minded scientists to exorcise from their ranks clergymen-scientists and lay scientists who regarded the study of physical nature as serving natural theology or as standing subordinate to theology and religious authority.

Since the seventeenth century the parson-naturalist and the academic clergyman-scientist had played a major and by no means inglorious role in British science, as the names of John Ray, Joseph Priestley, John Stevens Henslow, Adam Sedgwick, and William Whewell attest. Such scientists were often contributing members of the Royal Society and in some cases

---

[31] G. H. Lewes, *History of Philosophy from Thales to Comte* (4th ed.; London: Longmans, Green, 1871), Vol. I, p. xxxix. For further discussion of the character and function of this empirical epistemology, see Hull, *Darwin and His Critics*, pp. 37–67, and Turner, *Between Science and Religion*, pp. 17–23.

recipients of high awards for their work. During the 1830s the clerical scientists had joined the effort to found the British Association for the Advancement of Science and had served as its officers. For them natural science and natural theology, the clerical and the scientific callings, were not simply compatible, but complementary. From at least the 1840s onward, however, their position had become increasingly difficult. The naturalistic bent of theories in geology, biology, and physiological psychology drove deep wedges into existing reconciliations of scientific theory with revelation or theology. The faith that the truth of revelation and the truth of science must be the same had become severely strained. The place of humankind in nature particularly raised difficulties. Fewer lay scientists remained concerned with meshing science and religion.[32]

Besides urging a completely naturalistic view of nature and banishment of religious purposes and categories from scientific work, the drive by young lay scientists toward professionalization struck the clerical scientists on two other levels. The first was that of the degree of expertise that might qualify a person and his work for professional recognition and monetary support. In 1859 Huxley told Hooker in regard to a proposed research fund,

> If there is to be any fund raised at all, I am quite of your mind that it should be a scientific fund and not a mere naturalist's fund.... For the word 'Naturalist' unfortunately includes a far lower order of men than chemist, physicist, or mathematician. You don't call a man a mathematician because he has spent his life in getting as far as quadratics; but every fool who can make bad species and worse genera is a 'Naturalist.'[33]

Here was the cutting edge of the professionalizing spirit before which, as much as before the edge of objectivity, the amateur parson-naturalist fell. With or without the impact of Darwin and other new theories, the amateur's day as a 'man of science' was drawing to a close. As persons of Huxley's opinion and ambitions came to control the meager research funds administered by the Royal Society, the British Association, and other pro-

---

[32] Richard Westfall, *Science and Religion in Seventeenth Century England* (New Haven: Yale University Press, 1958); Gillispie, *Genesis and Geology, passim*; Walter F. Cannon, 'Scientists and Broad Churchmen: An Early Victorian Intellectual Network,' *Journal of British Studies*, 1964, *4*: 65–88; Michael Ruse, 'The Relationship between Science and Religion in Britain, 1830–1870,' *Church History*, 1975, *44*: 505–522; Milton Millhauser, 'The Scriptural Geologists: An Episode in the History of Opinion,' *Osiris*, 1954; *11*: 65–86; Robert M. Young, 'The Impact of Darwin on Conventional Thought,' in Anthony Symondson, ed., *The Victorian Crisis of Faith* (London: Society for Promoting Christian Knowledge, 1970), pp. 13–36.

[33] Leonard Huxley, *The Life and Letters of Thomas Henry Huxley* (New York: D. Appleton, 1900), Vol. I, p. 177.

fessional scientific societies, amateur scientists with marginal training and expertise could expect both less support and less recognition.

Second, the clerical scientists stood accused of dual loyalties that were incompatible with pursuit of thoroughly naturalistic science according to which theological, teleological, and metaphysical concerns stood banned both as matters for investigation and as principles of explanation. The emerging professional coterie considered 'scientifical-geological-theologians,' such as Hugh Miller and Adam Sedgwick, who continued to attempt to reconcile science and revelation, as public embarassments who resembled 'asses between bundles of hay, distorting their consciences to meet the double-call of their public profession.'[34] In the professional scientific community there would be little or no room for the person of two callings. Science and the scientist must serve the profession or community at large but not some particular religious doctrine, sect, or church to which scientific activity was subordinate. In this respect Philip Gosse and the Victoria Institute were as much a conclave of amateurs surviving into the dawn of the professional era as they were a group of orthodox theologians.

The professionalizers were not content merely to note or to ridicule the intellectual problems of the clerical scientist. In some cases they set out to prove that no clergyman could be a genuine man of science. Such an argument provided a secondary theme for Francis Galton's *English Men of Science: Their Nature and Nurture* (1872). This book was both a pioneering work of statistical inquiry and a professional manifesto that contended, 'The pursuit of science is uncongenial to the priestly character.'[35] To support this contention Galton noted that very few men whom he defined as scientists came from clerical homes. His own experience on scientific councils, he believed, confirmed his view of the incapacity of clergymen for serious scientific work. He explained that between 1850 and 1870 clergymen had occupied only 16 out of 660 positions on the councils of the major scientific societies, 'and they have in nearly every case been attached to those subdivisions of science which have the fewest salient points to scratch or jar against dogma.'[36] He quickly added, 'There is not a single biologist among them.'[37]

---

[34] L. Huxley, *Life and Letters of Hooker*, Vol. I, p. 520.

[35] Francis Galton, *English Men of Science: Their Nature and Nurture* (2nd ed.; London: Frank Cass, 1970), p. 24. See Victor L. Hilts, *A Guide to Francis Galton's* English Men of Science (Philadelphia: Transactions of the American Philosophical Society, 1975), N.S. 65, p. 5.

[36] Galton, *English Men of Science*, p. 26.

[37] *Ibid.* For this polemical passage Galton was compelled to fall back on his own experience with clergymen and scientists because the respondents to his questionnaire had overwhelmingly insisted the religious training of their youth and even their present religious convictions did not interfere with their scientific work. See *ibid.*, pp. 126–201, and Hilts, *Guide*, pp. 29–31.

Galton's tactic was a commonplace one within emerging professional groups edging out marginal members on the grounds of alleged indifference or incompetence. His real charge against the clergymen-scientists was that they were clergymen first, scientists second, and thus could not be good professionals as he and others had begun to define the term. Galton hoped to persuade his readers that since clergymen by virtue of their theological vocation could not be genuine scientists and could not honestly teach science, professional men of science seeking to serve the material needs of the entire community should occupy those positions of research and teaching in the universities and public schools presently occupied by clergy or persons appointed and controlled by clergy. The message was also relevant to the managers of the new school-board schools. Galton hoped those teaching positions as well as employment in government agencies would eventually 'give rise to the establishment of a sort of scientific priesthood throughout the kingdom, whose high duties would have reference to the health and well-being of the nation in its broadest sense, and whose emoluments would be made commensurate with the importance and variety of their functions.'[38] Banishment of clergymen from positions of influence in the scientific world and the abolishment of clerically dominated education were essential to that goal.

For inclusion in his data Galton had defined a 'man of science' with his professionalizing aims in mind. To qualify, a person had to have been elected to the Royal Society after 1850, that is, three years after the important membership reforms. Second, the scientist must have earned a medal for his work, presided over a learned society or section of the British Association, have been elected to the Council of the Royal Society, or occupied a professorship in an important college or university. These distinctly professional criteria effectively excluded both amateur aristocratic practitioners of science and the more notable of the clerical scientists, most of whom had been elected to the Royal Society prior to the reforms of 1847. Consequently, no matter what the quality of the work of the clerical scientists or the number of scientific honors and offices achieved, those people had almost no impact on Galton's data. Had he not so skewed his numbers by choosing the date of 1850, more clergymen would have been included. Moreover, some of those investigators would have been deeply involved with geology during a period when that science did indeed jar against dogma.[39]

---

[38] Galton, *English Men of Science*, p. 260.

[39] *Ibid.*, p. 4. In one case, that of Rev. John Stevens Henslow, Galton actually solicited information on a clergyman-scientist. Henslow was dead, but his son provided information. (The reasons for Galton's decision in this case are not known.) Hilts, *Guide*, pp. 13–14.

Galton's handling of his evidence in effect made prescriptive a steady decrease in the number of clergymen-scientists occupying significant positions in the scientific community. This process of clerical withdrawal from the world of science commenced in the third quarter of the century and is quite apparent in the figures recording the number of Anglican clergymen who were members of the Royal Society at various intervals during the last half of the century.[40]

Anglican clergymen members of the Royal Society, 1850–1900

Year	Total membership	Anglican clergy	Clerical percentage of total membership
1849	741	72	9.7
1859	636	57	8.96
1869	544	44	8.1
1879	488	27	5.5
1889	466	17	3.6
1899	449	14	3.1

During the entire lifetime of the Philosophical Club (1847–1901), the professionally oriented offshoot of the Royal Society, only two clergymen-scientists, Adam Sedgwick and Baden Powell, ever graced the membership roll.[41]

The figures for major participation by Anglican clergy in the British Association are equally striking. They are also perhaps even more indicative because the standards of the Association were less rigorous than those of the Royal Society.[42] From 1831 to 1865, the first thirty-five years of the Association's history, nine clergymen held the office of president, the last one in 1862. During the second thirty-five years of the Association's existence no clergyman was president. Prior to 1865 a total of fifty-two Anglican clergymen served in the rather honorary post of one of the Association's several vice presidents. From 1866 to 1900 the number fell to nineteen. A similar pattern occurred among the local secretaries of the Association who helped with the local arrangements for the annual meetings. During the first forty years (1831–1870) twenty-one clergymen attended to this task;

---

[40] The figures for this table have been calculated from the Royal Society membership lists published annually during the 19th century under the title of *The Royal Society*.

[41] See the membership lists and biographical sketches in Bonney, *Annals of the Philosophical Club*.

[42] These figures have been calculated from the officer lists published in the *Report of the Seventy-first Meeting of the British Association for the Advancement of Science* (London, 1901), pp. xl–lxxxiii.

between 1871 and 1900 only five clergymen did so. The number of Anglican clergymen presiding over the individual sections of the Association repeated the picture of clerical departure. In each case, clergymen gave way to lay professionals.

Anglican clergymen presiding over sections of the British Association for the Advancement of Science, 1831—1900

	1831–1865	1866–1900
Mathematics	15	2
Chemistry	4	0
Geology	6	0
Biology	8	1
Mechanical	8	0

This gradual severance of Anglican clergy from the world of British science reflected changes in the religious community as well as the harassment of the professionalizing scientists and the dispersion of theories incompatible with the Bible and natural theology. When early Victorian clerical scientists of stature, such as Sedgwick, Powell, and Whewell, died, there were few replacements from the ranks of the clergy. Many young clergymen not unnaturally had come to regard science as the enemy rather than the helpmate of religion. But reasons unrelated to developments in the scientific community also shaped this new attitude. A considerable body of clergy influenced by the Oxford Movement wanted the Anglican Church itself to become more autonomous from extra-ecclesiastical and extra–theological influences and to define its mission and character in terms of its own peculiar institutional and theological values. Most prominently they sought to liberate the Church of England from domination by the secular state. This movement also contained an intellectual component. The Bible and church tradition were to define doctrine and to serve as the foundation for religious truth and practice. Adjustment of theology for compatibility with science, such as had occurred in England since the age of Newton, implied a surrender of part of the intellectual and theological autonomy of the Church to nonreligious authority. Science, especially as defined by the professional man of science and as accepted by the contemporary liberal or Broad–Church theologian, was part and parcel of the liberalism rejected by the Tractarians and their followers.

As these clergymen — probably the most dynamic element in the mid-century Church — defined the priesthood in distinctly clerical, theological, and devotional terms, it became increasingly difficult for men who might wish to combine the priesthood and the scientific calling to do so. For professional scientists that double vocation seemed retrogressive, but for the high–church clergy it seemed too progressive and potentially rationalizing. Consequently, within the Church of England a clergyman–scientist confronted the choice of perpetuating traditional natural theology and risking ridicule by scientists or attempting further rationalization of theology in accord with science and encountering persecution by fellow clergymen.[43] The new rising clericalism in the Church gave further credibility to the stereotyped clergyman who disliked science and progressive thought generally.[44] The growing absence of clerical scientists seemed to prove that clergymen could not be scientists. Reform of the universities, removal of religious tests, and new opportunities for employment of scientifically trained persons in the government, school–board schools, the civic universities, and sometimes in industry meant that the Church and ecclesiastical patronage were no longer paths to the scientific career. By the third quarter of the century it had become increasingly clear that to be a scientist was one vocation and to be a clergyman was another. The professionalizing scientists seized upon these developments, not wholly of their own making, to effect an intellectual and social reorientation of the scientific community.

Yet fewer clergy in the ranks of the scientific world solved only part of the professional problem. Lay scientists, such as the powerful and much disliked Richard Owen, still retained active religious convictions, curried favor with the ecclesiastical hierarchy, and subordinated their intellectual enterprise to theological values.[45] This traditional and preprofessional outlook manifested itself in several British Association presidential addresses

---

[43] See n. 32 above and Chadwick, *The Victorian Church*, Vol. 1, pp. 309–324, 455–468, 476–480, 487–491; Kenneth A. Thompson, *Bureaucracy and Church Reform: The Organizational Response of the Church of England to Social Change, 1800–1965* (Oxford: Clarendon Press, 1970), pp. 26–55, 117–121; M. A. Crowther, *Church Embattled: Religious Controversy in Mid–Victorian England* (Hamden, Conn.: Archon Books, 1970), pp. 13–39, 138–240; Meacham, *Lord Bishop*, pp. 207–234; F. W. Farrar, 'The Church and Her Younger Members,' *Authorized Report of the Church Congress Held at Dublin* (Dublin: Hodges, Smith, and Foster, 1868), pp. 143–147. In regard to the changing character of the Anglican clergy during the third quarter of the century, the author wishes to acknowledge the aid of conversations with Prof. Josef Altholz of the University of Minnesota.

[44] 'The clergy have their ideal conception of men of science, and men of science have an equally ideal notion of the clergy. The ordinary parson creates an imaginary being bent on destroying the fact of a revelation, the truths of religion, and the difference between a man and a brute. This imaginary being he christens Professor Huxley. On the other hand, the man of science constructs an equally imaginary being who resists every step of physical research, who is blind to the most obvious facts, who has no sense to truth, and who is laboring to make others as blind and as untruthful as himself. This imaginary being he styles the English Parson.' J. R. Green, 'Professor Huxley on Science and the Clergy,' *The Saturday Review*, 1867, 24: 692. Such mutually distorting appeals to stereotypes are a common occurence during struggles over professionalization.

[45] Roy M. MacLeod, 'Evolutionism and Richard Owen, 1830–1868: An Episode in Darwin's Century,' *Isis*, 1965, *56*: 259–280.

during the sixties and early seventies and in the famous 'Scientists' Declaration' of 1865.[46] So long as this reverent spirit did not measurably interfere with a person's teaching, research, or peer evaluation, there was minimal professional difficulty. For example, despite his compromising with ecclesiastical authorities, his regular church attendance, and his reluctance to accept the antiquity of man and natural selection, no one really doubted Charles Lyell's professional loyalty. Nor did James Clerk Maxwell's theistic speculations based on the nature of molecules raise questions. The same was true of W. B. Carpenter, a distinguished Unitarian physiologist, who hoped that science might still provide some grounds for a personal theism. His faith was not professionally pernicious, and he stood more than ready to do battle with spiritualists and the antivivisectonists. All of these men generally succeeded in separating their religious faith from a critical approach to scientific research.[47]

There were, however, other more harmful cases of scientific allegiance to traditional religion. In 1875 P.G. Tait and Balfour Stewart published *The Unseen Universe*, in which they attempted to prove the validity of the Christian doctrine of immortality. These writers were answered and their speculations thoroughly criticized.[48] But the more significant target was any lay scientist who actually employed his scientific expertise to reconcile science with the doctrines of an ecclesiastical organization. Such a person had to be attacked frontally, for he was a remnant of those earlier scientific men who were, in Huxley's words, 'citizens of two states, in which mutually unintelligible languages were spoken and mutually incompatible laws were enforced.'[49] Professionally minded scientists would not tolerate persons who employed or seemed to employ science for ecclesiastical ends or in hope of ecclesiastical commendation.

St George Jackson Mivart, a Roman Catholic biologist, was just such a professional apostate who proved an irresistible and necessary target for

---

[46] Brock and MacLeod, "The 'Scientists' Declaration."

[47] Wilson, *Charles Lyell*, pp. 310–315; W. B. Carpenter, 'On Mind and Will in Nature,' *Contemporary Review*, 1872, *20*: 738–762, and *Mesmerism, Spiritualism, etc., Historically & Scientifically Considered* (New York: D. Appleton, 1877); James Clerk Maxwell, *Matter and Motion* (London: Society for Promoting Christian Knowledge, 1876); James Clerk Maxwell, 'Molecule,' *Encyclopedia Britannica*, 9th ed.; Lewis Campbell and William Garnett, *The Life of James Clerk Maxwell* (London: Macmillan, 1882).

[48] P. G. Tait and Balfour Stewart, *The Unseen Universe; or Physical Speculations on a Future State* (London: Macmillan, 1875); W. K. Clifford, *Lectures and Essays*, ed. Leslie Stephen and Frederick Pollock (London: Macmillan, 1901). Vol. I, pp. 268–300; P. M. Heimann, 'The Unseen Universe: Physics and the Philosophy of Nature in Victorian Britain,' *Brit. J. Hist. Sci.*, 1972, *6*: 73–79.

[49] T. H. Huxley, 'Past and Present,' *Nature*, 1894, *51*: 1.

professionalizing wrath. He had been a Huxley student, an adherent to natural selection, and a peripheral member of the Darwin circle. But in the late 1860s, Mivart came to entertain doubts (as did others at the time) about the sufficiency of natural selection alone to determine species. In the *Genesis of Species* (1871) he expressed his newly found skepticism and set forth supplementary explanations. The same year he also criticized an article on marriage and divorce written by George Darwin and did so in such a manner as to cast aspersions on the younger Darwin's moral character.[50] Each of these factors invited attack, but what particulatly aroused Huxley and required detailed refutation was Mivart's contention that evolution was perfectly compatible with the Church fathers and later Roman Catholic theologians. After numerous references to Augustine and Suarez, Mivart declared.

> It is then evident that ancient and most venerable theological author-
> ities distinctly assert *derivative* creation and thus harmonize with all
> that modern science can possibly require.... The various extracts
> given show clearly how far 'evolution' is from any necessary opposi-
> tion to the most orthodox theology.[51]

In this fashion Mivart hoped to reconcile the Roman Catholic Church of Pius IX to the general doctrines of modern science.

Mivart's immediate reward was perhaps the most scathing review essay ever to come from Huxley's pen. The proposed reconciliation might have saved evolution for the Church, but it would have directly undercut arguments for the pursuit of science oriented toward the profession and the community rather than toward the approval of ecclesiastical authorities. Mivart was also in effect suggesting that little difference separated religious and scientific epistemology. If sustained, Mivart's analysis would have perpetuated the dual citizenship in scientific work that Huxley and others of his opinion abhorred. To those of Huxley's professional persuasion, it was essential that evolution not be embraced by the Roman Catholic Church.

Consequently, Huxley spent several hours in an Edinburgh library reading Augustine and Suarez to assure himself, and later the readers of 'Mr Darwin's Critics' (1871), that the teaching of the Church was absolutely irreconcilable with evolution. Huxley also warned that no one should imagine that 'he is, or can be, both a true son of the Church and a loyal

---

[50] Jacob W. Gruber, *A Conscience in Conflict: The Life of St. George Jackson Mivart* (New York: Columbia University Press, 1960), pp. 52–114.

[51] St George Jackson Mivart, *The Genesis of Species* (New York: D. Appleton, 1871), p. 283.

soldier of science.'[52] That opinion came as a severe shock to the be-leaguered Mivart, who replied that 'it is not ... without surprise that I learned my one unpardonable sin ... the one great offense disqualifying me from being 'a loyal soldier of science' — was my attempt to show that there is no real antagonism between the Christian religion and evolution.'[53] Mivart, like most of the historians after him, assumed that the antagonism between science and religion related primarily to ideas, when in fact it was also profoundly involved with men and institutions. Still regarding physcial science as intimately related to natural theology, in good Baconian fashion, he had quite understandably failed to perceive that the issue at stake was not only the substance of theory but also the character of the scientific community and the right of its members to set the parameters of their thought, education, epistemology, employment, and social utility indepen-dent of considerations for religious doctrine or ecclesiastical organization.

Outside the boundaries of the scientific community the professionally minded scientists confronted further obstacles to their redefinition of the direction and role of science. As Peter Marsh has observed, 'Above Victo-rian England's nagging doubts, there was a thick layer of organized activity among all Christian denominations, thicker than at any time since the Civil War.'[54] This activity constituted the religious counterpart to the popular diffusion of science previously described by Clerk Maxwell. Between 1850 and 1880 ten new Anglican theological colleges were founded, and the number of priests rose from 17,320 in 1851 to 21,663 in 1881. From 1868 to 1880, approximately seventy new urban parishes were organized annually. In 1888 a spokesman at the Anglican Church Congress reported that between 1860 and 1885 over 80.5 million pounds had been expended on building and restoring churches, missions, charities, and education. The ritualist movement and the restoration of Anglican conventional life con-tinued to revitalize Anglo-Catholicism. In 1878 the Lambeth Conference approved reinstitution of auricular confession on a voluntary basis. Begin-ning in the late fifties and culminating in the seventies with the visit of the American evangelists Dwight Moody and Ira Sankey, revivals took place throughout the nation. Nonconformists and their preachers, such as Charles Spurgeon, were reaching the height of their influence. Under the leadership of Cardinal Manning, English Roman Catholicism made con-siderable headway among the poor. The third quarter of the century also

---

[52] Huxley, *Collected Essays*, Vol. II, p. 149.

[53] St George Jackson Mivart, *Essays and Criticisms* (London: James R. Osgood, McIlvaine, 1892), Vol. II, p. 60.

[54] P. T. Marsh, *The Victorian Church in Decline* (London: Routledge and Kegan Paul, 1969), p. 66.

witnessed a broad Roman Catholic religious revival in Ireland. These developments, as well as the launching of the Salvation Army, the intrusion of Spiritualism from America, and the spectacle of the miracle of Lourdes in France, proved fundamental to the scientists' perception of their situation in the general society and intellectual nation.[55] John Morley was not alone in his conviction that 'our age of science is also the age of deepening superstition and reviving sacerdotalism.'[56]

This climate of aggressive corporate and devotional religious revival, as much as their own naturalistic theories, brought the scientists into conflict with the clergy. Because of their friendships with liberal churchmen and their mutual resistance to theological excesses, unorthodox men of science have sometimes been portrayed as holding a position 'in which theological dogma was being attacked not for the sake of undercutting religious faith, but as a means of freeing that faith for what were regarded as nobler and more adequate forms in which it could find expression.'[57] This interpretation is largely, if not wholly, incorrect. It ignores the frequent disagreements between liberal theologians and advocates of science and obscures the social and professional goals of the professionalizing scientists.[58] The

---

[55] Kenneth Inglis, *The Churches and the Working Classes in Victorian England* (London: Routledge and Kegan Paul, 1964), pp. 27–28 41; George Kitson Clark, *The Making of Victorian England* (New York: Atheneum, 1971), pp. 169–171; J. Edwin Orr, *The Second Evangelical Awakening in Britain* (London: Marshall, Morgan, and Scott, 1949); Ralph W. Sockman, *The Revival of Conventional Life in the Church of England in the Nineteenth Century* (New York: W. D. Gray, 1917); Marsh, *The Victorian Church in Decline*, pp. 132–133; Emmet Larkin, 'The Devotional Revival in Ireland, 1850–1875,' *American Historical Review*, 1972, 77: 625–652.

[56] John Morley, *The Struggle for National Education* (2nd ed.; London: Chapman and Hall, 1873), p. 63.

[57] Maurice Mandelbaum, *History, Man and Reason: A Study in Nineteenth Century Thought* (Baltimore: Johns Hopkins University Press 1971), p. 30. For variations of this theme, see Walter Houghton, *The Victorian Frame of Mind, 1830–1870* (New Haven: Yale University Press, 1957), pp. 48–53, 70–71; William Irvine, *Apes, Angels, and Victorians: The Story of Darwin, Huxley, and Evolution* (New York: McGraw Hill, 1955), pp. 127–134, 339–341; Robert Young, 'The Impact of Darwin on Conventional Thought,' in Symondson, *The Victorian Crisis of Faith*, pp. 13–36.

[58] During the 1830s and 1840s certain scientists did see their work as leading to a higher, more rational conception of the deity. However, by the 1860s and later this impulse had become much more rare. Unorthodox scientists, such as Huxley, Tyndall, Galton, and Spencer, did repeatedly protest that they opposed ecclesiasticism and particular theological doctrines rather than religion itself; and they also allowed a limited role in personal life for inner emotional experiences which they, like contemporary religious liberals, classified as 'religious.' Such adherence to vague modes of liberal religion proved existentially useful to some of these scientists and also separated them from less respectable working-class atheists and secularists. But the critical scientists adamantly opposed religion as it was generally defined by religious authorities and spokesmen in their culture. Moreover, late Victorian religious liberals, such as Benjamin Jowett, James Martineau, and R. H. Hutton, understood that scientific naturalism was basically antithetical to both traditional and liberal Christianity. As the Broad-Church

latter sought to reform religion for the sake not of purifying religious life but of improving the lot of science in Victorian society. The intellectual authority frequently ascribed to the clergy, the Bible, and theological concepts such as divine providence exerted a pernicious influence on the practical affairs of everyday life. Traditional religious authority provided the justification for sabbatarianism, restrictive marriage laws, prayers to change the weather and to prevent disease, religiously dominated education, and other social practices that inhibited the discovery, diffusion, and application of scientific truth.[59] So long as that authority and those practices continued, the scientists could not achieve the cultural and social influence necessary for the establishment and improvement of their professional position.

Education provided the major arena for confrontation and conflict. In the mid–1860s liberal Bishop Connop Thirlwall shrewdly observed that much of the hostility between scientists and clergymen arose because 'Science is debarred its rightful share of influence in the education of the national mind.'[60] Penetration of the educational system at both the secondary and university levels would insure the dispersion of scientific knowledge and eventually lead to broader applications throughout the society. Achievement of a larger share of educational influence also meant to the professional scientific elite attainment of social legitimacy and prestige and of new areas of employment for students of science. The scientists' assault on the educational system necessarily required confrontation with the religious groups who controlled it and guided its curriculum. Acquiring professional inclusion in the major educational institutions involved attacking the sufficiency of strictly literary training, calling for removal of theological tests in the universities and informal requirements in the public schools, opposing denominational control of the school boards after the Education Act of 1870, and demanding that the science taught be science as

impulse came to have less and less influence within the church, the scientists made fewer and fewer accommodations. See n. 32 above and L. Huxley, *The Life and Letters of T. H. Huxley*, Vol. 1, pp. 233–239; Vol. II, p. 9: L. Huxley, *The Life and Letters of Hooker*, Vol. II, pp. 54–58; Tyndall, *Fragments of Science* (6th ed.; New York: D. Appleton, 1892), Vol. II, pp. 198–201; Karl Pearson, *The Life, Letters, and Labours of Francis Galton* (Cambridge: Cambridge University Press, 1930), Vol. IIIB, pp. 471–472; Herbert Spencer, *First Principles* (New York: P. F. Collier, n.d.), pp. 1–38; Evelyn Abbott and Lewis Campbell, eds., *Letters of Benjamin Jowett* (New York: E. P. Dutton, 1899), p. 190; James Martineau, *Essays, Reviews, and Addresses* (London: Longmans, Green, 1891), Vol, III, pp. 185–218; Vol. IV, pp. 165–268; Richard Holt Hutton. *Aspects of Religious and Scientific Thought*, ed. Elizabeth M. Roscoe (London: Macmillan, 1899).

[59] Frank M. Turner, 'Rainfall, Plagues, and the Prince of Wales: A Chapter in the Conflict of Religion and Science,' *J. Brit. Stud.*, 1974, *8*: 46–65.

[60] Connop Thirlwall, *Essays, Speeches, and Sermons*, ed. J. J. Stewart Perowne (London: Richard Bently, 1880), p. 287. Thirlwall drew his distinction between literary men and scientists rather than clergy and scientists, but from the essay it is clear that by literary men he meant clergy educated for their calling in the classics. For a direct challenge by a scientist to clerical

defined by professional scientists. This process involved more frequent clashes with Roman Catholics and Anglicans than with Protestant Nonconformists who in the seventies were themselves frequently calling for nonsectarian education.

A large measure of the scientists' complaint against religious influence over education and culture generally was reserved for Roman Catholicism, which Huxley described as 'our great antagonist' and 'that damnable perverter of mankind.'[61] Linking the advance of science to anticatholicism allowed the cause of the professional scientists to benefit from the widespread popular antipapist sentiment in Britain.[62] But much more was involved than anticatholicism. Under the pontificate of Pius IX the Roman Catholic Church epitomized the most extreme mode of religious authority and clerical pretension for control of intellectual life. The Church had specifically condemned the theory, methods, conclusions, and practice of modern science. However, as much as the general condemnation in the *Syllabus of Errors* (1864), the role of the Roman Catholic Church in Ireland accounted for the intense antipathy of the scientists. So long as Catholicism permeated Ireland and its hierarchy dominated the Catholic University, science and its practitioners could play no effective role in that nation. Ireland stood as an object lesson in the potential ecclesiastical blight of a nation; and the scientists, who were generally unionists, regarded Ireland as an integral part of Britain.[63]

educators, see John Tyndall, *Heat Considered as a Mode of Motion* (New York: D. Appleton, 1864), p. vi.

[61] T. H. Huxley, *Science and Education* (New York: D. Appleton, 1898), p. 120; L. Huxley, *Life and Letters of T. H. Huxley*, Vol. II, p. 242. During one session of the London School Board Huxley seems clearly to have used an appeal to anticatholicism to consolidate his position among other members who were otherwise somewhat unsympathetic to his general point of view. See *The Times*, Oct. 28, 1871, p. 11. Anticatholicism permeated the writings of the scientists and their allies. For examples of this sentiment, consult Edward B. Tylor, *Anahuac: or Mexico and the Mexicans, Ancient and Modern* (London, Longman, Green, Longman and Roberts, 1861), pp. 20, 126, 289; and W. K. Clifford, *Lectures and Essays*. Vol. II, pp. 233–234. In Draper's *History of the Conflict between Religion and Science*, as well as in the various editions of White's *Warfare of Science and Theology in Christendom*, the religion and theology in question were primarily Roman Catholic. Apparently outside Catholic journals few commentators noticed the anticatholic bias of the scientists. Three exceptions were Robert Buchanan, 'Lucretius and Modern Materialism,' *New Quarterly Review*, 1876, 6: 18: J. R. Seeley, *Natural Religion* (Boston: Roberts Brothers, 1882), *passim;* T. W. Marshall, *My Clerical Friends and Their Relations to Modern Thought* (London, 1873), pp. 263–270. Owen Chadwick in passing noted the problem of Catholicism for the scientists but did not emphasize it. However, a newspaper article which he cites as an example of interest in the conflict refers only to the problems of science with Roman Catholicism. Chadwick, *The Victorian Church*, Vol. II, pp. 2–3; *The Times*, May 25, 1864, pp. 8–9.

[62] G. F. A. Best, 'Popular Protestantism,' in Robert Robson, ed., *Ideas and Institutions of Victorian England* (London: Bell, 1967), pp. 115–142, and E. R. Norman, *Anti–Catholicism in Victorian England* (New York: Barnes and Noble, 1968).

[63] Gladstone's policy of Irish Home Rule and resentment over the fate of General Gordon were among the reasons for Huxley's debating Gladstone over Genesis. Huxley later explained, "It

It was against Irish Catholicism and more particularly against its impact on education that John Tyndall directed his notorious Belfast Address of 1874. In the course of his presidential address to the British Association Tyndall declared that men of science 'claim, and ... shall wrest from theology, the entire domain of cosmological theory. All schemes and systems which infringe upon the domain of science must, in so far as they do this, submit to its control, and relinquish all thought of controlling it.'[64] Probably no single incident in the conflict of religion and science raised so much furor. Most contemporaries interpreted Tyndall's remarks as applying to all churches. However, a careful reading of the address and of Tyndall's later 'Apology for the Belfast Address' (1874) reveals that by theology he meant Roman Catholicism in particular. A few months earlier the Irish Catholic hierarchy had refused the request of the laity for inclusion of physical science in the curriculum of the Catholic University. To a scientist with eyes to see, ecclesiasticism was alive, well, and prospering across the Irish Sea. Tyndall, who was an Anglo-Irishman, used his presidential address to chastise the Irish Catholic religious authorities.[65] But the widespread hostile criticism of the address throughout the British religious community suggested that Irish Catholic bishops were not the only religious authorities who aspired to limit the cosmological speculations of their flocks.

Within England the scientists were fighting a similar battle, although against a weaker mode of ecclesiasticism. Since the late thirties, provision of education for the nation had constituted the chief claim of the Church of England to social utility. Although the Education Act of 1870 destroyed the Anglican pretension to monopoly in that area, the Church continued to exercise widespread educational influence. Indeed the provisions of the Education Act served to stir new Anglican activity to avoid imposition of school-board schools.[66] However, probably at no time in modern history did the Anglican Church appear to be less of a *national* establishment. The ritualist controversy persuaded many people that the Church harbored potential or secret Roman Catholic clergy. The hostile reaction to *Essays and Reviews* discouraged hopes that the Church might become more liberal from within. The judicial actions taken against both the reviewers and the ritualists cast the Church of England in the role of a persecutor. In 1867 J. R. Green, the historian, complained, 'At present the breadth of the Church

---

was most important at the moment to shake him in the minds of sensible men." L. Huxley, *Life and Letters of T. H. Huxley*, Vol. II, p. 450; see also Vol. II, pp. 124, 130. Tyndall also attacked Gladstone on the Home Rule issue; see John Tyndall, *Mr. Gladstone and Home Rule* (2nd ed.; Edinburgh/London: William Blackwood, 1887).

[64] Tyndall, *Fragments of Science*, Vol. II, p. 197.

[65] *Ibid.*, Vol. II, pp. 196–197, 210–218. On the petition of the Irish Catholic laity, see *The Times*, Dec. 2, 1873, p. 7. Tyndall renewed his advice to Roman Catholics in the 'Prefatory Note'

is brought sharply out against the narrowness of the clergy. They do not even represent the Church. What then do they represent? Not the educated laity — the intelligence of England — but its unintelligence.'[67] Throughout the third quarter of the century the Anglican clergy appeared to the general public to be pursuing party goals within the Church and denominational ascendancy within the nation.

Such an institution in the eyes of many citizens seemed unfit to be the schoolmaster of the nation. Later the Church had to oppose raising standards of scientific education because the added cost would harm already tight budgets.[68] All of these conditions permitted the professional scientists not only to compare their rationalism with the faith of the clergy but also to contrast both implicitly and explicitly their own enlightened, practical, and unselfish goals with the apparently narrow, vested, dysfunctional, and denominational interests of the clergy. In opposition to Irish Catholic and Anglican ecclesiastical authorities who spurned the inclusion of science and other practical subjects favored by middle class parents, the scientists emerged as the educational party of national efficiency and imperial vision whose concerns and self-interest were at one with the medical, economic, military, and industrial requirements of the nation.

The internal ideology of much, though certainly not all, early Victorian science had been related to tracing the presence of the Creator in the creation. But that of the more nearly professionalized science in the second half of the century became the glorification and strengthening of the nation and its wealth. In 1870, during the Franco–Prussian War, Norman Lockyer argued,

> As there is little doubt that a scientific training for the young officer means large capabilities for combination and administration when that officer comes to command, we must not be surprised if the organization of our army, if it is to do its work with the minimum of science, will, at some future time, again break down as effectually as it did in the Crimea, or that our troops will find themselves over-matched should the time ever come when they will be matched with a foe who knows how to profit to the utmost from scientific aids.[69]

(1876) to White, *The Warfare of Science* (1876 ed.), pp. iii–iv.

[66] Marsh, *The Victorian Church in Decline*, pp. 72–81.

[67] Leslie Stephen, ed., *The Letters of J. R. Green* (New York: Macmillan, 1901), p. 142. About the same time Joseph Dalton Hooker told a correspondent, 'The worst of it is that the present condition of things prevents the rising talent and candid thinkers from entering the Church at all, and we shall be bepastored with fools, knaves, or imbeciles.' L. Huxley, *Life and Letters of Hooker*, Vol. II, p. 57.

[68] Marsh, *The Victorian Church in Decline*, pp. 79–81.

During the same period Henry Cole repeatedly pointed to the necessity for better scientific education as the key to Britain's continued economic supremacy. Edition after edition of *Nature* carried the same message. In 1875 the Devonshire Commission on which Huxley served and for which Lockyer was secretary declared that 'considering the increasing importance of Science to the Material Interests of the Country, we cannot but regard its almost total exclusion from the training of the upper and middle classes as little less than a national misfortune.'[70] The linking of the fortunes of science with the fate of the nation climaxed at the turn of the century when the elderly Lockyer lectured the British Association on 'The Influence of Brain Power in History' (1903) and when Karl Pearson in a whole series of books and articles proclaimed the necessity for scientists to advise the government and for politicians to pursue scientific policies and procedures in all areas of national life.[71] These were the arguments of concerned, patriotic Englishmen. But they were also the arguments of persons who understood that only by connecting in the public mind the future of their emerging profession with the welfare of the nation could they attain the financial support, employment, prestige, and public influence they desired.

Commenting in the mid–1920s on Draper's *History of the Conflict between Religion and Science*, Arthur Balfour observed, 'it is not perhaps surprising that the most interesting characteristic of Dr Draper's volume of 1873 is its total want of interest for readers in 1925.'[72] That development had not, however, come about because of any genuine intellectual reconciliation of science and religion. As David Lack has argued, 'The basic conflict is unresolved.'[73] Rather the social and professional context of science in Britain had changed. By World War I most Christian theologians had abandoned natural theology, and the clergy no longer seriously sought either to rival or complement scientists as interpreters of physical nature. From the standpoint of the scientists, their efforts to carve out for themselves an independent social and intellectual sphere had largely succeeded. The scientific community had become self-defining. Scientists had estab-

[69] Norman Lockyer, *Education and National Progress: Essays and Addresses, 1870–1905* (London: Macmillan, 1906), p. 4.

[70] *Sixth Report of the Royal Commission on Scientific Instruction and the Advancement of Science* (1875), *British Parliamentary Papers, Education: Science and Technical*, Vol. IV. p. 24.

[71] Lockyer, *Education and National Progress*, pp. 172–215. Karl Pearson, *The Ethic of Freethought* (London: T. F. Unwin, 1888), pp. 115–134; *National Life from the Standpoint of Science* (London: A. and C. Black, 1901); and *The Grammar of Science* (London: J. M. Dent, 1951), pp. 7–18. Bernard Semmel, *Imperialism and Social Reform: English Social-Imperial Thought 1895–1914* (Garden City, N. Y.: Doubleday, 1968), pp. 24–42.

[72] Lord Balfour, 'Introduction' in Needham, *Science, Religion, and Reality*, p. 4. Balfour alludes to Draper's preface of 1873; the book appeared in 1874.

lished themselves firmly throughout the educational system and could pursue research and teaching free from ecclesiastical interference. Science, as defined by the profession rather than for the profession, had become a part of national life. Politicians, such as Balfour and Haldane, though theists and authors of books on religious philosophy, no longer defended the Bible as had Gladstone. Rather they joined the chorus of spokesmen urging the national and imperial significance of science in light of the German economic and military threat.[74]

Asa Briggs once wrote, 'The conflict between science and religion petered out, giving way to new debates about the nature not of the Universe but of society.'[75] However, at its center much of the debate, including consideration of epistemological and scientific theory, had involved controversy about the social structure of the intellectual nation as well as about the structure of knowledge and of the universe. When the former set of issues had been resolved, many of the latter no longer furnished grounds for continued dispute. In this regard the Victorian conflict of science and religion represents one chapter in the still-to-be-written intellectual history of the emergence of the professionalized society in the West.

---

[73] David Lack, *Evolutionary Theory and Christian Belief* (London: Methuen, 1957), p. 9.

[74] Cardwell, *The Organization of Science in England*, pp. 156–187; George Haines, *Essays on German Influence upon English Education and Science 1850–1819* (Hamden, Conn.: Archon Books, 1969), pp. 47–48, 122–166; G. R. Searle, *The Quest for National Efficiency: A Study in British Politics and Political Thought, 1899–1914* (Oxford: Basil Blackwell, 1971), pp. 1–107.

[75] Asa Briggs, *The Age of Improvement, 1783–1867* (New York: David McKay, 1964), p. 488.

FRANK M. TURNER AND JEFFREY VON ARX

CHAPTER 10

VICTORIAN ETHICS OF BELIEF: A RECONSIDERATION

F OR one of his most successful assignments to undergraduates in his course on British and European intellectual history, Franklin Baumer in the late 1960s asked his students to compose a letter purportedly written in the 1870s by an English university student explaining to his father why he could not take Holy Orders. The twentieth-century students at first encountered some difficulty in comprehending why anyone should think twice about, let alone redirect his life over, the matter of the Virgin Birth unless the question were likely to appear on the entrance examination for medical school. However, the assignment produced exceedingly thoughtful papers. For, once their initial inhibitions had been overcome, the undergraduates realized that for most of those young Victorians the problem of religious belief was one of conscience. And the American undergraduate of the late 1960s, fully aware of the moral dimension of the great national debates of that decade, discovered a certain kinship of conscience with those troubled English students and scholars of a century ago.

Yet, we are by no means certain that today or a decade from now the epistolary assignment that Franklin Baumer employed with such success would continue to elicit good essays. It may be that the brotherhood of conscience between the young of our time and those of Britian's intellectual elite of a century ago may have diminished or vanished. We suspect that the students of the early 1980s may react to those troubled mid-Victorian consciences or the character of Robert Elsmere as John Maynard Keynes and his friends reacted to the demise of religious faith recounted in the biography of Henry Sidgwick when it appeared in 1906. Sidgwick had wrestled with the questions of what doctrines he could believe in good conscience throughout the 1860s. In 1869 he resigned his fellowship at Cambridge not because it required him to take Holy Orders but rather because its occupation presupposed acceptance of the Apostle's Creed. Reading about the early life of his one-time teacher, Keynes wrote to B. W. Swithinbank in March 1906:

> Have you read Sidgwick's Life? ... He never did anything but wonder whether Christianity was true and prove that it wasn't and hope that it was. He even learnt Arabic [*sic*] in order to read Genesis in the original, not trusting the authorized translators, which does

seem a little sceptical ... I wonder what he would have thought of us; and I wonder what we think of him. And then his conscience — incredible. There is no doubt about his moral goodness. And yet it is all so dreadfully depressing — no intimacy, no clear-cut crisp boldness. Oh, I suppose he was intimate but he didn't seem to have anything to be intimate about except his religious doubts. And he really ought to have got over that a little sooner; because he knew that the thing wasn't true perfectly well from the beginning.[1]

Perceptions as well as opinions do change. The pursuit of the dictates of conscience may be a necessary part of our humanity, but that pursuit does not necessarily manifest itself in the same way at all times or in all places. In the years separating Sidgwick's spiritual crisis and Keynes's letter a profound change had occurred among British intellectuals. Put quite simply, they had become more secular in their outlook. By the close of the century religious questions, concerns, and institutions troubled the inner lives of such people far less than they had in the 1860s. The debate over the ethics of belief, of which Sidgwick's doubts were a part, was a key engine of transition in that movement from religious to more nearly secular preoccupations among the British intellectual classes.

The issue of the ethics of belief arose in Britain during the late 1830s. Earlier in the century it had been assumed that to be an *honest Christian* was a problem of character and not one of intellect. That assumption received several challenges. First, the question arose of what it meant to be an honest Christian clergyman, and at a later point doubts were expressed as to whether one could be both an intellectually honest person and a Christian. The issue grew out of the Oxford movement and initially took the form of asking what did it mean on the part of a clergyman to indicate intellectual and religious acceptance of the Thirty-nine Articles of the Church of England? Did he interpret them in a Catholic manner as suggested by Newman's Tract 90 or in a more nearly Protestant manner? Was it morally right to accept them in the former fashion without so indicating publicly? By the late 1850s and 1860s the issue had largely redefined itself into a question of what meaning one ascribed to the Articles, the Creed, and the Bible? Could a clergyman or a layman who by virtue of his profession was presumed to accept those documents do so in a nonliteral manner or could he actually disbelieve a particular clause or portion of one of those documents? Again there arose the question of whether those reservations must be made public? Toward the end of the 1860s and throughout the 1870s, as

[1] Quoted in R. F. Harrod, *The Life of John Maynard Keynes* (London: Penguin Books, 1972) p. 135.

the clergy quarreled among themselves, agnostics, including T. H. Huxley, John Morley, and W. K. Clifford entered the fray. They raised the question of the morality of accepting or asserting the truth of any religious or philosophical statement on nonempirical evidence. Consequently, by the closing years of the century, when Keynes and his generation were coming of age, the problem of the truth of the interpretation of the Articles and the Bible seemed a much less significant issue than that of the perhaps fundamental incompatibility of maintaining both intellectual integrity and religious faith.

The question we wish to explore is what were some of the particular circumstances that caused or more properly allowed this debate over the ethics of belief to occur and that sustained it for so many years. Let us immediately caution that we are not contending that conscience itself was not a primary factor in the actions that men and women pursued in working through the ethics of belief for themselves and in making personal sacrifices, such as separation from their families and vocations. We believe, in other words, that they were sincere. However, we also believe that certain social, political, and ecclesiastical circumstances existed without which the debate either would not have occurred or would have taken a different direction.

Some of these circumstances were directly intellectual and related to books published and read or in vogue at a particular time. Religious and intellectual historians have been quite alert to these intellectual factors, such as the impact of Tract 90 upon the meaning of accepting the Thirty-nine Articles and the dissolvent influence upon religious faith of the works of Mill, Darwin, Spencer, and the higher critics of the Bible. However, in future studies we believe scholars of Victorian theology and religion must also address themselves to nonintellectual factors and must pose new, more skeptical questions to familiar documents. They must seek to understand the larger social and religious framework of ideas and institutions that both conditioned and channeled the personal responses to the dissolvent scientific and theological literature of the third quarter of the century. Both clergymen and laymen had experienced various modes of religious doubt and philosophic skepticism before this period, but only during these years did the experience take so collective a form and give rise to broad discussions and debate in essays, sermons, poetry, and novels.

In the remainder of this essay we will consider three conditions that made possible, though did not in and of themselves bring about, the Victorian manifestation of conscience in regard to the ethics of belief. They are *(a)* the religious revival of the first half of the century *(b)* the passage of the Clerical Disabilities Act of 1870, and *(c)* the political and social implications of different positions on the ethics of belief.

THE RELIGIOUS REVIVAL

It must never be forgotten that the immediate background and context for the years of theological doubt and scepticism was a period of ecclesiastical and devotional revival. The emergence of the problem of the ethics of belief was one by-product of the religious renewal within the Church of England. The leaven of Evangelicalism still touched the lives of young men and women coming of age in the 1840s and 1850s. The Tractarian influence continued to work its way even after the departures of Newman, Manning, and others to Rome. Moreover, the Broad Church party was stressing both a learned ministry and a heightened sense of social responsibility on the part of the Establishment. All of these developments meant that those people who were religious tended to regard both doctrine and devotion more seriously than in the first quarter of the century and that the ministry itself had come to be considered a more distinctly religious vocation. The problem of defining the ethics of belief was almost always closely related to the problem of vocation. And at the center of the crisis over the ethics of belief were young men about to enter the Anglican priesthood or recently ordained. The sense of the ministry as a religious vocation rather than one of social status was one result of the religious revival that had marked the Church of England in the first half of the century.

A letter written in 1816 by a young clergyman explaining the conditions of his acceptance of a particular curacy may serve to illustrate the contrast between Victorian clerical life and that which preceded it.

> The necessity of residing at Waterperry, did, I confess, at first make me hesitate from religious scruples, whether I ought to take the Curacy of it, that is, whether the kind of residence I meant was perfectly compatible with the full discharge of my pastoral duties in such a Parish. This led me to make enquiries, the results of which I am happy to say is satisfactory to me, principally on these two grounds; — first that the Parish is not so large as to require the constant residence of a Minister on the spot — and second, upon enquiring into the state of the Parish, I find such a system of education adopted under the liberal auspices of the Family presiding over it, as to render my daily attendance unnecessary, though I shall make it a point of duty to give it whenever I am in the parish. If I be asked what motives have induced me to divide my time between two places — I reply that it is certainly not done to unite the pecuniary advantages of both: — by sacrificing, as I shall do, those which I already possess by a constant residence here, I become a loser on point of income. My real and sole motive then, is this, to make myself as useful as I am

able to my Ministerial office, without giving up the advantages I derive from hence in point of Society. And now I think in the case under consideration that I may be permitted to unite the advantages without prejudice to either, lawfully and conscientiously.[2]

Even as they were written, these sentiments and the view of the ministry they implied were encountering grave difficulties. By 1816 the success of the Methodists, the growing vigor of the Nonconformists, and the ever-growing presence of rationalism, secularism, and Owenism stirred the Church of England from without as the efforts of the Evangelicals and later the Tractarians did from within. The Low Church stressed the preaching ministry, the High Church the sacramental ministry, and the Broad Church the socially responsible ministry. Each of the major ecclesiastical parties for its own particular reasons was reinterpreting the ministerial vocation from one of political and social patronage into one of devotional duty. All would have criticized the new curate of Waterperry.

The revival of the first half of the century stirred a new understanding of the Church of England as a corporate religious body and its priesthood as a devotional vocation actively supporting defined doctrine. The ethics of belief could become problematical only for clergymen or potential clergymen who had learned to take seriously and earnestly the life of the church and its theological foundations. Such was the state of mind of a significant number of vocal clergymen by the third quarter of the century. The Oxford movement had initially called forth a new religiosity and devotion on the part of the Anglican ministry. The theological extremes to which for better or worse some of its leaders carried their convictions elicited a reaction that sought to delineate more strictly and dogmatically the parameters of Anglican doctrine. As a result of this new awareness of devotion, doctrine, and religious duty, those people who grew up in either Evangelical or Tractarian homes during the 1840s and 1850s always viewed the Church of England primarily as a religious institution and its ministry as a body of men called to devotional service and theological loyalty. It was for such people, who became the articulate spokesmen of the 1860s, that the ethics of belief became problematical. It was for this reason that to the end of his life Sidgwick, himself an unbeliever, argued that the Anglican clergy must genuinely believe the doctrines of the Articles and the Creed. Unlike Matthew Arnold, the heir of the latitudinarian tradition, Sidgwick and others like him even in their unbelief could not regard the church merely as an institution of national culture.

This new sense of the church as a distinct corporate body clearly defined

---

[2] Quoted in D. McClatchey, *Oxfordshire Clergy, 1777–1869: A Study of the Established Church and of the Role of Its Clergy in Local Society* (Oxford: 1960), pp. 35–36.

by devotion, doctrine, and ministry also had the effect of exacerbating and hardening the differences between churchmen and doubters. When one group came increasingly to understand itself in terms of an exclusive clerical identity, for a person even to begin to doubt was to place himself beyond that charmed circle, and even over against it. When, for example, in 1862, the Reverend Leslie Stephen of Trinity Hall, Cambridge, began to entertain doubts about the literal truth of Noah's flood, he immediately concluded that he could no longer conduct the services in the college chapel that fell to him.[3] This decision in its turn precipitated a request from college authorities that he resign the position of tutor to undergraduates, which he held in virtue of being a fellow in orders. Soon thereafter, Stephen left Cambridge for London to embark on a career in journalism, never to return again in an academic capacity. Where once Stephen had been a liberal churchman, working from within the Anglican university system for moderate reforms, such as the admission of Dissenters to degrees, he very rapidly found himself thrust outside it. That he became a bitter opponent of any privileged place for the English Church in education was due in no small measure to this peculiar dialectic affecting doubt in a period of clerical resurgence: even to begin to question the accepted beliefs of the group had the ineluctable effect of excluding one from the fold.

Moreover, this same period witnessed both a new emphasis on the authority of the Bible and the Articles and a widespread disagreement over their interpretation. The more seriously the doctrines and documents of the faith were taken from the Tracts onward, the less agreement there existed over their meaning. The answer of the state to this impasse was to relieve the ecclesiastical authorities of their power of enforcing conformity and to impose theological pluralism through the major ecclesiastical judicial decisions and legislation of the 1850s and 1860s. This solution addressed the problem from an erastian point of view, but skirted the theological issues by failing to consider the Church of England as part of the Holy Catholic Church. And it was as part of the latter, whether in an Evangelical or Tractarian sense, that a large number of clergymen considered themselves ministers.

This heightened religiosity of the clergy meant that judicial decisions outlining legal conformity could not define the ethics of belief as Rowland

[3] See Stephen's account of his loss of faith in 'Some Early Impressions,' *Nation* 42 (October 1903), 70ff.; also in the 'Mausoleum Book,' an unpublished memoir Stephen wrote for his children, now in the British Library, BM AddMss 57920, especially p.4

[4] Rowland Williams, *Hints to My Counsel in the Court of Arches* (London: 1861–1862). Williams was concerned to separate a legalistic manner of avoiding conflict over the affirmation of the Thirty-nine Articles and a genuinely theological consideration of what such affirmation implied.

Williams, one of the contributors to *Essays and Reviews*, once explained to the consternation of Fitzjames Stephens, his counsel.[4] Consequently in a legally latitudinarian state church, the genuinely faithful and self-examining clergyman was thrown back upon no other support or authority for his theological integrity than his own conscience. As a nameless minister wrote the *Times* in 1862,

> Who at this day shall say what really is the doctrine, or where is to be found the defined discipline of the Church? People travel a good deal in the summer months, and it for ever happens that you find in one church different ceremonial, different preached doctrine from what you found in the place you last left.... We are at sea with compasses unadjusted, with no true chart, no real pilots ... What is next to heresy in one diocese is unorthodox in another; what is laid down in one parish as vital truth in the next is denounced as most opposed to it.[5]

Theological pluralism imposed by the state on an ecclesiastical body served by a clergy with a new distinctly religious and doctrinal conception of their vocation resulting from the years of devotional and ecclesiastical revival was the fundamental condition that made wholly problematical the ethics of belief.

THE CLERICAL DISABILITIES ACT (1870)

In 1862 criticizing the authors of *Essays and Reviews*, Bishop Samuel Wilberforce contended that men holding such liberal theological views 'cannot, consistently with moral honesty, maintain their posts as clergymen of the Established Church.'[6] It was all very well for Wilberforce to make this statement and for other people to entertain similar sentiments in silence. However, at the time when the bishop wrote, there existed no legal means whereby an Anglican clergyman might renounce his calling without encountering considerable social, legal, and financial obstacles. An Anglican priest could resign his offices and livings, but under Canon 76 he could not relinquish his vows and legally become a layman. Nor could a clergyman who had resigned his benefice enter any of the other learned professions, sit in the House of Commons, or serve as a member of a municipal corporation. Moreover, he could not without danger of prosecution in ecclesiastical courts become a protestant Nonconformist minister. As a writer in the *Quarterly Review* of 1850 explained the situation, clergymen might conceal

---

[5] *Times* (London), June 25, 1862, p. 9.

[6] Quoted in James C. Livingston, *The Ethics of Belief: An Essay on the Victorian Religious Conscience* (Tallahassee, Fla., 1974), p. 4. The authors are much indebted to this excellent monograph.

their disagreement with Anglican doctrine (in this context as that disagreement related to Nonconformity) or forego the exercise of their priestly functions,

> but if their own inward persuasion urges them to active and public exertion — nay, as it would seem, even if they become private or lay members of any religious sect — they are liable not only to censures properly ecclesiastical, as consisting in the deprivation of ecclesiastical privileges, but to monitions respecting their personal conduct, the disregard of which may entail the penalty of imprisonment.[7]

Paradoxically, the only calling that a resigned Anglican clergyman could undertake without danger of legal difficulties of any kind was the Roman Catholic priesthood, which the law protected from prosecution.

The Clerical Disabilities Act of 1870 removed these various prohibitions that had meant that only an Anglican clergyman with substantial private means could follow the dictates of conscience if he disagreed with doctrine. Yet the story of its passage illustrates how far the concerned members of Parliament stood from any real perception or understanding of the problem of the ethics of belief.

The matter originated in the mid-1840s in the diocese of Bishop Philpotts of Exeter when an Anglican priest by the name of Shore, being possessed of what seventeenth-century writers called a 'tender conscience,' wished to leave the ministry of the established church to serve a Nonconformist chapel in the same neighborhood. Mr Shore began his new ministry, but soon found himself in the Bishop's Court accused and then convicted of a violation of canon law. He was duly deprived of his offices and privileges. The bishop said that he had followed this course of action so that Mr Shore might properly move to his new congregation. The only meaningful penalty imposed on Mr Shore was court costs, which he refused to pay. For that refusal he was promptly imprisoned. Though Mr Shore was ultimately released, the upshot of his case was a formal decision by the Court of Queen's Bench that a clergyman of the Church of England could not relinquish his calling.[8]

The second result of the Shore case was a more than twenty-year sporadic effort to modify the laws binding the Anglican clergy to their occupation. A measure to this end first came before the House of Commons in 1848 but was only fully debated in 1849. On February 22, 1849, Edward Bouverie submitted a private bill that would have permitted an Anglican

---

[7] *Quarterly Review*, American ed., 87 (1850); 25.

[8] For further details of the Shore case, consult *Quarterly Review*, American ed., 87 (1850): 22–43.

clergyman to declare his dissent from the Church of England and then be permitted to enter the Nonconformist ministry. None of the debate on this measure touched directly on the ethics of belief. The first question posed to Bouverie was whether the resigned clergyman would be eligible to sit in the House of Commons. Bouverie replied in the affirmative. In the debate of March 14, 1849, a speaker voiced fear that there might be some clergy 'who would be induced to leave the Church, solely because they saw some good opportunity of holding a secular employment of profit and advantage either by death, or some other changes in their own families.'[9] Here the issue was that of younger sons who because of the death of an elder brother might inherit an estate and with it the possibility of a political career. Bouverie himself saw the chief problem as clergymen being compelled to preach insincerely or to face ecclesiastical penalties for preaching to a Nonconformist congregation. Throughout the debate the question was considered exclusively in terms of the relationship between the Establishment and Nonconformity. At no time did anyone raise the possibility that an Anglican clergyman might not simply dissent from the Articles but actually disbelieve them in a substantial theological rather than liturgical manner. The bill passed the Commons, but reached the Lords too late in the session for action before Parliament was prorogued.

Bouverie revived his effort in 1862. There was no clear reason for the long delay, but as before he seemed to have been responding as a private member to outside pressure. This time he emphasized that the new measure would aid both those clergymen who wished to become Nonconformists and those who for one reason or another wished to renounce the clerical vocation but still remain in the Church of England. He stressed that there were men of goodwill and genuine honesty who had quite simply changed their minds about their vocation since as young students they had taken Holy Orders. *In passing*, he also noted that men such as the authors of *Essays and Reviews* could not presently leave the church. He did not suggest whether or not they wished to leave or should leave.[10]

Opponents of the measure continued to avoid the matter of fundamental theological convictions. For example, William Heathcote suggested there were really very few people who would benefit from the measure. He raised the matter of membership in the House of Commons and also insisted that a distinction be drawn between those who wished to leave the ministry for sound reasons and

> others who might be tempted to enter the Church for the purpose of trying whether they should draw prizes or blanks, and who, if they

---

[9] *Hansard*, 3rd ser., 103 (1849): 697.

[10] *Ibid.*, 166 (1862): 718, 722–724.

should draw blanks would not hesitate to leave it to try their hand in some mercantile or legal occupation, or perhaps, to obtain seats in that House.[11]

Another opponent feared clergymen might take the opportunity of leaving the ministry to avoid prosecution in an ecclesiatical court for some grave moral offense. However, in the final debate Bouverie declared that 'unless some measure of the kind were passed, the clergy of the Church of England would remain the only people in the kingdom who were deprived of all liberty of conscience.'[12] Again the bill failed when its third reading was postponed past the date of the recess. There seems to have been no concerted effort to stop the measure, but as a private bill it simply became lost in the legislative shuffle. The need for passage did not yet seem acute.

During the rest of the 1860s even without the benefit of a clerical disabilities measure numerous clergymen or potential clergymen abandoned their vocation. Certain developments made this act of conscience (and in some cases an act of prudence) somewhat easier and in very meaningful ways reduced both the financial and social cost of the action. The growth of a liberal, industrial, secular state and society created new vocational opportunities for educated men and presented a constant panorama of change. During the 1860s it became possible from the standpoint of the Bar for an Anglican clergyman to enter the legal profession if he promised he would no longer pursue his clerical duties. The same decade also witnessed the expansion of the publishing industry with several new journals appearing in London. It will be recalled that earlier the editorship of *Fraser's* had provided employment for James Anthony Froude after he decided against the clerical vocation. Various journals in the 1860s did the same for Leslie Stephen. And, of course, the passage of the Education Act of 1870 opened new vocational opportunities in the teaching profession. Moreover, there must also have been academic figures or potential academic figures who realized that it would be only a matter of time until religious tests were removed from the universities as they finally were with certain exceptions in 1871. Yet the Anglican ministry remained a profession without the possibility of legal exit.

The Clerical Disabilities Act was enacted in 1870. The act originated again from a private bill, but one that enjoyed Gladstone's public blessing.[13] It permitted an Anglican clergyman to leave the ministry by registering a deed of relinquishment with the Chancery. After the passage of

---

[11] *Ibid.*, p. 728.

[12] *Ibid.*, 168 (1862): 92.

[13] *Times* (London), Feb. 9, 1870, p.12.

six months he again became a layman in the eyes of the law, possessing all the normal rights of a layman. The measure that had originally passed the Commons had also permitted the former clergyman to return to the ministry. This clause was removed in the Lords. There the bishop of London voiced anxiety that the two doors would allow a man who had failed in a secular career to return to the security of the church. Only the bishop of Llandaff supported the idea of re-entry, because he believed that certain men who entertained serious theological or vocational doubts would be able to return to their clerical calling after they had come to peace with themselves. The other bishops and lords were not so persuaded.[14] The Commons agreed to the change in order to save the bill from another parliamentary demise. On August 9, 1870, the Clerical Disabilities Act became law.

Only when such unhampered departure from the ministry became both legally and practically feasible was much of the discussion about the proper ethical behavior of the clergy in regard to the ethics of belief, such as Sidgwick's *Ethics of Subscription* of 1870, functionally valid. Only with this law on the books could one discuss whether a liberal clergyman should fight for his convictions within or without the Church of England. To depart over matters of conscientious theological disagreement was no longer tantamount to signing one's economic death warrant. This act in conjunction with new vocational opportunities for educated men allowed the Anglican clergy to afford to be conscientious. Moreover, the law also meant that the decision to stay within the church to fight for the liberalization of theology now became a decision that could stem from conscience rather than from economic or legal necessity. Finally, the knowledge on the part of church authorities that departure of clergy was freely possible may well have played a role in the gradual but steady liberalization of creedal requirements for the clergy. In effect, the act permitted conscience to be more liberally exercized and ultimately required that conscientious differences be recognized and tolerated.

CONCRETE IMPLICATIONS OF INTUITIVE AND EMPIRICIST EPISTEMOLOGY

From the appearance of Tract 90 until the late 1860s the debate over the ethical implications of belief remained primarily an intrachurch matter. But from the close of the 1860s until the early 1880s the ethics of belief became discussed in a wide public arena where questions and considerations other than those applying to the church and clergy were raised. The public discussion was largely the result of the existence of the Metaphysical Society and the work of enterprising editors who saw that many of the

[14] *Hansard*, 3rd ser., 203 (1870): 928, 1065–1068.

papers read before the society and issues debated there appeared in the new journals.[15] But both the activity of the society over more than a decade and the public interest in these ethical and epistemological debates as manifested in the success of the *Contemporary Review*, the *Fortnightly Review*, and the *Nineteenth Century* suggest that in the 1870s the participants and observers saw immediate matters of social, educational, and political policy, as well as existential issues of determining right and wrong, involved in these discussions. It is this public interest in these debates that differentiates them from the later discussions of the Aristotelian Society, where similar philosophical issues were aired.

There were at least three major national questions about which the epistemological issues debated at the Metaphysical Society carried immediate implications. The first of these was the direction of the Church of England and of those institutions that it controlled or influenced. It is often assumed that the controversy over the direction of the Church of England in the period under consideration continued to be principally an affair among factions within the church — of Ritualists, Broad Churchmen, and Evangelicals struggling for control of doctrine, discipline, and worship. Certainly it was true, as the career of someone like Archbishop Tait illustrates, that party conflict was the most pressing of all the issues confronting Anglican leadership in these decades.[16] If, for example, the parties of orthodoxy prevailed, whether of the Ritualist or the Evangelical variety, the intellectual life of the church as a national institution would be very different than if a moderate freedom of thought accommodating the church to science, criticism, and historical method won out. If the Church of England through its bishops, leading spokesmen, and clergy wrapped itself in the cloak of intuition, that institution would become a major roadblock to intellectual and educational progress and enlightenment. From the standpoint of liberal churchmen, such as A. P. Stanley or J. R. Seeley, who wanted the Anglican Establishment to survive as a sensible and moderately progressive institution, adherence to intuitive epistemology on the part of the clergy meant the church would cut itself off from the nation and ultimately from the future.

But what is less clearly perceived is the degree to which events within the church occupied the attention and set the terms for broader discourse about social issues among thinkers who viewed the church from without. The attitudes of these outsiders — who had left the church but who related

---

[15] See Alan Brown, *The Metaphysical Society: Victorian Minds in Conflict, 1869–1880* (London, 1947).

[16] See P. T. Marsh, *The Victorian Church in Decline: Archbishop Tait and the Church of England 1868–1882* (London, 1969).

to it from a stance of doubt — toward the question of belief was inevitably colored by their perception of what the social effects of ecclesiastical developments might be. One receives a striking impression of how large religious and ecclesiastical affairs could loom for a typical freethinker by looking at the journalistic output of Leslie Stephen between 1866 and 1873. During these years Stephen, who had for some time ceased to consider himself a Christian, published articles under the following titles: 'Ritualism,' 'Dr Pusey and Dr Temple,' 'The Broad Church,' 'The Religious Difficulty,' 'Matthew Arnold and the Church of England,' 'Mr Voysey and Mr Purchas' (in the matter of two clergymen, one a theological liberal, the other a Ritualist, both threatened with legal action), 'Religion as Fine Art,' 'Darwinism and Divinity,' and 'Are We Christians?'[17] At the same time, he contributed a fortnightly column on English affairs to the American magazine the *Nation*. These columns provided a continuous and detailed narrative of events and controversies affecting the church: the trials and tribulations of Ritualist clergymen, the latest heterodox publication by a theological liberal, the prospects of disestablishment. From a certain perspective, it is not surprising that an opponent of the church like Stephen should be concerned to follow so closely its fortunes. If indeed the progress of society depended on the liberation of the intellect from the constraints of theological doctrine, it was well to know the movements of the enemy. But this perspective on Stephen's interest in ecclesiastical affairs does not do justice to the way in which this preoccupation affected his outlook on many other things besides.

It is often assumed that, in the late 1860s and 1870s, the epistemology of religious belief was under serious attack, and that as a consequence the church was on the retreat on the social front as well. If men like Stephen took the time to write against the church, so this interpretation runs, it was to deliver telling blows against a staggering foe on behalf of a new world view that was scientific, secular, and progressive. However, if one looks closely at the theological and ecclesiastical writings of Stephen for this period, an interpretation that views them as the initiatives of aggressive freethought must be revised. Almost without exception, the articles cited above were written in reaction to some threat posed by one or another party in the church. In 'Ritualism,' for example, Stephen perceived two

---

[17] 'Ritualism,' *Macmillan's Magazine* 17 (1868), 479–494: 'Dr Pusey and Dr Temple,' *Fraser's Magazine* 80 (1869), 722–737; 'The Broad Church,' *Fraser's* NS 1 (1870), 311–325; 'The Religious Difficulty,' *Fraser's* (1870), 623–634; 'Matthew Arnold and the Church of England,' *Fraser's* 2 (1870), 414–432; 'Mr Voysey and Mr Purchas,' *Fraser's* 3 (1871), 457–468: 'Religion as Fine Art,' *Fraser's* 4 (1872), 156–168; 'Darwinism and Divinity,' *Fraser's* 5 (1872), 409–421; 'Are We Christians?' *Fortnightly Review* 19 (1873) 281–303.

grave dangers. First, the exaltation of the priesthood as a caste, which Stephen calls sacerdotalism, exploited the need of uneducated or unintelligent people — he notes the appeal of Ritualism to women and to the poor — for leaders in whom they could place their trust. Second, the use of gorgeous ceremonial responded to a widespread desire for 'embodiments in image of the spiritual aspirations of mankind.' Though he believed sacerdotalism and religious ceremonial were profoundly retrograde in their social tendency, he could not help wondering whether the upsurge of Ritualism represented 'the resuscitation of faiths which have suffered a temporary eclipse.'[18] Similarly, developments within the Broad Church party or liberal wing of the church filled Stephen with foreboding. The reinterpretation of dogmas on terms more acceptable to the modern mind by men like Matthew Arnold undercut efforts of freethinkers like Stephen to construct a new post-Christian intellectual synthesis. Moreover, the attempts of Broad Churchmen to achieve religious comprehension by these measures of theological accommodation threatened one of the strongest points in the secularist critique of the church: that Christianity inevitably tended toward sectarian exclusivism, and therefore could never serve as a firm basis for national unity.[19]

Finally, not only the terms, but even the structure, of discourse about the social implications of belief in this period were strongly influenced by events within the church. For Stephen as for other freethinkers like John Morley and Frederic Harrison, disestablishment became the key to a new direction in the development of society. Stephen conceived this new direction from a progressive point of view that owed much to Auguste Comte's law of the three stages. The goal of intellectual development, according to Comte's law, was a stage in which all phenomena, including social phenomena, could be understood according to scientific law. But in order for this positive stage to be reached, it was necessary first for the restrictions that supported an older, theological point of view to collapse. For this reason, Stephen scanned the signs of the times, looking for indications of the demise of the established church that would presage the emergence of a new, positive age. He followed with great interest the growing consensus among Ritualists that the freedom and autonomy of the church required the severance of its links with the state. When Evangelicals, upset by the reluctance of the courts to move against heterodoxy and ritualistic excesses, began agitating for disestablishment as well, Stephen took this as a sign

[18] See 'Ritualism,' 492, 480; also 'Religion as Fine Art,' 160, 162.

[19] See the articles 'The Broad Church' especially 318; and 'Matthew Arnold and the Church of England,' especially 427.

that the demise of the church had begun, and the new age was at hand.[20]

What Stephen did not realize was that these signs both permitted and received just the opposite interpretation. The agitation of Ritualists and Evangelicals for disestablishment, and the initiatives of Broad Churchmen could signify just as well an intensification of the sense of mission by groups within the church. Stephen borrowed from church parties, especially from the Ritualists, the conviction that new departures in the church's self-understanding were closely connected with the advent of a new age. Where churchmen viewed the connection eschatologically — a new age required new forms of witness — Stephen chose to see it from the perspectives of a developmental theory that equated progress with the decline of the church. From this perspective, the growing sense of clerical corporate identity and mission that led churchmen to reexamine — whether critically or positively — the link with the state, seemed to Stephen a symptom of collapse. Which perception of the significance of controversy within the church was accurate is not relevant to the purpose of this essay. More important is to recognize that for Stephen, social progress was a matter that depended on what he perceived to be the direction of the Church of England.

The second public issue on which epistemological questions had broad implications was education. From the mid-1860s through the mid-1870s (and really well beyond) the questions of the relationship of public education to church-supported schools and religious teaching was one of the most bitterly disputed of political topics.

One need only consider the controversies surrounding the Education Act of 1870 to see how the debate about belief carried over into the public arena. The Education Act, drawn up by W. E. Forster, vice-president of the Council Board on Education in Gladstone's first ministry, had been designed to meet one of the most pressing needs of an industrial democracy: an effective system of universal elementary education. However, in framing the act, Forster had to contend with two conflicting interests. On the one hand, the majority of already existing schools in the kingdom were controlled by the Church of England, which was not likely to surrender them to state control. On the other hand, the strongest advocates of universal compulsory education were Protestant Nonconformists, who demanded that any national system, especially one supported through the rates, be nonsectarian. To compromise these interests, Forster proposed what amounted to a mixed system. Voluntary schools that already existed, or that would be established in a certain period of time, would receive outright grants from Parliament. But wherever they were needed, local school boards could be

[20] See Stephen's columns in *Nation* (New York) for October 3, 1867; Jan. 23, 1868; July 2, 1868; Feb. 11, 1869; Dec. 23, 1869; July 14, 1870; Apr. 11, 1872; Nov. 21, 1872.

set up to run nonsectarian schools financed through the rates. Additionally, if parents wished to send their children to denominational schools, and could not afford the fees, these local boards might pay the fees from the rates.

This solution, though acceptable to Anglicans and Roman Catholics, met with strong opposition from Protestant Nonconformists and freethinkers. For not only did it leave an extensive system of religious education in place, but it even encouraged the Church of England to set up new schools, and provided them with new sources of revenue. A campaign to rescind or modify the act was undertaken by Joseph Chamberlain's Nonconformist National Education League. But this campaign was also the occasion for Nonconformists and freethinkers to unite against a common foe. After consultation with Chamberlain, John Morley, the editor of the *Fortnightly Review*, published a series on 'The Struggle for National Education,' probably the most effective piece of anti-Act propaganda.[21] Morley's series reveals some of the reasons freethinkers had for fearing the impact on public affairs of a religious motivation, especially within the established church. According to Morley, the church had decided to take advantage of the national consensus on the importance of education to extend its own influence. The National Society, the educational arm of the church, had been quite direct in announcing its intention to use the provisions of the new act to 'imbue ... the two-thirds of the voters of England under her direct teaching ... with her principles, and secure their allegiance to her cause.'[22] Morley saw the threat of clerical control over education as a Europewide phenomenon, and explicitly identified the cause of English secularists with that of Bismarck, then in the midst of the *Kulturkampf*. In 1873 he wrote,

> The expediency of entrusting the [Anglican] clergy and the Catholic priests — with the control of national instruction turns upon the same set of general considerations with reference to progress, enlightenment and the common weal as those which determine the expediency of allowing Jesuits and others to corrupt public spirit and weaken national life in Germany. This is really a true account of the matter, and it brings us to the root of the present dispute.[23]

[21] Morley to Chamberlain, July 4, 1873, Chamberlain Papers, Birmingham University Library.

[22] John Morley, quoting from the *Monthly Paper* of the National Society in *The Struggle for National Education* (London, 1873), 42–43.

[23] Ibid., 47–48.

The education controversy was therefore, from the perspective of a freethinker like Morley, only one aspect of a much broader and more serious problem that faced those countries where an expanded franchise was altering the condition of politics. This was the threat of political and religious reaction associated with the resurgence of clerical forces, and it is the third aspect from which many who had abandoned organized religion in the late 1860s and 1870s viewed its claims. It is a temptation for the modern reader to discount the fear so often voiced in the 1870s by thinkers like Morley and Stephen that the entrance of new classes into political life brought with it the danger of increased clerical domination. After all, these men had themselves favored a more democratic constitution as a way to break clerical and aristocratic power, and they had supported an expanded franchise in 1867. In addition, our subsequent convictions about unchurched masses and the inseparable link between the Church of England and the upper classes make talk about the alliance of church and democracy seem exaggerated. Against this impression it is important to recognize that in the 1870s, English freethinkers had before them what they believed were two striking examples of the very alliance they feared. On the one hand, Louis Napoleon had combined plebiscitary democracy with clerical support to create what English radicals considered one of the most oppressive regimes in Europe.[24] Closer to home, the militant Catholicism growing in Ireland in the late 1860s and 1870s appeared to have found political expression in Fenianism and in the growth of a Home Rule party. Even so experienced an observer of the Irish scene as the Anglo-Irish historian W. E. H. Lecky missed the bitter opposition of the Catholic hierarchy to Fenian agitators, and their refusal to endorse the goals of Isaac Butt's moderate Home Rule party. According to Lecky, the 'diseased state of public opinion in Ireland' was due to the joint action of ambitious clergy, who 'subordinated all ... questions to ecclesiastical interest,' and political demagogues, who felt 'only indifference to ... constitutional means,' and who were motivated by 'a blind persistent hatred of England.'[25]

Lecky's association of clerical ambition with political opportunism as the moving forces in Irish public life sounds a theme that recurs more than once in the political reflection of those who had come to question revealed religion. Several reasons help to illustrate and explain why the fear of clerical reaction in this decade should be linked to distaste for popular political movements. The Education Act itself was an instance of how a clerical interest group had been able to mobilize public support and exploit

[24] See, for example, Morley's two articles in the *Fortnightly Review*, 'France and Gemany,' 45 (September 1870), and 'England and the War,' 46 (October 1870).

[25] W. E. H. Lecky, *The Leaders of Public Opinion in Ireland* (London, 1871), x.

the weakness of the party system to achieve its own ends. It was particularly galling to radicals like Morley, Stephen, and Harrison that the act had been passed, not by Tories, but by a Liberal ministry under a leader from whom they had expected great things. Morley especially took the passage of the Education Act as a lesson in the inherent tendency of party government to compromise and temporize, to solve political problems by trying to gratify conflicting interests, in short, to act out of expediency rather than on principle.[26] While Gladstone's government wasted time and energy on an unacceptable Education Act, thinkers like Stephen and Morley became increasingly pessimistic about the ability of party government to frame progressive policies, or even to deal with national issues of pressing importance.[27] They attributed these failures to the ability of obstructive and reactionary forces — especially the clergy — to use the techniques of managing public opinion and manipulating party government for their own sectarian purposes.[28] After the fall of Gladstone's government, both men agreed that in view of this debacle, if reform were to have any future, it would be necessary to accomplish two things. First, the power of the church in national politics would have to be broken by ending its established status; second, party government must be replaced with a system of government by men of education and ability.[29]

The connection between the political ambitions of religious denominations and the evils of the party system became even clearer in the minds of English freethinkers with the emergence of a united Irish Nationalist party in the late 1870s. At first, Parnell and his followers were able, through their disruptive tactics, to thwart or delay legislation proposed by the ministry and desired by the English majority. As the party grew in strength through the early 1880s, its support or defection could make or break English gov-

---

[26] For his next political sally after *The Struggle for National Education*, Morley told Chamberlain he wished to write a manifesto against expediency in politics, 'as forceful and intrepid' as he could make it, castigating Liberal party leadership for 'deserting our principles' and making Liberalism into 'a catchword for parliamentary intrigues' (Morley to Chamberlain, March 12, 1874, Chamberlain Papers). In fact, Morley's *On Compromise* (London, 1874), published serially in the *Fortnightly* later that year was an effort to define the place of principles in politics, and the limits of compromise.

[27] For Morley on the failure of Gladstone's government to discern progressive forces, see *The Struggle for National Education*, 71; for Stephen's strictures on the inefficiency of party government see *Nation* (Sept. 28, 1871), 208.

[28] *On Compromise*, 33; Stephen, 'The Religious Difficulty,' 623–624.

[29] These were the two facets of a political program of action planned by Morley and Chamberlain in 1873–1874. See their correspondence from July 19, 1873, to March 12, 1874. For Stephen's awareness of the same two needs, see 'Matthew Arnold and the Church of England,' 426; also 'Social Macadamization,' *Fraser's Magazine* 6 (1872), 161–162.

ernments. When Gladstone finally decided to introduce a bill for home rule, his action was viewed by many English agnostics as surrendering the government of Ireland to priests, and he was suspected of having done so in exchange for the political support of the Irish Nationalist party.[30] Once again, observers in England assumed uncritically that the Catholic church and the Nationalist party were in close alliance. Lecky, for example, described the home rule bill as a plan 'to entrust the government of Ireland ... to the tender mercies of priests and Fenians and agitators.'[31]

Finally, it is impossible not to recognize that home rule encountered such widespread opposition among English freethinkers not just because it was home rule for the Irish, but because it was home rule for Irish Roman Catholics. Certainly in mid-Victorian Britian, one did not have to be agnostic to be anti-Catholic. However, almost all freethinkers who opposed home rule associated their opposition with vehement hatred of Catholicism.[32] This fear and hatred of Roman Catholicism was often inspired by the disturbing role of that church in the politics of other European countries: recall John Morley's approval of the *Kulturkampf*; and one can find similar concern over the conduct of the church in France, Belgium, Italy, and Austria in the writings of other English freethinkers. But it is also important to recognize how much the anti-Catholicism of English freethinkers was a reaction to the inroads made by Rome on English life in general, but especially on the Church of England. These inroads were not only the growth of the Roman church in England, nor the dramatic conversions, nor even the more extreme manifestations of Catholic revival among the Ritualists: the mass, auricular confession, religious orders. Of even greater concern to freethinkers were the more pervasive clericalizing tendencies mentioned earlier in this essay, which they discovered in every party in the church. The growth of clerical caste-consciousness — manifested, for example, in the prevalence of clerical dress among all groups of the clergy — the reassertion

---

[30] For reaction of English intellectuals to home rule, see Lewis P. Curtis, Jr., *Anglo-Saxons and Celts* (Bridgeport, Conn., 1968), 98–107. Goldwin Smith accused Gladstone of having 'flung himself into the arms of ... public plunder and treason' in order to maintain his parliamentary majority. See G. Smith, 'The Moral of the Late Crisis,' *Nineteenth Century* 20 (September 1886), 307.

[31] W. E. H. Lecky, letter to the *Times*, June 7, 1886.

[32] John Morley was an exception to the general opposition of English intellectuals to home rule. However, his reasons for supporting home rule were not unrelated to those of other thinkers for opposing it. He hoped by granting the Irish control over their own affairs to end the disturbing influence they had on English parties. Removing the temptation to play for partisan advantage on the religious passions aroused wherever Ireland was concerned might, Morley expected, purify English politics and open the way for disinterested statesmen to develop a truly national political consensus. See D. A. Hamer, *John Morley, Liberal Intellectual in Politics* (Oxford, 1968), pp. 183–194.

of the authority of ecclesiastical institutions, especially schools, over the minds of individuals; the new aggressiveness of the church in the political arena: all these developments were redolent to English agnostics of the theory and practice of Rome. If English freethinkers spent as much time as they did worrying and writing about the threat from Rome, it was because developments within the Church of England made this threat of clerical repression seem very real.

These and other concrete issues made the problem of belief much more than a problem of epistemology and infused such passion into debates and controversy on the subject. The theological and ethical arguments about belief carried on in books and periodicals had, not only for their authors, but also for those who read them, immediate ramifications for the way people lived and the authorities by which they guided their lives.

CONCLUSION

We hope that consideration of these three disconnected issues will illustrate how religious, legal, and political conditions, as well as the more familiar dissolvent literature, helped to foster the debate over the ethics of belief and led to the emergence of a secular frame of mind among British intellectuals. The ironic element in this situation was the role played by religion and by the religious revival itself, first in making the character of belief both more intense and problematical, and then by so strengthening the political and educational influence of religion so as to call forth a strongly secular response. The religious revival led to the deep divisions within the Church of England that prevented a uniform interpretation of the Articles and the Bible and that ultimately required the secular state to enforce theological pluralism. The novel mid-century rigor of definition of the clerical vocation eventually called forth passage of the Clerical Disabilities Act that sustained the debate over the ethics of belief by making departure from the ministry possible and reasonably simple. Finally, the role of ecclesiastical institutions in education and politics throughout the British Isles made the issues of the honesty of religious belief a powerful weapon for intellectual and political polemic. And it was a weapon that the religious community had given its enemies through its own internal quarrels. Once the discussion of what one could truthfully and honestly believe passed from religious circles to the intellectual nation at large it became a way of breaking the hold of the church and of religion over the culture as a whole.

INDEX